# Journey of Faith: Lessons from the Book of Numbers

Harper Nomad

# The Census of Israel

The Command to Number the People
**Numbers 1:1-19 (NIV)**

1. The Lord spoke to Moses in the tent of meeting in the Desert of Sinai on the first day of the second month of the second year after the Israelites came out of Egypt. He said:
2. "Take a census of the whole Israelite community by their clans and families, listing every man by name, one by one.
3. You and Aaron are to number by their divisions all the men in Israel twenty years old or more who are able to serve in the army.
4. One man from each tribe, each the head of his family, is to help you.
5. These are the names of the men who are to assist you: from Reuben, Elizur son of Shedeur;
6. from Simeon, Shelumiel son of Zurishaddai;
7. from Judah, Nahshon son of Amminadab;
8. from Issachar, Nethanel son of Zuar;
9. from Zebulun, Eliab son of Helon;
10. from the sons of Joseph: from Ephraim, Elishama son of Ammihud; from Manasseh, Gamaliel son of Pedahzur;
11. from Benjamin, Abidan son of Gideoni;
12. from Dan, Ahiezer son of Ammishaddai;
13. from Asher, Pagiel son of Okran;
14. from Gad, Eliasaph son of Deuel;

15. from Naphtali, Ahira son of Enan."

16. These were the men appointed from the community, the leaders of their ancestral tribes. They were the heads of the clans of Israel.

17. Moses and Aaron took these men whose names had been specified,

18. and they called the whole community together on the first day of the second month. The people registered their ancestry by their clans and families, and the names of all those twenty years old or more were listed by name, one by one,

19. as the Lord commanded Moses. And so he counted them in the Desert of Sinai.

**Theological Significance:**

- **Divine Command:** The census was initiated by God, emphasising that this was not merely an administrative task but a divine directive. It reflects God's sovereignty and His concern for the orderly organisation of His people.

- **Community Structure:** The enumeration by clans and families highlights the importance of family and tribal identity within the Israelite community. This structure was crucial for maintaining order and unity.

- **Preparation for Warfare:** Counting the men able to serve in the army underscores the practical need for preparedness in defending the nation and undertaking conquests as directed by God.

**Modern Interpretation:**

This passage teaches modern believers about the importance of organisation, preparation, and community identity. It underscores that God's directives often involve practical steps that require diligence and cooperation.

**Key Themes:**

- **Obedience to Divine Command:** The census was a direct command from God, showing the importance of obedience in even the most seemingly mundane tasks.
- **Community and Identity:** The emphasis on clans and families highlights the importance of maintaining strong communal ties and a sense of identity.
- **Preparation and Readiness:** The counting of those able to serve in the army reflects the need for preparation and readiness to face challenges.

**Modern-Day Examples:**

- **Church Organisation:** Just as the Israelites were organised by clans and families, modern churches benefit from clear organisational structures that help maintain unity and effective ministry.
- **Family and Community Identity:** Maintaining strong family and community ties within a church can help foster a sense of belonging and support.
- **Preparedness for Ministry:** Just as the Israelites prepared for warfare, modern believers should be prepared for spiritual battles and ready to serve in their communities.

**Questions for Reflection and Discussion:**

1. How does the census of the Israelites reflect the importance of obedience to God's commands?
2. In what ways can maintaining a sense of community and

identity strengthen modern churches and faith
communities?

3. How can believers prepare themselves to face spiritual and
practical challenges in their lives?

4. What lessons can we learn from the organisational
structure of the Israelite community that can be applied to
our own communities?

**Sermon Notes for Religious Leaders:**
**Title:** "Obedience, Community, and Preparation: Lessons from
the Census of Israel"
**Introduction:**

- Introduce the context of the census in Numbers 1, focusing
on its significance and the lessons it offers for modern
believers.
- Highlight the themes of obedience to divine command,
community identity, and preparation for challenges.

**Body:**

1. **Obedience to Divine Command:**
   - Discuss the importance of the census as a direct
command from God and the need for obedience
in all aspects of life.
   - Reflect on how this principle can be applied to
modern spiritual practices, encouraging believers
to seek and follow God's guidance in their daily
tasks.

2. **Community and Identity:**
   - Explore the emphasis on clans and families in the
census, highlighting the importance of
maintaining strong communal ties and a sense of

    identity.
- Encourage the congregation to foster a sense of belonging and support within their own communities.

3. **Preparation and Readiness:**
   - Discuss the practical aspect of counting those able to serve in the army, reflecting the need for preparation and readiness to face challenges.
   - Emphasise the importance of being prepared for spiritual battles and ready to serve in ministry and community service.

## Conclusion:

- Summarise the key lessons from the census of Israel, focusing on obedience, community identity, and preparation.
- Challenge the congregation to apply these principles in their modern spiritual practices and community life.
- Offer a prayer for guidance, unity, and readiness to follow God's commands and serve in His kingdom.

**Link to Modern-Day Problems:**

◇ **Church Organisation:** How can modern churches benefit from clear organisational structures that help maintain unity and effective ministry, inspired by the census of the Israelites?

◇ **Family and Community Identity:** In what ways can maintaining strong family and community ties within a church foster a sense of belonging and support?

◇ **Preparedness for Ministry:** How can believers prepare themselves to face spiritual and practical challenges in their lives, following the example of the Israelites' readiness for warfare?

◇ **Obedience to Divine Command:** How does the census of the Israelites reflect the importance of obedience to God's commands, and how can this principle be applied in modern spiritual practices?

**The Tribal Leaders and Their Duties**
**Numbers 1:20-46 (NIV)**

1. From the descendants of Reuben the firstborn son of Israel: all the men twenty years old or more who were able to serve in the army were listed by name, one by one, according to the records of their clans and families.
2. The number from the tribe of Reuben was 46,500.
3. From the descendants of Simeon: all the men twenty years old or more who were able to serve in the army were counted and listed by name, one by one, according to the records of their clans and families.
4. The number from the tribe of Simeon was 59,300.
5. From the descendants of Gad: all the men twenty years old or more who were able to serve in the army were listed by name, one by one, according to the records of their clans and families.
6. The number from the tribe of Gad was 45,650.
7. From the descendants of Judah: all the men twenty years old or more who were able to serve in the army were listed by name, one by one, according to the records of their clans and families.
8. The number from the tribe of Judah was 74,600.
9. From the descendants of Issachar: all the men twenty years old or more who were able to serve in the army were listed by name, one by one, according to the records of their clans and families.
10. The number from the tribe of Issachar was 54,400.

11. From the descendants of Zebulun: all the men twenty years old or more who were able to serve in the army were listed by name, one by one, according to the records of their clans and families.

12. The number from the tribe of Zebulun was 57,400.

13. From the sons of Joseph: from the descendants of Ephraim: all the men twenty years old or more who were able to serve in the army were listed by name, one by one, according to the records of their clans and families.

14. The number from the tribe of Ephraim was 40,500.

15. From the descendants of Manasseh: all the men twenty years old or more who were able to serve in the army were listed by name, one by one, according to the records of their clans and families.

16. The number from the tribe of Manasseh was 32,200.

17. From the descendants of Benjamin: all the men twenty years old or more who were able to serve in the army were listed by name, one by one, according to the records of their clans and families.

18. The number from the tribe of Benjamin was 35,400.

19. From the descendants of Dan: all the men twenty years old or more who were able to serve in the army were listed by name, one by one, according to the records of their clans and families.

20. The number from the tribe of Dan was 62,700.

21. From the descendants of Asher: all the men twenty years old or more who were able to serve in the army were listed by name, one by one, according to the records of their clans and families.

22. The number from the tribe of Asher was 41,500.

23. From the descendants of Naphtali: all the men twenty years old or more who were able to serve in the army were

listed by name, one by one, according to the records of their clans and families.

24. The number from the tribe of Naphtali was 53,400.

25. These were the men counted by Moses and Aaron and the twelve leaders of Israel, each one representing his family.

26. All the Israelites twenty years old or more who were able to serve in Israel's army were counted according to their families.

27. The total number was 603,550.

## Theological Significance:

- **Leadership and Representation:** The appointment of tribal leaders to assist in the census underscores the importance of leadership and representation in the community. These leaders acted as representatives of their tribes, ensuring that each tribe's interests were considered.

- **Divine Order and Structure:** The detailed enumeration of each tribe reflects God's desire for order and structure within His people. This orderliness is seen as an expression of divine wisdom and care.

- **Preparedness for Mission:** The focus on those able to serve in the army highlights the necessity of being prepared for the tasks and missions God assigns. It reflects a readiness to engage in spiritual and physical battles.

### Modern Interpretation:

This section of Numbers teaches modern believers about the importance of effective leadership, the value of structure and organisation, and the need for readiness in fulfiling God's missions.

### Key Themes:

- **Effective Leadership:** The role of tribal leaders emphasises the importance of effective leadership and representation in maintaining community unity and order.
- **Divine Order:** The meticulous counting and organisation reflect God's desire for orderliness and structure within His community.
- **Readiness for Mission:** The emphasis on counting those able to serve in the army highlights the need for readiness and preparedness in fulfiling God's missions.

**Modern-Day Examples:**

- **Church Leadership:** Modern churches can benefit from effective leadership and representation, ensuring that the needs and interests of all members are considered.
- **Organisational Structure:** Just as the Israelites were meticulously organised, modern faith communities can adopt structured approaches to ministry and service.
- **Readiness to Serve:** Believers should be prepared and ready to engage in the missions and tasks God assigns, whether spiritual or practical.

**Questions for Reflection and Discussion:**

1. How does the appointment of tribal leaders in the census highlight the importance of effective leadership and representation?
2. What can we learn from the detailed organisation of the Israelite tribes about the value of structure and order in our communities?
3. How can believers prepare themselves to be ready for the missions and tasks God assigns?

4.  In what ways can modern faith communities adopt structured approaches to ministry and service, inspired by the census of the Israelites?

**Sermon Notes for Religious Leaders:**
**Title:** "Leadership, Order, and Readiness: Lessons from the Tribal Leaders and Their Duties"
**Introduction:**

- Introduce the role of tribal leaders in the census, focusing on the importance of effective leadership, divine order, and readiness for mission.
- Highlight the themes of leadership and representation, divine order, and readiness for mission.

**Body:**

1.  **Effective Leadership and Representation:**
    - Discuss the appointment of tribal leaders to assist in the census, emphasising the importance of effective leadership and representation in maintaining community unity and order.
    - Reflect on how these principles can be applied to modern faith communities, encouraging the development of effective leadership structures.

2.  **Divine Order and Structure:**
    - Explore the meticulous counting and organisation of the Israelite tribes, highlighting the value of structure and order as expressions of divine wisdom and care.
    - Encourage the congregation to adopt structured approaches to ministry and service, recognising the importance of orderliness in fulfiling God's

purposes.

3. **Readiness for Mission:**
    ○ Discuss the focus on counting those able to serve in the army, reflecting the need for readiness and preparedness in fulfiling God's missions.
    ○ Emphasise the importance of being prepared to engage in the tasks and missions God assigns, whether spiritual or practical.

## Conclusion:

- Summarise the key lessons from the role of tribal leaders and their duties, focusing on effective leadership, divine order, and readiness for mission.
- Challenge the congregation to apply these principles in their modern spiritual practices and community life.
- Offer a prayer for guidance, order, and readiness to follow God's commands and serve in His kingdom.

### Link to Modern-Day Problems:

◇ **Church Leadership:** How can modern churches benefit from effective leadership and representation, ensuring that the needs and interests of all members are considered, inspired by the appointment of tribal leaders in the census?

◇ **Organisational Structure:** What steps can faith communities take to adopt structured approaches to ministry and service, recognising the value of order and structure in fulfiling God's purposes?

◇ **Readiness to Serve:** How can believers prepare themselves to be ready for the missions and tasks God assigns, following the example of the Israelites' readiness for warfare?

◇ **Effective Leadership and Representation:** In what ways can effective leadership and representation be fostered within faith communities to maintain unity and order, inspired by the role of tribal leaders in the census?

**Exclusion of the Levites**

**Numbers 1:47-54 (NIV)**

1. The ancestral tribe of the Levites, however, was not counted along with the others.
2. The Lord had said to Moses:
3. "You must not count the tribe of Levi or include them in the census of the other Israelites.
4. Instead, appoint the Levites to be in charge of the tabernacle of the covenant law—over all its furnishings and everything belonging to it. They are to carry the tabernacle and all its furnishings; they are to take care of it and encamp around it.
5. Whenever the tabernacle is to move, the Levites are to take it down, and whenever the tabernacle is to be set up, the Levites shall do it. Anyone else who approaches it is to be put to death.
6. The Israelites are to set up their tents by divisions, each of them in their own camp under their standard.
7. The Levites, however, are to set up their tents around the tabernacle of the covenant law so that my wrath will not fall on the Israelite community. The Levites are to be responsible for the care of the tabernacle of the covenant law."
8. The Israelites did all this just as the Lord commanded Moses.

**Theological Significance:**

- **Special Role of the Levites:** The exclusion of the Levites from the census and their appointment to care for the tabernacle underscores their unique role and responsibilities within the Israelite community. This highlights the concept of sacred duties and the importance of specialised roles in religious service.

- **Sanctity of Worship:** The Levites' responsibility for the tabernacle emphasises the sanctity of worship and the need for careful stewardship of holy spaces and objects. Their role was vital in maintaining the holiness of the worship environment.

- **Divine Protection:** By surrounding the tabernacle, the Levites acted as a buffer between the sacred space and the rest of the community, preventing unauthorised access and protecting the community from divine wrath.

**Modern Interpretation:**

This section of Numbers teaches modern believers about the importance of recognising and respecting specialised roles within the faith community, the sanctity of worship spaces, and the need for stewardship and protection of holy things.

**Key Themes:**

- **Specialised Roles in Service:** The passage highlights the importance of recognising and respecting specialised roles within the faith community, emphasising the unique responsibilities of those called to serve in particular ways.

- **Sanctity of Worship:** The emphasis on the Levites' role in caring for the tabernacle underscores the need to maintain the sanctity of worship spaces and objects.

- **Stewardship and Protection:** The role of the Levites as protectors of the tabernacle highlights the importance of stewardship and protecting what is holy.

## Modern-Day Examples:

- **Specialised Ministry Roles:** Modern churches can benefit from recognising and respecting specialised roles within their communities, ensuring that individuals are called and equipped to serve in specific capacities.
- **Maintaining Worship Spaces:** The emphasis on the sanctity of worship spaces can inspire believers to care for and maintain their places of worship, recognising them as holy and set apart.
- **Stewardship and Protection:** Believers can adopt practices of stewardship and protection for what is holy, ensuring that sacred spaces and objects are treated with respect and care.

## Questions for Reflection and Discussion:

1. How does the exclusion of the Levites from the census highlight the importance of specialised roles within the faith community?
2. What can we learn from the Levites' responsibilities for the tabernacle about maintaining the sanctity of worship spaces and objects?
3. How can believers practice stewardship and protection of what is holy in their own lives and communities?
4. In what ways can modern faith communities recognise and respect specialised roles within their congregations, inspired by the Levites' unique responsibilities?

## Sermon Notes for Religious Leaders:

**Title:** "Specialised Roles and Sanctity: Lessons from the Exclusion of the Levites"

**Introduction:**

- Introduce the exclusion of the Levites from the census and their appointment to care for the tabernacle, focusing on the significance of specialised roles, sanctity of worship, and stewardship.
- Highlight the themes of specialised roles in service, sanctity of worship, and stewardship and protection.

**Body:**

1. **Specialised Roles in Service:**
   - Discuss the importance of recognising and respecting specialised roles within the faith community, as illustrated by the exclusion of the Levites from the census and their unique responsibilities.
   - Reflect on how these principles can be applied to modern spiritual practices, encouraging the development and support of specialised ministry roles.

2. **Sanctity of Worship:**
   - Explore the Levites' responsibilities for the tabernacle, emphasising the need to maintain the sanctity of worship spaces and objects.
   - Encourage the congregation to care for and maintain their places of worship, recognising them as holy and set apart.

3. **Stewardship and Protection:**
   - Discuss the role of the Levites as protectors of the tabernacle, highlighting the importance of stewardship and protecting what is holy.
   - Emphasise the need for believers to adopt

practices of stewardship and protection for sacred spaces and objects in their own lives and communities.

**Conclusion:**

- Summarise the key lessons from the exclusion of the Levites, focusing on specialised roles in service, sanctity of worship, and stewardship and protection.
- Challenge the congregation to apply these principles in their modern spiritual practices and community life.
- Offer a prayer for guidance, respect for specialised roles, and a deeper commitment to maintaining the sanctity of worship and stewardship of what is holy.

**Link to Modern-Day Problems:**

◇ **Specialised Ministry Roles:** How can modern churches benefit from recognising and respecting specialised roles within their communities, ensuring that individuals are called and equipped to serve in specific capacities, inspired by the exclusion of the Levites from the census?

◇ **Maintaining Worship Spaces:** What steps can believers take to care for and maintain their places of worship, recognising them as holy and set apart, inspired by the Levites' responsibilities for the tabernacle?

◇ **Stewardship and Protection:** How can believers practice stewardship and protection of what is holy in their own lives and communities, ensuring that sacred spaces and objects are treated with respect and care, inspired by the role of the Levites?

◇ **Specialised Roles in Service:** In what ways can modern faith communities recognise and respect specialised roles within their congregations, inspired by the unique responsibilities of the Levites?

**The Significance of the Census**

**Numbers 1:54 (NIV)**

1.  The Israelites did all this just as the Lord commanded
    Moses.

**Theological Significance:**

- **Obedience to God's Command:** The census and the
  organisation of the Israelite community were done in strict
  obedience to God's command. This underscores the
  importance of following divine instructions precisely.
- **Foundation for Future Narratives:** The census laid the
  foundation for the rest of the Book of Numbers, as well as
  the historical and theological narrative of the Israelites. It
  provided a detailed record of the community's structure
  and readiness for the journey ahead.
- **Symbol of Commitment:** The successful completion of
  the census symbolises the Israelites' commitment to God's
  plan and their readiness to follow His guidance.

**Modern Interpretation:**

This final verse of the chapter teaches modern believers about
the importance of obedience, the significance of foundational work
for future endeavours, and the symbolism of commitment to God's
plans.

**Key Themes:**

- **Obedience to God:** The passage highlights the
  importance of obedience to God's commands in all aspects
  of life.
- **Foundational Work:** The census provided a necessary
  foundation for future narratives and events, emphasising

the importance of thorough preparation.

- **Commitment to God's Plan:** The successful completion
  of the census symbolises the Israelites' commitment to
  God's plan and their readiness to follow His guidance.

## Modern-Day Examples:

- **Obedience in Daily Life:** Modern believers can strive to
  follow God's commands in their daily lives, recognising the
  importance of obedience in all aspects of life.
- **Laying Foundations:** Just as the census laid the
  foundation for future narratives, believers can focus on
  laying solid foundations in their spiritual practices and
  community work.
- **Commitment to God's Plan:** The completion of tasks
  assigned by God can symbolise a believer's commitment to
  His plan and readiness to follow His guidance.

## Questions for Reflection and Discussion:

1. How does the completion of the census highlight the
   importance of obedience to God's commands?
2. What can we learn from the census about the significance
   of foundational work for future endeavours?
3. How can believers demonstrate their commitment to
   God's plan in their daily lives and community work?
4. In what ways can modern believers focus on laying solid
   foundations in their spiritual practices and community
   work, inspired by the census of the Israelites?

## Sermon Notes for Religious Leaders:

**Title:** "Obedience, Foundations, and Commitment: Lessons from the Significance of the Census"

**Introduction:**

- Introduce the significance of the census in Numbers 1, focusing on the importance of obedience, foundational work, and commitment to God's plan.
- Highlight the themes of obedience to God, foundational work, and commitment to God's plan.

**Body:**

1. **Obedience to God:**
    - Discuss the importance of the census as an act of obedience to God's command, highlighting the need for obedience in all aspects of life.
    - Reflect on how these principles can be applied to modern spiritual practices, encouraging believers to strive for obedience in their daily lives.
2. **Foundational Work:**
    - Explore the significance of the census as a foundational work for future narratives and events, emphasising the importance of thorough preparation.
    - Encourage the congregation to focus on laying solid foundations in their spiritual practices and community work, recognising the importance of preparation for future endeavours.
3. **Commitment to God's Plan:**
    - Discuss the successful completion of the census as a symbol of the Israelites' commitment to God's plan and their readiness to follow His guidance.
    - Emphasise the importance of demonstrating

commitment to God's plan in daily life and
community work, recognising the symbolism of
completing tasks assigned by God.

**Conclusion:**

- Summarise the key lessons from the significance of the census, focusing on obedience, foundational work, and commitment to God's plan.
- Challenge the congregation to apply these principles in their modern spiritual practices and community life.
- Offer a prayer for guidance, obedience, and a deeper commitment to following God's commands and laying solid foundations for future endeavours.

**Link to Modern-Day Problems:**

◈ **Obedience in Daily Life:** How can modern believers strive to follow God's commands in their daily lives, recognising the importance of obedience in all aspects of life, inspired by the completion of the census?

◈ **Laying Foundations:** What steps can believers take to focus on laying solid foundations in their spiritual practices and community work, recognising the significance of foundational work for future endeavours?

◈ **Commitment to God's Plan:** How can believers demonstrate their commitment to God's plan in their daily lives and community work, following the example of the Israelites' completion of the census?

◈ **Obedience to God:** In what ways can modern believers focus on obedience to God's commands and laying solid foundations in their spiritual practices and community work, inspired by the significance of the census in Numbers 1?

# The Arrangement of the Camp

The Camp of Judah
**Numbers 2:1-9 (NIV)**

1. The Lord said to Moses and Aaron:
2. "The Israelites are to camp around the tent of meeting some distance from it, each of them under their standard and holding the banners of their family."
3. On the east, toward the sunrise, the divisions of the camp of Judah are to encamp under their standard. The leader of the people of Judah is Nahshon son of Amminadab.
4. His division numbers 74,600.
5. The tribe of Issachar will camp next to them. The leader of the people of Issachar is Nethanel son of Zuar.
6. His division numbers 54,400.
7. The tribe of Zebulun will be next. The leader of the people of Zebulun is Eliab son of Helon.
8. His division numbers 57,400.
9. All the men assigned to the camp of Judah, according to their divisions, number 186,400. They will set out first.

**Theological Significance:**

- **Order and Structure:** The arrangement of the tribes around the tent of meeting reflects God's desire for order and structure among His people. This orderly arrangement is a physical representation of divine organisation.

- **Leadership and Responsibility:** The mention of specific leaders and their tribes underscores the importance of leadership and responsibility within the community. Each leader is accountable for their tribe, highlighting the need for organised leadership.
- **Symbolism of East:** The east, where the camp of Judah is positioned, often symbolises new beginnings and hope. This positioning underscores the prominence and leadership role of the tribe of Judah, from which King David and ultimately Jesus Christ would come.

**Modern Interpretation:**

This passage teaches modern believers about the importance of order and structure within their communities, the value of strong leadership, and the symbolic significance of positioning in relation to spiritual matters.

**Key Themes:**

- **Divine Order:** The meticulous arrangement around the tent of meeting underscores the importance of divine order in the community of believers.
- **Leadership:** The role of tribal leaders is crucial in maintaining order and responsibility within the community.
- **Symbolism of Direction:** Positioning within the camp has symbolic significance, reflecting roles and spiritual meanings.

**Modern-Day Examples:**

- **Church Organisation:** Modern churches can benefit from

clear organisational structures that reflect divine order, ensuring that each member and leader understands their role and responsibilities.

- **Effective Leadership:** Just as tribal leaders were responsible for their people, modern church leaders should embody responsibility and accountability.
- **Symbolic Positioning:** The symbolic significance of positioning can be reflected in church traditions and practices, recognising the deeper meanings behind actions and placements.

## Questions for Reflection and Discussion:

1. How does the arrangement of the tribes around the tent of meeting highlight the importance of divine order and structure?
2. What can we learn from the specific roles and responsibilities of tribal leaders about effective leadership in our communities?
3. How can believers incorporate the symbolic significance of positioning and direction into their spiritual practices and community life?
4. In what ways can modern churches reflect the principles of order, leadership, and symbolism seen in the arrangement of the camp of Judah?

**Sermon Notes for Religious Leaders:**
**Title:** "Order, Leadership, and Symbolism: Lessons from the Camp of Judah"
**Introduction:**

- Introduce the arrangement of the camp of Judah in

Numbers 2, focusing on the significance of order,
leadership, and symbolic positioning.

- Highlight the themes of divine order, leadership, and
  symbolism of direction.

**Body:**

1. **Divine Order and Structure:**
   - Discuss the importance of the orderly
     arrangement around the tent of meeting,
     reflecting God's desire for structure and
     organisation.
   - Reflect on how these principles can be applied to
     modern spiritual practices, encouraging believers
     to maintain order and structure in their
     communities.
2. **Leadership and Responsibility:**
   - Explore the roles of tribal leaders, emphasising the
     importance of leadership and responsibility
     within the community.
   - Encourage the congregation to support and
     respect their leaders, recognising their roles in
     maintaining community order.
3. **Symbolism of Direction:**
   - Discuss the symbolic significance of the tribe of
     Judah's position to the east, relating it to themes
     of new beginnings and hope.
   - Emphasise the importance of understanding
     symbolic actions and placements within spiritual
     practices and traditions.

**Working Example for Religious Leaders:**
**Example:** "Envisioning Our Church's Future"

- **Scenario:** Imagine your church is planning a major outreach event. Just as the tribes were strategically positioned around the tent of meeting, you will organise different teams for various tasks: welcoming visitors, setting up the venue, managing logistics, and providing spiritual support.
- **Action:** Assign leaders to each team, making sure they understand their responsibilities and the significance of their roles.
- **Symbolism:** Position the welcome team at the entrance, symbolising new beginnings and hospitality, much like Judah's position to the east.
- **Outcome:** By clearly organising and symbolically positioning your teams, you create an orderly, welcoming, and spiritually significant event, reflecting the principles from the arrangement of the camp of Judah.

**Conclusion:**

- Summarise the key lessons from the arrangement of the camp of Judah, focusing on divine order, leadership, and symbolic significance.
- Challenge the congregation to apply these principles in their modern spiritual practices and community life.
- Offer a prayer for guidance, order, and a deeper understanding of symbolic actions and placements in their spiritual journey.

**Link to Modern-Day Problems:**

◈ **Church Organisation:** How can modern churches benefit from clear organisational structures that reflect divine order, ensuring that each member and leader understands their role and responsibilities, inspired by the arrangement of the camp of Judah?

◈ **Effective Leadership:** What steps can faith communities take to support and respect their leaders, recognising the importance of leadership and responsibility in maintaining community order?

◈ **Symbolic Positioning:** How can believers incorporate the symbolic significance of positioning and direction into their spiritual practices and community life, recognising the deeper meanings behind actions and placements?

◈ **Divine Order and Structure:** In what ways can modern churches reflect the principles of order, leadership, and symbolism seen in the arrangement of the camp of Judah, ensuring that their communities are organised and spiritually meaningful?

**The Camp of Reuben**
**Numbers 2:10-16 (NIV)**

1. On the south will be the divisions of the camp of Reuben under their standard. The leader of the people of Reuben is Elizur son of Shedeur.
2. His division numbers 46,500.
3. The tribe of Simeon will camp next to them. The leader of the people of Simeon is Shelumiel son of Zurishaddai.
4. His division numbers 59,300.
5. The tribe of Gad will be next. The leader of the people of Gad is Eliasaph son of Deuel.
6. His division numbers 45,650.
7. All the men assigned to the camp of Reuben, according to their divisions, number 151,450. They will set out second.

**Theological Significance:**

- **Unity and Cooperation:** The arrangement of the camp of Reuben, along with Simeon and Gad, reflects the need for unity and cooperation among different tribes. Each tribe, while distinct, contributes to the overall strength and function of the community.

- **Strategic Positioning:** The south position of the camp highlights strategic planning in the organisation of the tribes, ensuring that each division is properly placed for the journey and potential conflicts ahead.
- **Divine Instruction:** The detailed instructions for camp arrangement underscore the importance of following God's directives precisely, ensuring that the community functions smoothly and effectively.

**Modern Interpretation:**

The camp of Reuben teaches modern believers about the importance of unity, strategic planning, and adherence to divine instructions within their communities.

**Key Themes:**

- **Unity in Diversity:** The passage highlights the importance of unity and cooperation among diverse groups within the community.
- **Strategic Planning:** The strategic positioning of the tribes reflects the need for careful planning and organisation in community life.
- **Obedience to Divine Instructions:** The detailed arrangement underscores the importance of following God's instructions precisely for the smooth functioning of the community.

**Modern-Day Examples:**

- **Unity in Church Diversity:** Modern churches can foster

unity among diverse groups within their congregations, recognising the strength that comes from cooperation.

- **Strategic Church Planning:** Just as the tribes were strategically positioned, churches can benefit from careful planning and organisation in their ministries and activities.
- **Following Divine Guidance:** Believers should strive to follow God's instructions in their personal and communal lives, recognising the importance of obedience for effective functioning.

## Questions for Reflection and Discussion:

1. How does the arrangement of the camp of Reuben highlight the importance of unity and cooperation among diverse groups within the community?
2. What can we learn from the strategic positioning of the tribes about the need for careful planning and organisation in our communities?
3. How can believers practise unity and strategic planning in their modern spiritual practices and community life?
4. In what ways can modern churches foster unity among diverse groups, ensuring that cooperation strengthens the community?

## Sermon Notes for Religious Leaders:

**Title:** "Unity, Strategy, and Obedience: Lessons from the Camp of Reuben"

**Introduction:**

- Introduce the arrangement of the camp of Reuben in Numbers 2, focusing on the significance of unity, strategic planning, and obedience to divine instructions.

- Highlight the themes of unity in diversity, strategic planning, and obedience to divine guidance.

**Body:**

1. **Unity in Diversity:**
    - Discuss the importance of unity and cooperation among diverse groups within the community, as illustrated by the arrangement of the camp of Reuben.
    - Reflect on how these principles can be applied to modern spiritual practices, encouraging believers to foster unity and cooperation in their communities.
2. **Strategic Planning:**
    - Explore the strategic positioning of the tribes, highlighting the need for careful planning and organisation in community life.
    - Encourage the congregation to engage in strategic planning in their ministries and activities, recognising the importance of thoughtful organisation.
3. **Obedience to Divine Instructions:**
    - Discuss the detailed instructions for camp arrangement, emphasising the importance of following God's directives precisely.
    - Emphasise the need for believers to strive for obedience to divine guidance in their personal and communal lives.

**Working Example for Religious Leaders:**
**Example:** "Organising a Church Retreat"

- **Scenario:** Imagine planning a church retreat that includes different activities like worship sessions, workshops, and fellowship times. Each activity requires careful planning and coordination.
- **Action:** Assign leaders to each activity, ensuring they understand their roles and responsibilities. Emphasise the need for unity among diverse groups participating in the retreat.
- **Strategy:** Position workshops strategically within the schedule to maximise participation and engagement, similar to the strategic positioning of the tribes.
- **Outcome:** By fostering unity, careful planning, and following divine guidance, the retreat becomes a cohesive and spiritually enriching experience for all participants, reflecting the principles from the arrangement of the camp of Reuben.

## Conclusion:

- Summarise the key lessons from the arrangement of the camp of Reuben, focusing on unity in diversity, strategic planning, and obedience to divine instructions.
- Challenge the congregation to apply these principles in their modern spiritual practices and community life.
- Offer a prayer for guidance, unity, and a deeper commitment to following God's instructions and planning strategically.

**Link to Modern-Day Problems:**

◇ **Unity in Church Diversity:** How can modern churches foster unity among diverse groups within their congregations, recognising the strength that comes from cooperation, inspired by the arrangement of the camp of Reuben?

◈ **Strategic Church Planning:** What steps can faith communities take to engage in strategic planning and organisation in their ministries and activities, recognising the importance of careful planning?

◈ **Following Divine Guidance:** How can believers practise obedience to divine instructions in their personal and communal lives, recognising the importance of following God's guidance for effective functioning?

◈ **Unity and Strategy:** In what ways can modern churches foster unity among diverse groups and engage in strategic planning, ensuring that cooperation and careful organisation strengthen the community?

**The Camp of Ephraim**
**Numbers 2:18-24 (NIV)**

1. On the west will be the divisions of the camp of Ephraim under their standard. The leader of the people of Ephraim is Elishama son of Ammihud.
2. His division numbers 40,500.
3. The tribe of Manasseh will be next to them. The leader of the people of Manasseh is Gamaliel son of Pedahzur.
4. His division numbers 32,200.
5. The tribe of Benjamin will be next. The leader of the people of Benjamin is Abidan son of Gideoni.
6. His division numbers 35,400.
7. All the men assigned to the camp of Ephraim, according to their divisions, number 108,100. They will set out third.

**Theological Significance:**

- **Significance of Ephraim:** The placement of Ephraim's

camp to the west, along with the tribes of Manasseh and
Benjamin, reflects their significance within the Israelite
community. Ephraim, being the larger tribe from Joseph's
lineage, holds a prominent position.

- **Symbolic Direction:** The west often symbolises rest and
completion, aligning with Ephraim's role in providing
stability and support within the community.
- **Coordination Among Tribes:** The coordination among
the tribes of Ephraim, Manasseh, and Benjamin highlights
the importance of cooperation and mutual support within
the community, ensuring effective movement and
functioning.

**Modern Interpretation:**

The camp of Ephraim teaches modern believers about the
importance of recognising significant roles within the community,
the symbolic meanings behind directions and placements, and the
need for cooperation and support among community members.

**Key Themes:**

- **Significance of Roles:** The passage highlights the
importance of recognising and respecting significant roles
within the community, as seen in the placement of
Ephraim's camp.
- **Symbolic Direction:** The westward placement of
Ephraim's camp carries symbolic meaning, reflecting
themes of rest, stability, and completion.
- **Coordination and Support:** The coordination among the
tribes underscores the need for mutual support and
cooperation within the community.

**Modern-Day Examples:**

- **Recognising Roles in Church:** Modern churches can benefit from recognising and respecting significant roles within their communities, ensuring that all members contribute effectively.
- **Symbolic Placement:** Understanding the symbolic meanings behind actions and placements can enrich spiritual practices and traditions within the church.
- **Cooperation and Support:** Just as the tribes coordinated and supported each other, modern believers can practise mutual support and cooperation in their community activities.

**Questions for Reflection and Discussion:**

1. How does the placement of Ephraim's camp highlight the importance of recognising significant roles within the community?
2. What can we learn from the symbolic direction of the west about themes of rest, stability, and completion?
3. How can believers practise coordination and mutual support in their modern spiritual practices and community life?
4. In what ways can modern churches recognise and respect significant roles within their communities, ensuring effective cooperation and support?

**Sermon Notes for Religious Leaders:**
**Title:** "Significance, Symbolism, and Support: Lessons from the Camp of Ephraim"
**Introduction:**

- Introduce the arrangement of the camp of Ephraim in

Numbers 2, focusing on the significance of roles, symbolic direction, and the importance of coordination and support within the community.

- Highlight the themes of significance of roles, symbolic direction, and coordination and support.

**Body:**

1. **Significance of Roles:**
    - Discuss the importance of recognising and respecting significant roles within the community, as illustrated by the placement of Ephraim's camp.
    - Reflect on how these principles can be applied to modern spiritual practices, encouraging believers to recognise and respect significant roles within their communities.

2. **Symbolic Direction:**
    - Explore the westward placement of Ephraim's camp, highlighting the symbolic meanings of rest, stability, and completion.
    - Encourage the congregation to understand and appreciate the symbolic meanings behind actions and placements within their spiritual practices.

3. **Coordination and Support:**
    - Discuss the coordination among the tribes of Ephraim, Manasseh, and Benjamin, emphasising the importance of mutual support and cooperation within the community.
    - Emphasise the need for believers to practise coordination and mutual support in their community activities, recognising the strength that comes from cooperation.

**Working Example for Religious Leaders:**
**Example:** "Building a Supportive Church Community"

- **Scenario:** Imagine your church is working on a community outreach project, such as a food bank. Different teams will handle various aspects: collection, distribution, and community engagement.
- **Action:** Recognise and assign significant roles to individuals based on their strengths and capabilities, ensuring that each role is respected and valued.
- **Symbolism:** Use symbolic actions such as dedicating the west corner of the church for community support activities, symbolising stability and completion.
- **Outcome:** By recognising roles, appreciating symbolism, and fostering coordination, the outreach project becomes a successful and cohesive effort, reflecting the principles from the arrangement of the camp of Ephraim.

**Conclusion:**

- Summarise the key lessons from the arrangement of the camp of Ephraim, focusing on the significance of roles, symbolic direction, and coordination and support.
- Challenge the congregation to apply these principles in their modern spiritual practices and community life.
- Offer a prayer for guidance, recognition of significant roles, and a deeper commitment to practising coordination and support within the community.

**Link to Modern-Day Problems:**
◈ **Recognising Roles in Church:** How can modern churches benefit from recognising and respecting significant roles within their

communities, ensuring that all members contribute effectively, inspired by the placement of Ephraim's camp?

◈ **Symbolic Placement:** What steps can believers take to understand and appreciate the symbolic meanings behind actions and placements within their spiritual practices and traditions?

◈ **Cooperation and Support:** How can believers practise coordination and mutual support in their modern spiritual practices and community life, recognising the importance of cooperation for effective functioning?

◈ **Significance and Symbolism:** In what ways can modern churches recognise and respect significant roles within their communities and understand the symbolic meanings behind actions and placements, inspired by the arrangement of the camp of Ephraim?

**The Camp of Dan and Conclusion**
**Numbers 2:25-34 (NIV)**

1. On the north will be the divisions of the camp of Dan under their standard. The leader of the people of Dan is Ahiezer son of Ammishaddai.
2. His division numbers 62,700.
3. The tribe of Asher will camp next to them. The leader of the people of Asher is Pagiel son of Okran.
4. His division numbers 41,500.
5. The tribe of Naphtali will be next. The leader of the people of Naphtali is Ahira son of Enan.
6. His division numbers 53,400.
7. All the men assigned to the camp of Dan number 157,600. They will set out last, under their standards.
8. These are the Israelites, counted according to their families. All the men in the camps, by their divisions, number 603,550.

9.  The Levites, however, were not counted along with the other Israelites, as the Lord commanded Moses.
10. So the Israelites did everything the Lord commanded Moses; that is the way they encamped under their standards, and that is the way they set out, each of them with their clan and family.

**Theological Significance:**

- **Guardianship and Defence:** The placement of the camp of Dan to the north, along with Asher and Naphtali, underscores their role as guardians and defenders of the community. The north, often seen as a direction of threat, is strategically protected.
- **Completeness and Order:** The detailed enumeration and arrangement of all the tribes reflect the completeness and order that God desires for His people. This order ensures that each tribe has a specific place and role.
- **Obedience to Divine Instructions:** The meticulous following of God's commands in the arrangement of the camp underscores the importance of obedience and the blessings that come from adhering to divine instructions.

**Modern Interpretation:**
The camp of Dan and the conclusion of the census teach modern believers about the importance of guardianship and defence, the value of completeness and order, and the necessity of obedience to God's instructions.

**Key Themes:**

- **Guardianship and Defence:** The strategic placement of the camp of Dan highlights the importance of protecting and defending the community.

- **Completeness and Order:** The detailed arrangement of the tribes reflects the value of completeness and order within the community.
- **Obedience to Divine Instructions:** The careful adherence to God's commands emphasises the importance of obedience and the resulting blessings.

**Modern-Day Examples:**

- **Community Guardianship:** Modern churches can benefit from appointing guardians and defenders within their communities to ensure safety and security.
- **Order in Church Life:** Just as the tribes were meticulously arranged, modern faith communities can adopt practices that promote order and completeness.
- **Following God's Instructions:** Believers should strive to follow God's instructions in their personal and communal lives, recognising the importance of obedience for spiritual well-being.

**Questions for Reflection and Discussion:**

1. How does the placement of the camp of Dan highlight the importance of guardianship and defence within the community?
2. What can we learn from the detailed arrangement of the tribes about the value of completeness and order in our communities?
3. How can believers practise guardianship and promote order in their modern spiritual practices and community life?

4.  In what ways can modern churches adopt practices that
    promote order and completeness, inspired by the
    arrangement of the Israelite camps?

**Sermon Notes for Religious Leaders:**
**Title:** "Guardianship, Order, and Obedience: Lessons from the
Camp of Dan and Conclusion of the Census"
**Introduction:**

- Introduce the arrangement of the camp of Dan and the
  conclusion of the census in Numbers 2, focusing on the
  significance of guardianship, completeness and order, and
  obedience to divine instructions.
- Highlight the themes of guardianship and defence,
  completeness and order, and obedience to divine
  instructions.

**Body:**

1.  **Guardianship and Defence:**
    - Discuss the importance of the camp of Dan's
      strategic placement to the north, highlighting the
      role of guardianship and defence within the
      community.
    - Reflect on how these principles can be applied to
      modern spiritual practices, encouraging believers
      to appoint guardians and defenders within their
      communities.
2.  **Completeness and Order:**
    - Explore the detailed arrangement of the tribes,
      highlighting the value of completeness and order
      in community life.
    - Encourage the congregation to adopt practices

that promote order and completeness, recognising the importance of structure in fulfiling God's purposes.

3. **Obedience to Divine Instructions:**
   - Discuss the meticulous following of God's commands in the arrangement of the camp, emphasising the importance of obedience and the resulting blessings.
   - Emphasise the need for believers to strive for obedience to divine instructions in their personal and communal lives.

**Working Example for Religious Leaders:**

**Example:** "Establishing Safety and Order in Church Activities"

- **Scenario:** Imagine your church is planning a large community event. To ensure safety and smooth operation, different teams will handle security, logistics, and hospitality.
- **Action:** Assign individuals to security roles, placing them strategically to guard entrances and key areas, similar to the placement of the camp of Dan.
- **Order:** Implement detailed plans for logistics and hospitality, ensuring every task is assigned and every area is covered, reflecting the order and completeness of the tribal arrangements.
- **Outcome:** By focusing on guardianship, detailed planning, and obedience to guidelines, the event runs smoothly and safely, embodying the principles from the arrangement of the camp of Dan.

**Conclusion:**

- Summarise the key lessons from the arrangement of the camp of Dan and the conclusion of the census, focusing on guardianship and defence, completeness and order, and obedience to divine instructions.
- Challenge the congregation to apply these principles in their modern spiritual practices and community life.
- Offer a prayer for guidance, guardianship, and a deeper commitment to following God's instructions and promoting order within their communities.

**Link to Modern-Day Problems:**

◇ **Community Guardianship:** How can modern churches benefit from appointing guardians and defenders within their communities to ensure safety and security, inspired by the placement of the camp of Dan?

◇ **Order in Church Life:** What steps can faith communities take to adopt practices that promote order and completeness, recognising the value of detailed arrangement and structure in fulfiling God's purposes?

◇ **Following God's Instructions:** How can believers practise obedience to divine instructions in their personal and communal lives, recognising the importance of obedience for spiritual well-being, inspired by the meticulous following of God's commands in the arrangement of the camp?

◇ **Guardianship, Order, and Obedience:** In what ways can modern churches adopt practices that promote guardianship, order, and completeness within their communities, ensuring that they are organised and spiritually meaningful, inspired by the arrangement of the Israelite camps?

# The Levites and Their Duties

The Appointment of the Levites
### Numbers 3:1-13 (NIV)

1. This is the account of the family of Aaron and Moses at the time the Lord spoke to Moses at Mount Sinai.
2. The names of the sons of Aaron were Nadab the firstborn and Abihu, Eleazar and Ithamar.
3. Those were the names of Aaron's sons, the anointed priests, who were ordained to serve as priests.
4. Nadab and Abihu, however, died before the Lord when they made an offering with unauthorised fire before him in the Desert of Sinai. They had no sons, so Eleazar and Ithamar served as priests during the lifetime of their father Aaron.
5. The Lord said to Moses,
6. "Bring the tribe of Levi and present them to Aaron the priest to assist him.
7. They are to perform duties for him and for the whole community at the tent of meeting by doing the work of the tabernacle.
8. They are to take care of all the furnishings of the tent of meeting, fulfiling the obligations of the Israelites by doing the work of the tabernacle.
9. Give the Levites to Aaron and his sons; they are the Israelites who are to be given wholly to him.

10. Appoint Aaron and his sons to serve as priests; anyone else who approaches the sanctuary is to be put to death."
11. The Lord also said to Moses,
12. "I have taken the Levites from among the Israelites in place of the first male offspring of every Israelite woman. The Levites are mine,
13. for all the firstborn are mine. When I struck down all the firstborn in Egypt, I set apart for myself every firstborn in Israel, whether human or animal. They are to be mine. I am the Lord."

**Theological Significance:**

- **Divine Choice:** The selection of the Levites to serve in the tabernacle highlights God's sovereignty in choosing who will serve Him. This choice is a reminder that divine callings are purposeful and significant.
- **Substitution and Redemption:** The Levites are taken in place of the firstborn of Israel, signifying a form of substitution and redemption. This prefigures the concept of redemption that is fully realised in the New Testament.
- **Holiness and Service:** The dedication of the Levites to the service of the tabernacle underscores the importance of holiness and dedicated service in the life of believers.

**Modern Interpretation:**

This passage teaches modern believers about the significance of divine calling, the importance of understanding spiritual substitution and redemption, and the necessity of dedicated service in their spiritual lives.

**Key Themes:**

- **Divine Calling:** The passage underscores the importance of recognising and responding to God's calling in one's life.
- **Substitution and Redemption:** The Levites' role in place of the firstborn highlights themes of substitution and redemption that are central to Christian theology.
- **Holiness and Service:** The dedication of the Levites to the tabernacle service emphasises the need for holiness and committed service in the life of every believer.

**Modern-Day Examples:**

- **Recognising Calling:** Modern believers can seek to understand and follow God's calling in their lives, recognising the significance of divine purpose.
- **Embracing Redemption:** Understanding the concept of spiritual substitution and redemption can deepen one's faith and appreciation of Jesus' sacrifice.
- **Dedicated Service:** Just as the Levites were dedicated to tabernacle service, believers can commit themselves to serving in their communities and churches with dedication and holiness.

**Questions for Reflection and Discussion:**

1. How does the selection of the Levites highlight the importance of divine calling and purpose in one's life?
2. What can we learn from the concept of substitution and redemption as seen in the Levites' role in place of the firstborn?
3. How can believers practise dedicated service and holiness in their modern spiritual practices and community life?
4. In what ways can modern Christians recognise and

respond to God's calling in their lives, inspired by the appointment of the Levites?

**Sermon Notes for Religious Leaders:**
**Title:** "Divine Calling, Redemption, and Service: Lessons from the Appointment of the Levites"
**Introduction:**

- Introduce the appointment of the Levites in Numbers 3, focusing on the significance of divine calling, substitution and redemption, and dedicated service.
- Highlight the themes of divine calling, spiritual substitution and redemption, and holiness and service.

**Body:**

1. **Divine Calling:**
   - Discuss the importance of recognising and responding to God's calling in one's life, as illustrated by the selection of the Levites.
   - Reflect on how these principles can be applied to modern spiritual practices, encouraging believers to seek and follow God's purpose for their lives.
2. **Substitution and Redemption:**
   - Explore the concept of substitution and redemption as seen in the Levites' role in place of the firstborn, highlighting its theological significance.
   - Emphasise the importance of understanding and embracing the concept of spiritual redemption in one's faith journey.
3. **Holiness and Service:**
   - Discuss the dedication of the Levites to the

service of the tabernacle, emphasising the need for holiness and committed service in the life of believers.
  - Encourage the congregation to commit themselves to serving in their communities and churches with dedication and holiness.

**Working Example for Religious Leaders:**
**Example:** "Responding to God's Call in Our Lives"

- **Scenario:** Imagine a member of your congregation feels a calling to start a new ministry, such as a community outreach programme.
- **Action:** Help them recognise and affirm this calling by providing support, guidance, and resources. Encourage them to understand their role in God's plan, much like the Levites were chosen for a specific purpose.
- **Redemption:** Use this opportunity to teach about spiritual redemption, highlighting how their service reflects the broader theme of substitution and redemption in the Bible.
- **Outcome:** By recognising and responding to God's calling, the new ministry flourishes and becomes a vital part of the church's mission, reflecting the principles from the appointment of the Levites.

**Conclusion:**

- Summarise the key lessons from the appointment of the Levites, focusing on divine calling, substitution and redemption, and dedicated service.
- Challenge the congregation to apply these principles in

their modern spiritual practices and community life.

- Offer a prayer for guidance, recognition of God's calling, and a deeper commitment to holiness and service.

**Link to Modern-Day Problems:**

◇ **Recognising Calling:** How can modern believers seek to understand and follow God's calling in their lives, recognising the significance of divine purpose, inspired by the selection of the Levites?

◇ **Embracing Redemption:** What steps can believers take to deepen their understanding of spiritual substitution and redemption, recognising its importance in their faith journey?

◇ **Dedicated Service:** How can believers commit themselves to serving in their communities and churches with dedication and holiness, inspired by the dedication of the Levites to the tabernacle service?

◇ **Divine Calling and Service:** In what ways can modern Christians recognise and respond to God's calling in their lives, ensuring that they live out their purpose with dedication and holiness, inspired by the appointment of the Levites?

**Duties of the Levites**

**Numbers 3:14-32 (NIV)**

1. The Lord said to Moses in the Desert of Sinai,
2. "Count the Levites by their families and clans. Count every male a month old or more."
3. So Moses counted them, as he was commanded by the word of the Lord.
4. These were the names of the sons of Levi: Gershon, Kohath and Merari.
5. These were the names of the Gershonite clans: Libni and Shimei.
6. The Kohathite clans: Amram, Izhar, Hebron and Uzziel.

7.  The Merarite clans: Mahli and Mushi. These were the
    Levite clans, according to their families.

8.  To Gershon belonged the clans of the Libnites and
    Shimeites; these were the Gershonite clans.

9.  The number of all the males a month old or more who
    were counted was 7,500.

10. The Gershonite clans were to camp on the west, behind the
    tabernacle.

11. The leader of the families of the Gershonites was Eliasaph
    son of Lael.

12. At the tent of meeting the Gershonites were responsible
    for the care of the tabernacle and tent, its coverings, the
    curtain at the entrance to the tent of meeting,

13. the curtains of the courtyard, the curtain at the entrance to
    the courtyard surrounding the tabernacle and altar, and the
    ropes—and everything related to their use.

14. To Kohath belonged the clans of the Amramites, Izharites,
    Hebronites and Uzzielites; these were the Kohathite clans.

15. The number of all the males a month old or more was
    8,600. The Kohathites were responsible for the care of the
    sanctuary.

16. The Kohathite clans were to camp on the south side of the
    tabernacle.

17. The leader of the families of the Kohathite clans was
    Elizaphan son of Uzziel.

18. They were responsible for the care of the ark, the table, the
    lampstand, the altars, the articles of the sanctuary used in
    ministering, the curtain, and everything related to their
    use.

19. The chief leader of the Levites was Eleazar son of Aaron,
    the priest. He was appointed over those who were
    responsible for the care of the sanctuary.

**Theological Significance:**

- **Specific Roles and Responsibilities:** The division of duties among the Levite clans underscores the importance of specific roles and responsibilities within the community. Each clan had a unique role to play, ensuring the proper functioning of the tabernacle.
- **Attention to Detail:** The meticulous listing of duties reflects the importance of attention to detail in service to God. Every task, no matter how small, is significant in the context of divine service.
- **Holiness of Service:** The roles assigned to the Levites highlight the sacred nature of their duties. Caring for the tabernacle and its furnishings was not just a task but a holy service.

**Modern Interpretation:**

This passage teaches modern believers about the importance of recognising and fulfiling specific roles within their communities, the value of attention to detail in service, and the sacredness of all forms of service to God.

**Key Themes:**

- **Specific Roles:** The passage highlights the importance of recognising and fulfiling specific roles within the community, ensuring that every task is done efficiently and effectively.
- **Attention to Detail:** The meticulous detailing of duties underscores the value of attention to detail in service to God.
- **Holiness of Service:** The sacred nature of the Levites' duties emphasises the importance of viewing all forms of

service as holy and significant.

**Modern-Day Examples:**

- **Recognising Roles:** Modern believers can strive to
  understand and fulfil their specific roles within their
  communities, recognising the importance of each task.
- **Attention to Detail:** Emphasising the importance of
  attention to detail in all forms of service can enhance the
  quality and effectiveness of community and church
  activities.
- **Sacred Service:** Viewing all forms of service, no matter
  how small, as holy can inspire greater dedication and
  commitment among believers.

**Questions for Reflection and Discussion:**

1. How does the division of duties among the Levite clans
   highlight the importance of recognising and fulfiling
   specific roles within the community?
2. What can we learn from the meticulous detailing of duties
   about the value of attention to detail in service to God?
3. How can believers practise recognising and fulfiling their
   specific roles within their modern spiritual practices and
   community life?
4. In what ways can modern Christians view all forms of
   service as holy and significant, inspired by the roles
   assigned to the Levites?

**Sermon Notes for Religious Leaders:**
**Title:** "Roles, Details, and Holiness: Lessons from the Duties of
the Levites"
**Introduction:**

- Introduce the duties of the Levites in Numbers 3, focusing on the significance of specific roles, attention to detail, and the holiness of service.
- Highlight the themes of recognising specific roles, attention to detail, and viewing service as sacred.

**Body:**

1. **Recognising Specific Roles:**
   - Discuss the importance of recognising and fulfiling specific roles within the community, as illustrated by the division of duties among the Levite clans.
   - Reflect on how these principles can be applied to modern spiritual practices, encouraging believers to understand and fulfil their specific roles within their communities.

2. **Attention to Detail:**
   - Explore the meticulous detailing of duties, highlighting the value of attention to detail in service to God.
   - Encourage the congregation to emphasise the importance of attention to detail in all forms of service, recognising its impact on the quality and effectiveness of their efforts.

3. **Holiness of Service:**
   - Discuss the sacred nature of the Levites' duties, emphasising the importance of viewing all forms of service as holy and significant.
   - Emphasise the need for believers to approach all forms of service with dedication and commitment, recognising their sacred nature.

**Working Example for Religious Leaders:**
**Example:** "Fulfiling Our Roles in Church Ministry"

- **Scenario:** Imagine organising a church event where different teams handle various aspects like setup, hospitality, and worship.
- **Action:** Assign specific roles to individuals, ensuring they understand the significance of their tasks. Emphasise the importance of attention to detail in their preparations.
- **Holiness:** Encourage everyone to view their roles as sacred service, recognising that each task contributes to the overall success of the event.
- **Outcome:** By recognising roles, focusing on details, and viewing service as holy, the event runs smoothly and becomes a meaningful experience for all, reflecting the principles from the duties of the Levites.

## Conclusion:

- Summarise the key lessons from the duties of the Levites, focusing on recognising specific roles, attention to detail, and the holiness of service.
- Challenge the congregation to apply these principles in their modern spiritual practices and community life.
- Offer a prayer for guidance, dedication, and a deeper commitment to recognising roles, focusing on details, and viewing service as sacred.

**Link to Modern-Day Problems:**
◈ **Recognising Roles:** How can modern believers strive to understand and fulfil their specific roles within their communities,

recognising the importance of each task, inspired by the division of duties among the Levite clans?

◈ **Attention to Detail:** What steps can believers take to emphasise the importance of attention to detail in all forms of service, enhancing the quality and effectiveness of community and church activities?

◈ **Sacred Service:** How can believers practise viewing all forms of service, no matter how small, as holy and significant, inspired by the roles assigned to the Levites?

◈ **Roles, Details, and Holiness:** In what ways can modern Christians recognise and fulfil their specific roles, focus on attention to detail, and view all forms of service as holy and significant, inspired by the duties of the Levites?

**The Gershonites, Kohathites, and Merarites**
**Numbers 3:33-39 (NIV)**

1. To Merari belonged the clans of the Mahlites and the Mushites; these were the Merarite clans.
2. The number of all the males a month old or more who were counted was 6,200.
3. The leader of the families of the Merarite clans was Zuriel son of Abihail. They were to camp on the north side of the tabernacle.
4. The Merarites were appointed to take care of the frames of the tabernacle, its crossbars, posts, bases, all its equipment, and everything related to their use,
5. as well as the posts of the surrounding courtyard with their bases, tent pegs and ropes.
6. Moses and Aaron and his sons were to camp to the east of the tabernacle, toward the sunrise, in front of the tent of meeting. They were responsible for the care of the sanctuary on behalf of the Israelites. Anyone else who

approached the sanctuary was to be put to death.

7.  The total number of Levites counted at the Lord's command by Moses and Aaron according to their clans, including every male a month old or more, was 22,000.

## Theological Significance:

- **Varied Responsibilities:** The specific tasks assigned to the Gershonites, Kohathites, and Merarites highlight the diversity of roles within the community. Each clan had a unique and essential function, contributing to the overall operation and maintenance of the tabernacle.
- **Family and Community:** The detailed listing of family leaders and their responsibilities underscores the importance of family units in the functioning of the community. Each family played a vital role in the communal worship and service to God.
- **Guarding the Sacred:** The instruction that anyone who approached the sanctuary unlawfully would be put to death emphasises the seriousness of guarding the sacred. This underscores the holiness of the tabernacle and the importance of maintaining its sanctity.

## Modern Interpretation:

This passage teaches modern believers about the importance of diverse roles within the community, the significance of family units in communal worship, and the seriousness of guarding what is sacred.

## Key Themes:

- **Diverse Roles:** The passage highlights the importance of recognising and fulfiling diverse roles within the community, ensuring that every task is done efficiently and effectively.

- **Family and Community:** The detailed listing of family leaders underscores the significance of family units in communal worship and service to God.
- **Guarding the Sacred:** The instruction to guard the sanctuary emphasises the importance of maintaining the sanctity of worship spaces and practices.

**Modern-Day Examples:**

- **Recognising Diverse Roles:** Modern believers can strive to understand and fulfil their diverse roles within their communities, recognising the importance of each task.
- **Family Worship:** Emphasising the role of family units in communal worship can strengthen the overall spiritual life of the community.
- **Guarding Sacred Spaces:** Viewing worship spaces and practices as sacred can inspire greater dedication and respect among believers.

**Questions for Reflection and Discussion:**

1. How does the division of tasks among the Gershonites, Kohathites, and Merarites highlight the importance of diverse roles within the community?
2. What can we learn from the detailed listing of family leaders about the significance of family units in communal worship and service to God?
3. How can believers practise recognising and fulfiling their diverse roles within their modern spiritual practices and community life?

4. In what ways can modern Christians view worship spaces and practices as sacred, inspired by the instruction to guard the sanctuary?

**Sermon Notes for Religious Leaders:**

**Title:** "Diversity, Family, and Sanctity: Lessons from the Gershonites, Kohathites, and Merarites"

**Introduction:**

- Introduce the roles of the Gershonites, Kohathites, and Merarites in Numbers 3, focusing on the significance of diverse roles, family units, and guarding the sacred.
- Highlight the themes of recognising diverse roles, the importance of family in worship, and maintaining sanctity.

**Body:**

1. **Recognising Diverse Roles:**
   - Discuss the importance of recognising and fulfiling diverse roles within the community, as illustrated by the tasks assigned to the Gershonites, Kohathites, and Merarites.
   - Reflect on how these principles can be applied to modern spiritual practices, encouraging believers to understand and fulfil their diverse roles within their communities.

2. **Family and Community:**
   - Explore the detailed listing of family leaders, highlighting the significance of family units in communal worship and service to God.
   - Encourage the congregation to emphasise the role of family in worship, recognising its impact on the overall spiritual life of the community.

3. **Guarding the Sacred:**
    - Discuss the instruction to guard the sanctuary, emphasising the importance of maintaining the sanctity of worship spaces and practices.
    - Emphasise the need for believers to approach worship with dedication and respect, recognising the sacredness of their practices.

**Working Example for Religious Leaders:**
**Example:** "Building a Spiritually Strong Community"

- **Scenario:** Imagine your church is developing a new initiative to involve families in various ministries. Each family will take on specific roles, such as hospitality, teaching, and maintenance.
- **Action:** Assign roles to each family, ensuring they understand the significance of their tasks. Emphasise the importance of family involvement in communal worship.
- **Sanctity:** Encourage families to approach their roles with dedication and respect, viewing their tasks as sacred service to God.
- **Outcome:** By recognising diverse roles, involving families, and maintaining a sense of sanctity, the initiative strengthens the overall spiritual life of the community, reflecting the principles from the roles of the Gershonites, Kohathites, and Merarites.

**Conclusion:**

- Summarise the key lessons from the roles of the Gershonites, Kohathites, and Merarites, focusing on recognising diverse roles, the importance of family in worship, and maintaining sanctity.

- Challenge the congregation to apply these principles in their modern spiritual practices and community life.
- Offer a prayer for guidance, dedication, and a deeper commitment to recognising diverse roles, involving families, and guarding the sanctity of worship.

**Link to Modern-Day Problems:**

◈ **Recognising Diverse Roles:** How can modern believers strive to understand and fulfil their diverse roles within their communities, recognising the importance of each task, inspired by the division of tasks among the Gershonites, Kohathites, and Merarites?

◈ **Family Worship:** What steps can faith communities take to emphasise the role of family units in communal worship, strengthening the overall spiritual life of the community?

◈ **Guarding Sacred Spaces:** How can believers practise viewing worship spaces and practices as sacred, inspiring greater dedication and respect among community members?

◈ **Diversity, Family, and Sanctity:** In what ways can modern Christians recognise and fulfil their diverse roles, involve families in worship, and maintain the sanctity of their practices, inspired by the roles of the Gershonites, Kohathites, and Merarites?

**The Redemption of the Firstborn**
**Numbers 3:40-51 (NIV)**

1. The Lord said to Moses, "Count all the firstborn Israelite males who are a month old or more and make a list of their names.
2. Take the Levites for me in place of all the firstborn of the Israelites, and the livestock of the Levites in place of all the firstborn of the livestock of the Israelites. I am the Lord."
3. So Moses counted all the firstborn of the Israelites, as the

Lord commanded him.

4. The total number of firstborn males a month old or more, listed by name, was 22,273.

5. The Lord also said to Moses,

6. "Take the Levites in place of all the firstborn of Israel and the livestock of the Levites in place of their livestock. The Levites are to be mine. I am the Lord.

7. To redeem the 273 firstborn Israelites who exceed the number of the Levites,

8. collect five shekels for each one, according to the sanctuary shekel, which weighs twenty gerahs.

9. Give the money for the redemption of the additional Israelites to Aaron and his sons."

10. So Moses collected the redemption money from those who exceeded the number redeemed by the Levites.

11. From the firstborn of the Israelites he collected silver weighing 1,365 shekels, according to the sanctuary shekel.

12. Moses gave the redemption money to Aaron and his sons, as he was commanded by the word of the Lord.

**Theological Significance:**

- **Redemption and Substitution:** The redemption of the firstborn highlights the themes of substitution and redemption, illustrating God's provision and care for His people. The Levites take the place of the firstborn, symbolising God's claim over them.

- **Value of Life:** The specific monetary value placed on the redemption of the firstborn underscores the value of life and the importance of recognising God's ownership over all creation.

- **Divine Ownership:** The repeated assertion that the

Levites and the firstborn belong to God emphasises His sovereignty and ownership over His people.

**Modern Interpretation:**

This passage teaches modern believers about the importance of understanding spiritual redemption and substitution, the value of life, and recognising God's ownership over all creation.

**Key Themes:**

- **Redemption and Substitution:** The passage highlights the importance of understanding spiritual redemption and substitution in the context of faith.
- **Value of Life:** The monetary value placed on redemption underscores the inherent value of life and the need to recognise God's ownership.
- **Divine Ownership:** The repeated assertion of God's ownership over the Levites and the firstborn emphasises His sovereignty over all creation.

**Modern-Day Examples:**

- **Understanding Redemption:** Modern believers can deepen their faith by understanding and appreciating the concept of spiritual redemption and substitution.
- **Valuing Life:** Emphasising the value of life can inspire greater respect for the sanctity of life and a deeper commitment to protecting and nurturing it.
- **Recognising God's Ownership:** Recognising God's ownership over all creation can inspire believers to live with a greater sense of stewardship and responsibility.

**Questions for Reflection and Discussion:**

1. How does the redemption of the firstborn highlight the themes of substitution and redemption in the context of faith?
2. What can we learn from the monetary value placed on redemption about the inherent value of life and God's ownership?
3. How can believers deepen their understanding and appreciation of spiritual redemption and substitution in their modern spiritual practices?
4. In what ways can modern Christians recognise and live out the concept of God's ownership over all creation?

**Sermon Notes for Religious Leaders:**
**Title:** "Redemption, Value, and Ownership: Lessons from the Redemption of the Firstborn"
**Introduction:**

- Introduce the redemption of the firstborn in Numbers 3, focusing on the significance of redemption and substitution, the value of life, and recognising God's ownership.
- Highlight the themes of understanding spiritual redemption, valuing life, and recognising divine ownership.

**Body:**

1. **Redemption and Substitution:**
   - Discuss the importance of understanding spiritual redemption and substitution, as illustrated by the redemption of the firstborn.
   - Reflect on how these principles can deepen one's faith and appreciation of God's provision and

care.

2.  **Value of Life:**
    - ○ Explore the monetary value placed on the
      redemption of the firstborn, highlighting the
      inherent value of life and God's ownership.
    - ○ Encourage the congregation to emphasise the
      sanctity of life and commit to protecting and
      nurturing it.

3.  **Recognising God's Ownership:**
    - ○ Discuss the repeated assertion of God's ownership
      over the Levites and the firstborn, emphasising
      His sovereignty over all creation.
    - ○ Emphasise the need for believers to recognise and
      live out the concept of God's ownership, inspiring
      a greater sense of stewardship and responsibility.

**Working Example for Religious Leaders:**
**Example:** "Living Out Redemption and Stewardship"

- **Scenario:** Imagine a church initiative focused on
  environmental stewardship, recognising God's ownership
  over creation. Each member is encouraged to take practical
  steps to care for the environment.
- **Action:** Teach about the concept of redemption and
  substitution, drawing parallels to the importance of caring
  for God's creation. Assign specific roles and tasks to
  members, similar to the redemption and substitution of
  the firstborn.
- **Value of Life:** Emphasise the inherent value of life and the
  importance of protecting and nurturing it, extending this
  principle to environmental stewardship.
- **Outcome:** By understanding and living out the concepts

of redemption, valuing life, and recognising God's ownership, the initiative fosters a greater sense of responsibility and stewardship among members, reflecting the principles from the redemption of the firstborn.

**Conclusion:**

- Summarise the key lessons from the redemption of the firstborn, focusing on understanding spiritual redemption, valuing life, and recognising divine ownership.
- Challenge the congregation to apply these principles in their modern spiritual practices and community life.
- Offer a prayer for guidance, appreciation of redemption, and a deeper commitment to valuing life and recognising God's ownership.

**Link to Modern-Day Problems:**

◇ **Understanding Redemption:** How can modern believers deepen their faith by understanding and appreciating the concept of spiritual redemption and substitution, inspired by the redemption of the firstborn?

◇ **Valuing Life:** What steps can believers take to emphasise the value of life, recognising the inherent value and God's ownership over all creation?

◇ **Recognising God's Ownership:** How can believers practise recognising and living out the concept of God's ownership over all creation, inspiring a greater sense of stewardship and responsibility?

◇ **Redemption, Value, and Ownership:** In what ways can modern Christians understand and appreciate spiritual redemption, value life, and recognise divine ownership, inspired by the redemption of the firstborn?

# Duties of the Kohathites, Gershonites, and Merarites

D uties of the Kohathites
Numbers 4:1-20 (NIV)

1. The Lord said to Moses and Aaron:
2. "Take a census of the Kohathite branch of the Levites by their clans and families.
3. Count all the men from thirty to fifty years of age who come to serve in the work at the tent of meeting.
4. This is the work of the Kohathites at the tent of meeting: the care of the most holy things.
5. When the camp is to move, Aaron and his sons are to go in and take down the shielding curtain and put it over the ark of the covenant law.
6. Then they are to cover the curtain with durable leather, spread a cloth of solid blue over that and put the poles in place.
7. Over the table of the Presence they are to spread a blue cloth and put on it the plates, dishes and bowls, and the jars for drink offerings; the bread that is continually there is to remain on it.
8. They are to spread a scarlet cloth over them, cover that with durable leather and put the poles in place.
9. They are to take a blue cloth and cover the lampstand that is for light, together with its lamps, its wick trimmers and

trays, and all its jars for the oil used to supply it.

10. Then they are to wrap it and all its accessories in a covering of durable leather and put it on a carrying frame.

11. Over the gold altar they are to spread a blue cloth and cover that with durable leather and put the poles in place.

12. They are to take all the articles used for ministering in the sanctuary, wrap them in a blue cloth, cover that with durable leather and put them on a carrying frame.

13. They are to remove the ashes from the bronze altar and spread a purple cloth over it.

14. Then they are to place on it all the utensils used for ministering at the altar, including the firepans, meat forks, shovels and sprinkling bowls. Over it they are to spread a covering of durable leather and put the poles in place.

15. After Aaron and his sons have finished covering the holy furnishings and all the holy articles, and when the camp is ready to move, only then are the Kohathites to come and do the carrying. But they must not touch the holy things or they will die. The Kohathites are to carry those things that are in the tent of meeting.

16. Eleazar son of Aaron, the priest, is to have charge of the oil for the light, the fragrant incense, the regular grain offering and the anointing oil. He is to be in charge of the entire tabernacle and everything in it, including its holy furnishings and articles."

17. The Lord said to Moses and Aaron,

18. "See that the Kohathite tribal clans are not cut off from the Levites.

19. So that they may live and not die when they come near the most holy things, do this for them: Aaron and his sons are to go into the sanctuary and assign to each man his work and what he is to carry.

20. But the Kohathites must not go in to look at the holy things, even for a moment, or they will die."

**Theological Significance:**

- **Holy Responsibilities:** The Kohathites were assigned the care of the most holy things, emphasising the importance and sacredness of their duties. Handling these sacred objects required great reverence and precision.
- **Order and Precision:** The detailed instructions for packing and covering the sacred objects underscore the importance of order and precision in worship and service to God.
- **Life and Death:** The stipulation that the Kohathites must not touch or even look at the holy things lest they die highlights the seriousness of approaching God's holiness improperly. This teaches the reverence and caution required in sacred duties.

**Modern Interpretation:**

This passage teaches modern believers about the importance of reverence and precision in their spiritual duties, the seriousness of approaching God's holiness, and the need for careful obedience to divine instructions.

**Key Themes:**

- **Reverence in Service:** The duties of the Kohathites highlight the importance of reverence and carefulness in serving God.
- **Order and Precision:** The detailed instructions for handling sacred objects underscore the value of order and precision in worship.

- **Holiness and Life:** The consequences of improper handling of holy things teach the seriousness of approaching God's holiness with the right attitude and respect.

**Modern-Day Examples:**

- **Reverence in Worship:** Modern believers can approach their worship and service with reverence and carefulness, recognising the sacredness of their duties.
- **Attention to Detail:** Emphasising the importance of order and precision in spiritual practices can enhance the quality and reverence of worship.
- **Respect for Holiness:** Recognising the seriousness of approaching God's holiness can inspire greater respect and caution in spiritual matters.

**Questions for Reflection and Discussion:**

1. How does the care of the most holy things assigned to the Kohathites highlight the importance of reverence and precision in serving God?
2. What can we learn from the detailed instructions for packing and covering the sacred objects about the value of order and precision in worship?
3. How can believers practise reverence and carefulness in their modern spiritual duties and worship practices?
4. In what ways can modern Christians recognise and respect the seriousness of approaching God's holiness, inspired by the instructions given to the Kohathites?

**Sermon Notes for Religious Leaders:**

**Title:** "Reverence, Order, and Holiness: Lessons from the Duties of the Kohathites"

**Introduction:**

- Introduce the duties of the Kohathites in Numbers 4, focusing on the significance of reverence, order, and the seriousness of approaching God's holiness.
- Highlight the themes of reverence in service, order and precision, and holiness and life.

**Body:**

1. **Reverence in Service:**
   - Discuss the importance of reverence and carefulness in serving God, as illustrated by the duties of the Kohathites.
   - Reflect on how these principles can be applied to modern spiritual practices, encouraging believers to approach their worship and service with reverence.

2. **Order and Precision:**
   - Explore the detailed instructions for handling sacred objects, highlighting the value of order and precision in worship.
   - Encourage the congregation to emphasise the importance of order and precision in their spiritual practices, recognising its impact on the quality and reverence of worship.

3. **Holiness and Life:**
   - Discuss the seriousness of approaching God's holiness improperly, as seen in the stipulation that the Kohathites must not touch or look at the holy things lest they die.

- ○ Emphasise the need for believers to recognise and respect the seriousness of approaching God's holiness, inspiring greater respect and caution in spiritual matters.

**Working Example for Religious Leaders:**
**Example:** "Approaching God's Holiness with Reverence"

- **Scenario:** Imagine your church is preparing for a significant worship service, such as Easter or Christmas. Each detail must be carefully planned and executed.
- **Action:** Assign specific roles to individuals, ensuring they understand the importance of reverence and precision in their tasks. Emphasise the sacredness of the service and the need for carefulness.
- **Holiness:** Encourage everyone involved to approach their roles with a deep sense of reverence and respect for God's holiness, recognising the significance of their service.
- **Outcome:** By approaching the service with reverence, order, and precision, the worship experience becomes deeply meaningful and spiritually enriching for all, reflecting the principles from the duties of the Kohathites.

**Conclusion:**

- Summarise the key lessons from the duties of the Kohathites, focusing on reverence in service, order and precision, and the seriousness of approaching God's holiness.
- Challenge the congregation to apply these principles in their modern spiritual practices and worship.
- Offer a prayer for guidance, reverence, and a deeper

commitment to approaching God's holiness with respect and caution.

**Link to Modern-Day Problems:**

◇ **Reverence in Worship:** How can modern believers approach their worship and service with reverence and carefulness, recognising the sacredness of their duties, inspired by the duties of the Kohathites?

◇ **Attention to Detail:** What steps can believers take to emphasise the importance of order and precision in their spiritual practices, enhancing the quality and reverence of worship?

◇ **Respect for Holiness:** How can believers recognise the seriousness of approaching God's holiness with the right attitude and respect, inspired by the instructions given to the Kohathites?

◇ **Reverence, Order, and Holiness:** In what ways can modern Christians practise reverence in service, order and precision, and respect for God's holiness, inspired by the duties of the Kohathites?

**Duties of the Gershonites**
**Numbers 4:21-28 (NIV)**

1. The Lord said to Moses,
2. "Take a census also of the Gershonites by their families and clans.
3. Count all the men from thirty to fifty years of age who come to serve in the work at the tent of meeting.
4. This is the service of the Gershonite clans in their carrying and their other work:
5. They are to carry the curtains of the tabernacle, that is, the tent of meeting, its covering and its outer covering of durable leather, the curtains for the entrance to the tent of meeting,
6. the curtains of the courtyard surrounding the tabernacle and altar, the curtain for the entrance to the courtyard, the

ropes, and all the equipment used in its service. The Gershonites are to do all that needs to be done with these things.

7.  All their service, whether carrying or doing other work, is to be done under the direction of Aaron and his sons. You shall assign to them as their responsibility all they are to carry.

8.  This is the service of the Gershonite clans at the tent of meeting. Their duties are to be under the direction of Ithamar son of Aaron, the priest.

**Theological Significance:**

- **Service and Support:** The duties of the Gershonites highlight the importance of service and support roles within the community. Though their tasks might seem less prominent than those of the Kohathites, they were essential for the functioning of the tabernacle.

- **Divine Assignment:** The specific tasks assigned to the Gershonites by God, through Moses, underscore the importance of each person's role in the divine plan. Every task, no matter how seemingly small, is significant when it contributes to the overall purpose.

- **Obedience and Direction:** The Gershonites were to perform their duties under the direction of Aaron and his sons, highlighting the importance of obedience and following leadership in service to God.

**Modern Interpretation:**

This passage teaches modern believers about the significance of service and support roles, the value of every task in God's plan, and the importance of obedience and direction in spiritual duties.

## Key Themes:

- **Service and Support:** The duties of the Gershonites emphasise the importance of service and support roles within the community.
- **Value of Every Task:** The specific tasks assigned to the Gershonites highlight the value of every task in God's plan, no matter how seemingly small.
- **Obedience and Direction:** The importance of obedience and following leadership in service to God is underscored by the Gershonites' duties under the direction of Aaron and his sons.

## Modern-Day Examples:

- **Recognising Support Roles:** Modern believers can recognise and appreciate the significance of support roles within their communities, understanding that every task contributes to the overall purpose.
- **Valuing Every Task:** Emphasising the value of every task in God's plan can inspire greater dedication and commitment among believers, recognising that all service is significant.
- **Following Leadership:** Practising obedience and following leadership in spiritual duties can enhance the effectiveness and harmony of community service.

## Questions for Reflection and Discussion:

1. How do the duties of the Gershonites highlight the importance of service and support roles within the community?

2. What can we learn from the specific tasks assigned to the Gershonites about the value of every task in God's plan?

3. How can believers practise recognising and appreciating support roles within their modern spiritual practices and community life?

4. In what ways can modern Christians emphasise the importance of obedience and following leadership in their spiritual duties, inspired by the Gershonites' service?

**Sermon Notes for Religious Leaders:**

**Title:** "Service, Value, and Obedience: Lessons from the Duties of the Gershonites"

**Introduction:**

- Introduce the duties of the Gershonites in Numbers 4, focusing on the significance of service and support roles, the value of every task, and the importance of obedience and direction in spiritual duties.
- Highlight the themes of recognising support roles, valuing every task, and following leadership.

**Body:**

1. **Service and Support:**
    - Discuss the importance of service and support roles within the community, as illustrated by the duties of the Gershonites.
    - Reflect on how these principles can be applied to modern spiritual practices, encouraging believers to recognise and appreciate support roles within their communities.

2. **Value of Every Task:**
    - Explore the specific tasks assigned to the

Gershonites, highlighting the value of every task in God's plan, no matter how seemingly small.

- Encourage the congregation to recognise the significance of every task in their service, inspiring greater dedication and commitment.

3. **Obedience and Direction:**
    - Discuss the importance of obedience and following leadership in spiritual duties, as seen in the Gershonites' service under the direction of Aaron and his sons.
    - Emphasise the need for believers to practise obedience and follow leadership in their spiritual duties, enhancing the effectiveness and harmony of community service.

**Working Example for Religious Leaders:**
**Example:** "Recognising and Valuing Support Roles"

- **Scenario:** Imagine your church is organising a community event where various support roles are crucial for its success, such as setup, hospitality, and logistics.
- **Action:** Assign specific support roles to individuals, ensuring they understand the significance of their tasks. Emphasise the importance of each role in the overall success of the event.
- **Obedience:** Encourage everyone involved to follow the direction of the event leaders, recognising the importance of obedience and leadership in their service.
- **Outcome:** By recognising and valuing support roles, and practising obedience and following leadership, the event runs smoothly and becomes a meaningful experience for all, reflecting the principles from the duties of the

Gershonites.

**Conclusion:**

- Summarise the key lessons from the duties of the Gershonites, focusing on recognising support roles, valuing every task, and following leadership.
- Challenge the congregation to apply these principles in their modern spiritual practices and community life.
- Offer a prayer for guidance, dedication, and a deeper commitment to recognising and valuing support roles, and following leadership in their service.

**Link to Modern-Day Problems:**

◇ **Recognising Support Roles:** How can modern believers recognise and appreciate the significance of support roles within their communities, understanding that every task contributes to the overall purpose, inspired by the duties of the Gershonites?

◇ **Valuing Every Task:** What steps can believers take to emphasise the value of every task in God's plan, inspiring greater dedication and commitment among community members?

◇ **Following Leadership:** How can believers practise obedience and following leadership in their spiritual duties, recognising the importance of leadership in enhancing the effectiveness and harmony of community service?

◇ **Service, Value, and Obedience:** In what ways can modern Christians recognise and value support roles, emphasise the importance of every task, and follow leadership in their spiritual duties, inspired by the Gershonites' service?

**Duties of the Merarites**
**Numbers 4:29-33 (NIV)**

1.  "Count the Merarites by their clans and families.

2. Count all the men from thirty to fifty years of age who
   come to serve in the work at the tent of meeting.
3. As part of all their service at the tent, they are to carry the
   frames of the tabernacle, its crossbars, posts and bases,
4. as well as the posts of the surrounding courtyard with their
   bases, tent pegs, ropes, all their equipment and everything
   related to their use. Assign to each man the specific things
   he is to carry.
5. This is the service of the Merarite clans as they work at the
   tent of meeting under the direction of Ithamar son of
   Aaron, the priest."

## Theological Significance:

- **Physical Labour and Service:** The duties of the Merarites
  highlight the importance of physical labour in the service
  of God. Carrying the heavy structures of the tabernacle
  required strength and dedication.
- **Teamwork and Organisation:** The detailed assignments
  for each man emphasise the importance of teamwork and
  organisation in accomplishing tasks. Each person had a
  specific role that contributed to the overall function of the
  tabernacle.
- **Divine Assignment:** The specific tasks assigned to the
  Merarites underscore the importance of fulfiling God-
  given responsibilities. Every role, including those involving
  physical labour, is valuable in the service of God.

### Modern Interpretation:

This passage teaches modern believers about the significance of
physical labour in service to God, the importance of teamwork and
organisation, and the value of fulfiling God-given responsibilities.

**Key Themes:**

- **Physical Labour in Service:** The passage highlights the importance of physical labour in the service of God, recognising it as valuable and significant.
- **Teamwork and Organisation:** The detailed assignments emphasise the importance of teamwork and organisation in accomplishing tasks effectively.
- **Divine Assignment:** The specific tasks assigned to the Merarites underscore the importance of fulfiling God-given responsibilities, recognising the value of every role.

**Modern-Day Examples:**

- **Valuing Physical Labour:** Modern believers can recognise and appreciate the significance of physical labour in their service, understanding its value in the broader context of worship and community service.
- **Practising Teamwork:** Emphasising the importance of teamwork and organisation in spiritual practices can enhance the effectiveness and harmony of community efforts.
- **Fulfiling Responsibilities:** Encouraging believers to fulfil their God-given responsibilities can inspire greater dedication and commitment to their roles.

**Questions for Reflection and Discussion:**

1. How do the duties of the Merarites highlight the importance of physical labour in the service of God?
2. What can we learn from the detailed assignments for the Merarites about the value of teamwork and organisation in

accomplishing tasks?

3.  How can believers practise recognising and valuing physical labour in their modern spiritual practices and community life?

4.  In what ways can modern Christians emphasise the importance of fulfiling God-given responsibilities, inspired by the duties of the Merarites?

**Sermon Notes for Religious Leaders:**

**Title:** "Labour, Teamwork, and Responsibility: Lessons from the Duties of the Merarites"

**Introduction:**

- Introduce the duties of the Merarites in Numbers 4, focusing on the significance of physical labour, teamwork, and fulfiling God-given responsibilities.
- Highlight the themes of recognising the value of physical labour, practising teamwork, and fulfiling responsibilities.

**Body:**

1.  **Physical Labour in Service:**
    - Discuss the importance of physical labour in the service of God, as illustrated by the duties of the Merarites.
    - Reflect on how these principles can be applied to modern spiritual practices, encouraging believers to recognise and value physical labour in their service.

2.  **Teamwork and Organisation:**
    - Explore the detailed assignments for the Merarites, highlighting the value of teamwork and organisation in accomplishing tasks effectively.

- Encourage the congregation to practise teamwork and organisation in their spiritual practices, recognising its impact on the effectiveness and harmony of their efforts.

3. **Fulfiling Responsibilities:**
   - Discuss the importance of fulfiling God-given responsibilities, as seen in the specific tasks assigned to the Merarites.
   - Emphasise the need for believers to fulfil their responsibilities with dedication and commitment, recognising the value of every role in the service of God.

**Working Example for Religious Leaders:**
**Example:** "Valuing Physical Labour in Church Projects"

- **Scenario:** Imagine your church is undertaking a significant building project, such as constructing a new community centre. Physical labour is crucial for its success.
- **Action:** Assign specific tasks to individuals, ensuring they understand the importance of their roles. Emphasise the value of physical labour in the broader context of the project.
- **Teamwork:** Encourage teamwork and organisation among those involved, recognising that each person's efforts contribute to the overall success.
- **Outcome:** By recognising the value of physical labour, practising teamwork, and fulfiling responsibilities, the project progresses smoothly and becomes a testament to the community's dedication, reflecting the principles from the duties of the Merarites.

**Conclusion:**

- Summarise the key lessons from the duties of the Merarites, focusing on recognising the value of physical labour, practising teamwork, and fulfiling responsibilities.
- Challenge the congregation to apply these principles in their modern spiritual practices and community life.
- Offer a prayer for guidance, dedication, and a deeper commitment to valuing physical labour, practising teamwork, and fulfiling responsibilities in their service.

**Link to Modern-Day Problems:**

◇ **Valuing Physical Labour:** How can modern believers recognise and appreciate the significance of physical labour in their service, understanding its value in the broader context of worship and community service, inspired by the duties of the Merarites?

◇ **Practising Teamwork:** What steps can believers take to emphasise the importance of teamwork and organisation in their spiritual practices, enhancing the effectiveness and harmony of community efforts?

◇ **Fulfiling Responsibilities:** How can believers practise fulfiling their God-given responsibilities with dedication and commitment, recognising the value of every role in the service of God, inspired by the Merarites' duties?

◇ **Labour, Teamwork, and Responsibility:** In what ways can modern Christians recognise the value of physical labour, practise teamwork, and fulfil responsibilities in their spiritual duties, inspired by the duties of the Merarites?

**Conclusion of Duties and Census of the Levites**
**Numbers 4:34-49 (NIV)**

1. Moses, Aaron, and the leaders of the community counted the Kohathites by their clans and families.

2. All the men from thirty to fifty years of age who came to serve in the work at the tent of meeting were counted by clans.

3. The number of all the men from thirty to fifty years of age was 2,750.

4. This was the total of all those in the Kohathite clans who served at the tent of meeting. Moses and Aaron counted them according to the Lord's command through Moses.

5. The Gershonites were counted by their clans and families.

6. All the men from thirty to fifty years of age who came to serve in the work at the tent of meeting

7. were counted by their clans and families. The number was 2,630.

8. This was the total of those in the Gershonite clans who served at the tent of meeting. Moses and Aaron counted them according to the Lord's command.

9. The Merarites were counted by their clans and families.

10. All the men from thirty to fifty years of age who came to serve in the work at the tent of meeting

11. were counted by their clans. The number was 3,200.

12. This was the total of those in the Merarite clans. Moses and Aaron counted them according to the Lord's command through Moses.

13. So Moses, Aaron, and the leaders of Israel counted all the Levites by their clans and families.

14. All the men from thirty to fifty years of age who came to do the work of serving and carrying the tent of meeting

15. numbered 8,580.

16. At the Lord's command through Moses, each was assigned his work and told what to carry. Thus they were counted, as the Lord commanded Moses.

**Theological Significance:**

- **Divine Order and Structure:** The detailed census and assignment of duties to the Levites reflect God's desire for order and structure in worship and service. Each person had a specific role, contributing to the overall functioning of the tabernacle.
- **Collective Responsibility:** The census underscores the collective responsibility of the Levites in serving God. Each clan and family had a part to play, highlighting the importance of community effort in spiritual service.
- **Obedience to God's Command:** The meticulous following of God's instructions for counting and assigning duties to the Levites emphasises the importance of obedience to divine commands.

**Modern Interpretation:**

This passage teaches modern believers about the importance of divine order and structure in spiritual service, the significance of collective responsibility, and the necessity of obedience to God's commands.

**Key Themes:**

- **Divine Order and Structure:** The passage highlights the importance of order and structure in worship and service, ensuring that each person's role contributes to the overall functioning.
- **Collective Responsibility:** The census underscores the significance of collective responsibility in spiritual service, recognising the importance of each person's contribution.
- **Obedience to God's Command:** The meticulous following of God's instructions emphasises the importance

of obedience in spiritual practices.

## Modern-Day Examples:

- **Promoting Order and Structure:** Modern believers can emphasise the importance of order and structure in their spiritual practices, recognising its value in ensuring effective service and worship.
- **Encouraging Collective Responsibility:** Highlighting the significance of collective responsibility can inspire greater community effort and dedication in spiritual service.
- **Practising Obedience:** Encouraging obedience to God's commands in all aspects of spiritual life can enhance the effectiveness and harmony of community efforts.

## Questions for Reflection and Discussion:

1. How does the detailed census and assignment of duties to the Levites highlight the importance of divine order and structure in spiritual service?
2. What can we learn from the collective responsibility of the Levites about the significance of community effort in serving God?
3. How can believers practise promoting order and structure in their modern spiritual practices and community life?
4. In what ways can modern Christians emphasise the importance of obedience to God's commands in their spiritual duties, inspired by the meticulous following of instructions for the Levites?

## Sermon Notes for Religious Leaders:

**Title:** "Order, Responsibility, and Obedience: Lessons from the Census of the Levites"

**Introduction:**

- Introduce the conclusion of the duties and census of the Levites in Numbers 4, focusing on the significance of divine order and structure, collective responsibility, and obedience to God's commands.
- Highlight the themes of promoting order and structure, encouraging collective responsibility, and practising obedience.

**Body:**

1. **Divine Order and Structure:**
   - Discuss the importance of order and structure in worship and service, as illustrated by the detailed census and assignment of duties to the Levites.
   - Reflect on how these principles can be applied to modern spiritual practices, encouraging believers to promote order and structure in their communities.

2. **Collective Responsibility:**
   - Explore the collective responsibility of the Levites in serving God, highlighting the significance of each person's contribution to the overall functioning.
   - Encourage the congregation to recognise the importance of community effort and dedication in spiritual service.

3. **Obedience to God's Command:**
   - Discuss the meticulous following of God's instructions for counting and assigning duties to

the Levites, emphasising the importance of
obedience in spiritual practices.

- ○ Emphasise the need for believers to practise
  obedience to God's commands in all aspects of
  their spiritual life, enhancing the effectiveness and
  harmony of their efforts.

**Working Example for Religious Leaders:**
**Example:** "Promoting Order and Responsibility in Church Service"

- **Scenario:** Imagine your church is planning a series of outreach programmes, involving various teams and activities. Each team must work together harmoniously to ensure success.
- **Action:** Assign specific roles and tasks to each team, emphasising the importance of order and structure in their activities. Encourage collective responsibility, recognising that each person's contribution is vital.
- **Obedience:** Stress the importance of following the church's guidelines and instructions for the programmes, ensuring that everyone understands their roles and responsibilities.
- **Outcome:** By promoting order and structure, encouraging collective responsibility, and practising obedience, the outreach programmes run smoothly and become a testament to the church's dedication, reflecting the principles from the census and duties of the Levites.

**Conclusion:**

- Summarise the key lessons from the conclusion of the

duties and census of the Levites, focusing on promoting order and structure, encouraging collective responsibility, and practising obedience.

- Challenge the congregation to apply these principles in their modern spiritual practices and community life.
- Offer a prayer for guidance, dedication, and a deeper commitment to promoting order and structure, encouraging collective responsibility, and practising obedience in their service.

**Link to Modern-Day Problems:**

◈ **Promoting Order and Structure:** How can modern believers emphasise the importance of order and structure in their spiritual practices, recognising its value in ensuring effective service and worship, inspired by the census and duties of the Levites?

◈ **Encouraging Collective Responsibility:** What steps can believers take to highlight the significance of collective responsibility in their communities, inspiring greater community effort and dedication in spiritual service?

◈ **Practising Obedience:** How can believers practise obedience to God's commands in all aspects of their spiritual life, enhancing the effectiveness and harmony of community efforts, inspired by the meticulous following of instructions for the Levites?

◈ **Order, Responsibility, and Obedience:** In what ways can modern Christians promote order and structure, encourage collective responsibility, and practise obedience in their spiritual duties, inspired by the census and duties of the Levites?

# Purity in the Camp

## Exclusion from the Camp
### Numbers 5:1-4 (NIV)

1. The Lord said to Moses,
2. "Command the Israelites to send away from the camp anyone who has a defiling skin disease or a discharge of any kind, or who is ceremonially unclean because of a dead body.
3. Send away male and female alike; send them outside the camp so they will not defile their camp, where I dwell among them."
4. The Israelites did so; they sent them outside the camp. They did just as the Lord had instructed Moses.

**Theological Significance:**

- **Holiness and Purity:** The command to exclude those who are ceremonially unclean underscores the importance of holiness and purity within the community of God's people. It highlights the need to maintain a space that is clean and worthy of God's presence.
- **Community Responsibility:** The directive applies to all members of the community, reflecting a collective responsibility to uphold the standards of purity. It demonstrates that maintaining holiness is a communal

effort.

- **God's Presence:** The emphasis on the camp being where God dwells among His people underscores the sacred nature of the community. The presence of God demands a high standard of purity and holiness.

**Modern Interpretation:**

This passage teaches modern believers about the importance of maintaining spiritual and moral purity within their communities, the collective responsibility to uphold these standards, and the recognition of God's presence in their midst.

**Key Themes:**

- **Spiritual and Moral Purity:** The passage highlights the importance of maintaining purity within the community of believers.
- **Collective Responsibility:** It emphasises the communal effort required to uphold standards of holiness and purity.
- **God's Presence:** The recognition of God's presence in the community calls for a high standard of purity and reverence.

**Modern-Day Examples:**

- **Maintaining Purity:** Modern believers can strive to maintain spiritual and moral purity in their personal lives and within their communities.
- **Community Standards:** Emphasising the collective responsibility to uphold standards of holiness can strengthen community bonds and accountability.
- **Reverence for God's Presence:** Recognising the presence of God in their midst can inspire believers to maintain

high standards of purity and reverence.

**Questions for Reflection and Discussion:**

1.  How does the command to exclude those who are ceremonially unclean highlight the importance of maintaining spiritual and moral purity within the community?
2.  What can we learn from the collective responsibility to uphold standards of holiness and purity?
3.  How can believers practise maintaining purity and reverence in their modern spiritual practices and community life?
4.  In what ways can modern Christians recognise and respond to the presence of God in their midst, inspired by the command to maintain a pure camp?

**Sermon Notes for Religious Leaders:**
**Title:** "Purity, Responsibility, and God's Presence: Lessons from Exclusion from the Camp"
**Introduction:**

- Introduce the command to exclude those who are ceremonially unclean in Numbers 5, focusing on the significance of spiritual and moral purity, collective responsibility, and recognising God's presence.
- Highlight the themes of maintaining purity, communal standards, and reverence for God's presence.

**Body:**

1.  **Spiritual and Moral Purity:**
    - Discuss the importance of maintaining spiritual

and moral purity within the community of believers, as illustrated by the command to exclude those who are ceremonially unclean.
   - Reflect on how these principles can be applied to modern spiritual practices, encouraging believers to strive for purity in their personal lives and within their communities.

2. **Collective Responsibility:**
   - Explore the communal effort required to uphold standards of holiness and purity, highlighting the significance of collective responsibility in maintaining these standards.
   - Encourage the congregation to emphasise community standards of holiness, strengthening bonds and accountability among members.

3. **God's Presence:**
   - Discuss the recognition of God's presence in the community, emphasising the need for high standards of purity and reverence.
   - Emphasise the importance of maintaining reverence for God's presence, inspiring believers to uphold purity and holiness in their spiritual practices and community life.

**Working Example for Religious Leaders:**
**Example:** "Maintaining Purity and Reverence in Church Life"

- **Scenario:** Imagine your church is addressing issues of moral and spiritual purity within the community. Each member is encouraged to reflect on their personal and communal standards.
- **Action:** Conduct a series of teachings and discussions on

the importance of maintaining purity and holiness. Emphasise the collective responsibility to uphold these standards.

- **Reverence:** Encourage the congregation to recognise and respond to the presence of God in their midst, inspiring a renewed commitment to purity and reverence.
- **Outcome:** By addressing issues of purity and emphasising collective responsibility, the community grows stronger and more united in their commitment to holiness, reflecting the principles from the command to exclude the ceremonially unclean.

**Conclusion:**

- Summarise the key lessons from the command to exclude those who are ceremonially unclean, focusing on maintaining purity, communal standards, and reverence for God's presence.
- Challenge the congregation to apply these principles in their modern spiritual practices and community life.
- Offer a prayer for guidance, dedication, and a deeper commitment to maintaining purity, upholding community standards, and reverencing God's presence.

**Link to Modern-Day Problems:**

◇ **Maintaining Purity:** How can modern believers strive to maintain spiritual and moral purity in their personal lives and within their communities, inspired by the command to exclude the ceremonially unclean?

◇ **Community Standards:** What steps can believers take to emphasise the collective responsibility to uphold standards of holiness, strengthening community bonds and accountability?

◈ **Reverence for God's Presence:** How can believers recognise and respond to the presence of God in their midst, inspiring a renewed commitment to purity and reverence in their spiritual practices and community life?

◈ **Purity, Responsibility, and God's Presence:** In what ways can modern Christians practise maintaining purity, uphold community standards, and reverence God's presence, inspired by the command to exclude the ceremonially unclean?

**Restitution for Wrongs**
**Numbers 5:5-10 (NIV)**

1. The Lord said to Moses,
2. "Say to the Israelites: 'Any man or woman who wrongs another in any way and so is unfaithful to the Lord is guilty
3. and must confess the sin they have committed. They must make full restitution for the wrong they have done, add a fifth of the value to it and give it all to the person they have wronged.
4. But if that person has no close relative to whom restitution can be made, for the wrong done, it belongs to the Lord and must be given to the priest, along with the ram with which atonement is made for the wrongdoer.
5. All the sacred contributions the Israelites bring to a priest will belong to him.
6. Sacred things belong to their owners, but what they give to the priest will belong to the priest.'"

**Theological Significance:**

- **Confession and Restitution:** The requirement for confession and restitution for wrongs committed highlights the importance of acknowledging one's sins and making amends. This process is crucial for restoring relationships and maintaining justice within the community.

- **Atonement and Repentance:** The inclusion of a ram for atonement underscores the need for repentance and seeking forgiveness from God. It emphasises the spiritual aspect of restitution and the importance of being right with God.
- **Sacred Contributions:** The directive that sacred contributions belong to the priests underscores the sanctity of offerings and the role of the priests in mediating between God and the people.

**Modern Interpretation:**

This passage teaches modern believers about the importance of confessing sins and making restitution, the need for repentance and atonement, and the sanctity of offerings in spiritual life.

**Key Themes:**

- **Confession and Restitution:** The passage highlights the importance of acknowledging sins and making amends for wrongs committed.
- **Repentance and Atonement:** The requirement for atonement underscores the need for repentance and seeking forgiveness from God.
- **Sanctity of Offerings:** The directive that sacred contributions belong to the priests emphasises the sanctity of offerings and the role of spiritual leaders in mediating between God and the people.

**Modern-Day Examples:**

- **Practising Confession:** Modern believers can practise

confessing their sins and making restitution for wrongs committed, recognising the importance of maintaining justice and restoring relationships.

- **Seeking Forgiveness:** Emphasising the need for repentance and atonement can inspire believers to seek forgiveness and maintain a right relationship with God.
- **Honouring Offerings:** Recognising the sanctity of offerings and supporting spiritual leaders can enhance the spiritual life of the community.

## Questions for Reflection and Discussion:

1. How does the requirement for confession and restitution highlight the importance of acknowledging sins and making amends?
2. What can we learn from the inclusion of a ram for atonement about the need for repentance and seeking forgiveness from God?
3. How can believers practise confessing sins and making restitution in their modern spiritual practices and community life?
4. In what ways can modern Christians recognise and honour the sanctity of offerings, inspired by the directive that sacred contributions belong to the priests?

**Sermon Notes for Religious Leaders:**
**Title:** "Confession, Restitution, and Atonement: Lessons from Restitution for Wrongs"
**Introduction:**

- Introduce the requirement for confession and restitution in Numbers 5, focusing on the significance of acknowledging sins, making amends, and seeking atonement.

- Highlight the themes of practising confession, seeking forgiveness, and honouring offerings.

**Body:**

1. **Confession and Restitution:**
    - Discuss the importance of acknowledging sins and making restitution for wrongs committed, as illustrated by the requirement for confession and restitution.
    - Reflect on how these principles can be applied to modern spiritual practices, encouraging believers to practise confessing their sins and making amends.
2. **Repentance and Atonement:**
    - Explore the inclusion of a ram for atonement, highlighting the need for repentance and seeking forgiveness from God.
    - Encourage the congregation to seek forgiveness and maintain a right relationship with God through repentance and atonement.
3. **Sanctity of Offerings:**
    - Discuss the directive that sacred contributions belong to the priests, emphasising the sanctity of offerings and the role of spiritual leaders in mediating between God and the people.
    - Emphasise the importance of recognising and honouring the sanctity of offerings in spiritual life.

**Working Example for Religious Leaders:**

**Example:** "Practising Confession and Restitution in Church Life"

- **Scenario:** Imagine your church is addressing issues of unresolved conflicts and wrongs committed within the community. Each member is encouraged to reflect on their actions and seek reconciliation.
- **Action:** Conduct a series of teachings and discussions on the importance of confession and restitution. Encourage members to confess their sins and make amends for wrongs committed.
- **Atonement:** Emphasise the need for repentance and seeking forgiveness from God, incorporating rituals or prayers for atonement.
- **Outcome:** By addressing issues of confession and restitution and emphasising the need for atonement, the community grows stronger and more united in their commitment to justice and forgiveness, reflecting the principles from the requirement for confession and restitution.

**Conclusion:**

- Summarise the key lessons from the requirement for confession and restitution, focusing on practising confession, seeking forgiveness, and honouring offerings.
- Challenge the congregation to apply these principles in their modern spiritual practices and community life.
- Offer a prayer for guidance, dedication, and a deeper commitment to practising confession, seeking forgiveness, and honouring offerings in their spiritual life.

**Link to Modern-Day Problems:**

◇ **Practising Confession:** How can modern believers practise confessing their sins and making restitution for wrongs committed, recognising the importance of maintaining justice and restoring relationships, inspired by the requirement for confession and restitution?

◇ **Seeking Forgiveness:** What steps can believers take to emphasise the need for repentance and atonement, inspiring a deeper commitment to seeking forgiveness and maintaining a right relationship with God?

◇ **Honouring Offerings:** How can believers recognise and honour the sanctity of offerings, supporting spiritual leaders and enhancing the spiritual life of the community, inspired by the directive that sacred contributions belong to the priests?

◇ **Confession, Restitution, and Atonement:** In what ways can modern Christians practise confession, seek forgiveness, and honour offerings in their spiritual life, inspired by the requirement for confession and restitution?

**The Test for an Unfaithful Wife**
**Numbers 5:11-31 (NIV)**

1.  Then the Lord said to Moses,
2.  "Speak to the Israelites and say to them: 'If a man's wife goes astray and is unfaithful to him
3.  so that another man has sexual relations with her, and this is hidden from her husband and her impurity is undetected (since there is no witness against her and she has not been caught in the act),
4.  and if feelings of jealousy come over her husband and he suspects his wife and she is impure—or if he is jealous and suspects her even though she is not impure—
5.  then he is to take his wife to the priest. He must also take

an offering of a tenth of an ephah of barley flour on her behalf. He must not pour olive oil on it or put incense on it, because it is a grain offering for jealousy, a reminder-offering to draw attention to wrongdoing.

6. "'The priest shall bring her and have her stand before the Lord.

7. Then he shall take some holy water in a clay jar and put some dust from the tabernacle floor into the water.

8. After the priest has had the woman stand before the Lord, he shall loosen her hair and place in her hands the reminder-offering, the grain offering for jealousy, while he himself holds the bitter water that brings a curse.

9. Then the priest shall put the woman under oath and say to her, "If no other man has had sexual relations with you and you have not gone astray and become impure while married to your husband, may this bitter water that brings a curse not harm you.

10. But if you have gone astray while married to your husband and you have made yourself impure by having sexual relations with a man other than your husband"—

11. here the priest is to put the woman under this curse—"may the Lord cause you to become a curse among your people when he makes your womb miscarry and your abdomen swell.

12. May this water that brings a curse enter your body so that your abdomen swells or your womb miscarries." "'Then the woman is to say, "Amen. So be it."

13. "'The priest is to write these curses on a scroll and then wash them off into the bitter water.

14. He shall make the woman drink the bitter water that brings a curse, and this water that brings a curse and causes bitter suffering will enter her.

15. The priest is to take from her hands the grain offering for jealousy, wave it before the Lord and bring it to the altar.

16. The priest is then to take a handful of the grain offering as a memorial offering and burn it on the altar; after that, he is to have the woman drink the water.

17. If she has made herself impure and been unfaithful to her husband, this will be the result: When she is made to drink the water that brings a curse and causes bitter suffering, it will enter her, her abdomen will swell and her womb will miscarry, and she will become a curse.

18. If, however, the woman has not made herself impure but is clean, she will be cleared of guilt and will be able to have children.

19. "'This, then, is the law of jealousy when a woman goes astray and makes herself impure while married to her husband,

20. or when feelings of jealousy come over a man because he suspects his wife. The priest is to have her stand before the Lord and is to apply this entire law to her.

21. The husband will be innocent of any wrongdoing, but the woman will bear the consequences of her sin.'"

**Theological Significance:**

- **Jealousy and Justice:** The test for an unfaithful wife addresses issues of jealousy and justice within marriage. It seeks to provide a divine resolution to suspicions of infidelity.

- **Divine Judgment:** The ritual underscores the belief in divine judgment and the role of God in revealing hidden truths. It emphasises that ultimate justice comes from God.

- **Sanctity of Marriage:** The passage highlights the

importance of marital fidelity and the seriousness of accusations of infidelity, reinforcing the sanctity of the marital bond.

**Modern Interpretation:**

This passage teaches modern believers about the importance of addressing issues of jealousy and justice within relationships, the role of divine judgment in revealing truths, and the sanctity of marriage.

**Key Themes:**

- **Addressing Jealousy and Justice:** The passage highlights the importance of addressing jealousy and ensuring justice within relationships.
- **Divine Judgment:** It underscores the belief in divine judgment and the role of God in revealing hidden truths.
- **Sanctity of Marriage:** The importance of marital fidelity and the seriousness of accusations of infidelity are emphasised, reinforcing the sanctity of marriage.

**Modern-Day Examples:**

- **Dealing with Jealousy:** Modern believers can seek to address jealousy and ensure justice within their relationships, recognising the importance of trust and communication.
- **Belief in Divine Judgment:** Emphasising the role of divine judgment in revealing truths can inspire believers to seek God's guidance and justice in their lives.
- **Upholding Marital Fidelity:** Recognising the sanctity of marriage and the seriousness of accusations of infidelity can strengthen marital bonds and commitment.

**Questions for Reflection and Discussion:**

1. How does the test for an unfaithful wife address issues of jealousy and justice within relationships?
2. What can we learn from the emphasis on divine judgment and the role of God in revealing hidden truths?
3. How can believers practise addressing jealousy and ensuring justice within their modern relationships?
4. In what ways can modern Christians uphold the sanctity of marriage and the seriousness of accusations of infidelity, inspired by the test for an unfaithful wife?

**Sermon Notes for Religious Leaders:**

**Title:** "Jealousy, Justice, and Fidelity: Lessons from the Test for an Unfaithful Wife"

**Introduction:**

- Introduce the test for an unfaithful wife in Numbers 5, focusing on the significance of addressing jealousy and justice, the role of divine judgment, and the sanctity of marriage.
- Highlight the themes of dealing with jealousy, believing in divine judgment, and upholding marital fidelity.

**Body:**

1. **Addressing Jealousy and Justice:**
   - Discuss the importance of addressing jealousy and ensuring justice within relationships, as illustrated by the test for an unfaithful wife.
   - Reflect on how these principles can be applied to modern relationships, encouraging believers to seek trust and communication.

2. **Belief in Divine Judgment:**
    - Explore the role of divine judgment in revealing hidden truths, highlighting the importance of seeking God's guidance and justice.
    - Encourage the congregation to believe in and seek divine judgment in their lives, recognising the ultimate justice that comes from God.
3. **Sanctity of Marriage:**
    - Discuss the importance of marital fidelity and the seriousness of accusations of infidelity, reinforcing the sanctity of the marital bond.
    - Emphasise the need for believers to uphold the sanctity of marriage and strengthen their commitment to marital fidelity.

**Working Example for Religious Leaders:**
**Example:** "Addressing Jealousy and Strengthening Marital Bonds"

- **Scenario:** Imagine your church is addressing issues of jealousy and trust within marriages. Each couple is encouraged to reflect on their relationship and seek reconciliation.
- **Action:** Conduct a series of teachings and discussions on the importance of addressing jealousy and ensuring justice within relationships. Encourage couples to seek trust and communication.
- **Divine Judgment:** Emphasise the role of divine judgment in revealing truths and seeking God's guidance in their relationships.
- **Outcome:** By addressing issues of jealousy and emphasising the importance of marital fidelity, couples

strengthen their bonds and commitment, reflecting the principles from the test for an unfaithful wife.

**Conclusion:**

- Summarise the key lessons from the test for an unfaithful wife, focusing on addressing jealousy and justice, believing in divine judgment, and upholding marital fidelity.
- Challenge the congregation to apply these principles in their modern relationships and spiritual practices.
- Offer a prayer for guidance, trust, and a deeper commitment to addressing jealousy, seeking justice, and upholding the sanctity of marriage in their lives.

**Link to Modern-Day Problems:**

◇ **Dealing with Jealousy:** How can modern believers address jealousy and ensure justice within their relationships, recognising the importance of trust and communication, inspired by the test for an unfaithful wife?

◇ **Belief in Divine Judgment:** What steps can believers take to emphasise the role of divine judgment in revealing truths, inspiring a deeper commitment to seeking God's guidance and justice in their lives?

◇ **Upholding Marital Fidelity:** How can believers practise upholding the sanctity of marriage and the seriousness of accusations of infidelity, strengthening their marital bonds and commitment, inspired by the test for an unfaithful wife?

◇ **Jealousy, Justice, and Fidelity:** In what ways can modern Christians address jealousy and justice, believe in divine judgment, and uphold marital fidelity in their relationships, inspired by the test for an unfaithful wife?

**The Conclusion of Purity Laws**
**Numbers 5:1-31 (NIV)**

1. The Lord said to Moses,
2. "Command the Israelites to send away from the camp anyone who has a defiling skin disease or a discharge of any kind, or who is ceremonially unclean because of a dead body.
3. Send away male and female alike; send them outside the camp so they will not defile their camp, where I dwell among them."
4. The Israelites did so; they sent them outside the camp. They did just as the Lord had instructed Moses.

**Theological Significance:**

- **Holiness and Purity:** The command to exclude those who are ceremonially unclean underscores the importance of holiness and purity within the community of God's people. It highlights the need to maintain a space that is clean and worthy of God's presence.
- **Community Responsibility:** The directive applies to all members of the community, reflecting a collective responsibility to uphold the standards of purity. It demonstrates that maintaining holiness is a communal effort.
- **God's Presence:** The emphasis on the camp being where God dwells among His people underscores the sacred nature of the community. The presence of God demands a high standard of purity and holiness.

**Modern Interpretation:**
This passage teaches modern believers about the importance of maintaining spiritual and moral purity within their communities,

the collective responsibility to uphold these standards, and the recognition of God's presence in their midst.

**Key Themes:**

- **Spiritual and Moral Purity:** The passage highlights the importance of maintaining purity within the community of believers.
- **Collective Responsibility:** It emphasises the communal effort required to uphold standards of holiness and purity.
- **God's Presence:** The recognition of God's presence in the community calls for a high standard of purity and reverence.

**Modern-Day Examples:**

- **Maintaining Purity:** Modern believers can strive to maintain spiritual and moral purity in their personal lives and within their communities.
- **Community Standards:** Emphasising the collective responsibility to uphold standards of holiness can strengthen community bonds and accountability.
- **Reverence for God's Presence:** Recognising the presence of God in their midst can inspire believers to maintain high standards of purity and reverence.

**Questions for Reflection and Discussion:**

1. How does the command to exclude those who are ceremonially unclean highlight the importance of maintaining spiritual and moral purity within the community?
2. What can we learn from the collective responsibility to

uphold standards of holiness and purity?

3. How can believers practise maintaining purity and reverence in their modern spiritual practices and community life?

4. In what ways can modern Christians recognise and respond to the presence of God in their midst, inspired by the command to maintain a pure camp?

**Sermon Notes for Religious Leaders:**

**Title:** "Purity, Responsibility, and God's Presence: Lessons from Exclusion from the Camp"

**Introduction:**

- Introduce the command to exclude those who are ceremonially unclean in Numbers 5, focusing on the significance of spiritual and moral purity, collective responsibility, and recognising God's presence.
- Highlight the themes of maintaining purity, communal standards, and reverence for God's presence.

**Body:**

1. **Spiritual and Moral Purity:**
   - Discuss the importance of maintaining spiritual and moral purity within the community of believers, as illustrated by the command to exclude those who are ceremonially unclean.
   - Reflect on how these principles can be applied to modern spiritual practices, encouraging believers to strive for purity in their personal lives and within their communities.
2. **Collective Responsibility:**
   - Explore the communal effort required to uphold

standards of holiness and purity, highlighting the significance of collective responsibility in maintaining these standards.

- ◦ Encourage the congregation to emphasise community standards of holiness, strengthening bonds and accountability among members.

3. **God's Presence:**
   - ◦ Discuss the recognition of God's presence in the community, emphasising the need for high standards of purity and reverence.
   - ◦ Emphasise the importance of maintaining reverence for God's presence, inspiring believers to uphold purity and holiness in their spiritual practices and community life.

**Working Example for Religious Leaders:**
**Example:** "Maintaining Purity and Reverence in Church Life"

- **Scenario:** Imagine your church is addressing issues of moral and spiritual purity within the community. Each member is encouraged to reflect on their personal and communal standards.
- **Action:** Conduct a series of teachings and discussions on the importance of maintaining purity and holiness. Emphasise the collective responsibility to uphold these standards.
- **Reverence:** Encourage the congregation to recognise and respond to the presence of God in their midst, inspiring a renewed commitment to purity and reverence.
- **Outcome:** By addressing issues of purity and emphasising collective responsibility, the community grows stronger and more united in their commitment to holiness,

reflecting the principles from the command to exclude the ceremonially unclean.

## Conclusion:

- Summarise the key lessons from the command to exclude those who are ceremonially unclean, focusing on maintaining purity, communal standards, and reverence for God's presence.
- Challenge the congregation to apply these principles in their modern spiritual practices and community life.
- Offer a prayer for guidance, dedication, and a deeper commitment to maintaining purity, upholding community standards, and reverencing God's presence.

**Link to Modern-Day Problems:**

◇ **Maintaining Purity:** How can modern believers strive to maintain spiritual and moral purity in their personal lives and within their communities, inspired by the command to exclude the ceremonially unclean?

◇ **Community Standards:** What steps can believers take to emphasise the collective responsibility to uphold standards of holiness, strengthening community bonds and accountability?

◇ **Reverence for God's Presence:** How can believers recognise and respond to the presence of God in their midst, inspiring a renewed commitment to purity and reverence in their spiritual practices and community life?

◇ **Purity, Responsibility, and God's Presence:** In what ways can modern Christians practise maintaining purity, uphold community standards, and reverence God's presence, inspired by the command to exclude the ceremonially unclean?

# The Nazirite Vow and Priestly Blessing

The Nazirite Vow
**Numbers 6:1-12 (NIV)**

1. The Lord said to Moses,
2. "Speak to the Israelites and say to them: 'If a man or woman wants to make a special vow, a vow of dedication to the Lord as a Nazirite,
3. they must abstain from wine and other fermented drink and must not drink vinegar made from wine or other fermented drink. They must not drink grape juice or eat grapes or raisins.
4. As long as they remain under their Nazirite vow, they must not eat anything that comes from the grapevine, not even the seeds or skins.
5. "'During the entire period of their Nazirite vow, no razor may be used on their head. They must be holy until the period of their dedication to the Lord is over; they must let their hair grow long.
6. "'Throughout the period of their dedication to the Lord, the Nazirite must not go near a dead body.
7. Even if their own father or mother or brother or sister dies, they must not make themselves ceremonially unclean on account of them, because the symbol of their dedication to God is on their head.
8. Throughout the period of their dedication, they are

consecrated to the Lord.

9. "'If someone dies suddenly in the Nazirite's presence, thus defiling the hair that symbolises their dedication, they must shave their head on the seventh day—the day of their cleansing.

10. Then on the eighth day they must bring two doves or two young pigeons to the priest at the entrance to the tent of meeting.

11. The priest is to offer one as a sin offering and the other as a burnt offering to make atonement for the Nazirite because they sinned by being in the presence of the dead body. That same day they are to consecrate their head again.

12. They must rededicate themselves to the Lord for the same period of dedication and must bring a year-old male lamb as a guilt offering. The previous days do not count, because they became defiled during their period of dedication.

## Theological Significance:

- **Dedication to God:** The Nazirite vow represents a voluntary act of dedication to God. It signifies a deeper level of commitment and consecration to the Lord.

- **Separation and Holiness:** The requirements of the vow, such as abstaining from certain foods and not cutting hair, symbolise separation and holiness. These acts distinguish the Nazirite as someone set apart for God's purposes.

- **Purity and Cleansing:** The instructions for purification in case of defilement underscore the importance of maintaining purity and the process of cleansing and rededication.

## Modern Interpretation:

This passage teaches modern believers about the significance of voluntary dedication to God, the importance of living a life of separation and holiness, and the need for purity and cleansing in one's spiritual journey.

**Key Themes:**

- **Voluntary Dedication:** The Nazirite vow highlights the importance of voluntary acts of dedication and commitment to God.
- **Separation and Holiness:** The requirements of the vow symbolise the need for separation from worldly influences and living a holy life.
- **Purity and Cleansing:** The process of purification and rededication underscores the importance of maintaining spiritual purity and the steps required for cleansing.

**Modern-Day Examples:**

- **Voluntary Acts of Dedication:** Modern believers can seek ways to voluntarily dedicate themselves to God, such as through fasting, special prayers, or acts of service.
- **Living a Holy Life:** Emphasising the importance of separation from worldly influences and living a holy life can inspire believers to commit to God's standards.
- **Maintaining Purity:** Recognising the need for spiritual purity and the process of cleansing can help believers remain dedicated and focused on their spiritual journey.

**Questions for Reflection and Discussion:**

1. How does the Nazirite vow highlight the importance of voluntary acts of dedication and commitment to God?

2. What can we learn from the requirements of the Nazirite vow about the need for separation and holiness in our spiritual lives?

3. How can believers practise voluntary acts of dedication and commitment in their modern spiritual practices and community life?

4. In what ways can modern Christians recognise the importance of maintaining purity and the process of cleansing, inspired by the instructions for the Nazirite vow?

**Sermon Notes for Religious Leaders:**

**Title:** "Dedication, Holiness, and Purity: Lessons from the Nazirite Vow"

**Introduction:**

- Introduce the Nazirite vow in Numbers 6, focusing on the significance of voluntary dedication to God, the importance of separation and holiness, and the need for purity and cleansing.
- Highlight the themes of voluntary acts of dedication, living a holy life, and maintaining spiritual purity.

**Body:**

1. **Voluntary Dedication:**
   - Discuss the importance of voluntary acts of dedication and commitment to God, as illustrated by the Nazirite vow.
   - Reflect on how these principles can be applied to modern spiritual practices, encouraging believers to seek ways to dedicate themselves to God voluntarily.

2.  **Separation and Holiness:**
    - Explore the requirements of the Nazirite vow, highlighting the need for separation from worldly influences and living a holy life.
    - Encourage the congregation to commit to God's standards and live a life of holiness, recognising the importance of being set apart for God's purposes.
3.  **Purity and Cleansing:**
    - Discuss the process of purification and rededication in case of defilement, emphasising the importance of maintaining spiritual purity.
    - Emphasise the need for believers to recognise the importance of purity and the steps required for cleansing and rededication in their spiritual journey.

**Working Example for Religious Leaders:**
**Example:** "Voluntary Acts of Dedication in Modern Faith"

- **Scenario:** Imagine encouraging your congregation to participate in a voluntary act of dedication, such as a community fasting period or special prayer sessions.
- **Action:** Organise a series of teachings and discussions on the significance of voluntary dedication, separation, and holiness. Encourage members to commit to a period of fasting or prayer.
- **Purity:** Emphasise the importance of maintaining purity during this period and provide guidance on the process of cleansing and rededication.
- **Outcome:** By encouraging voluntary acts of dedication and emphasising the importance of holiness and purity, the

community grows stronger in their commitment to God, reflecting the principles from the Nazirite vow.

**Conclusion:**

- Summarise the key lessons from the Nazirite vow, focusing on voluntary acts of dedication, living a holy life, and maintaining spiritual purity.
- Challenge the congregation to apply these principles in their modern spiritual practices and community life.
- Offer a prayer for guidance, dedication, and a deeper commitment to voluntary acts of dedication, holiness, and purity in their spiritual journey.

**Link to Modern-Day Problems:**

◇ **Voluntary Acts of Dedication:** How can modern believers seek ways to voluntarily dedicate themselves to God, recognising the significance of such acts in their spiritual journey, inspired by the Nazirite vow?

◇ **Living a Holy Life:** What steps can believers take to emphasise the importance of separation from worldly influences and living a holy life, committing to God's standards?

◇ **Maintaining Purity:** How can believers recognise the need for spiritual purity and the process of cleansing, ensuring they remain dedicated and focused on their spiritual journey?

◇ **Dedication, Holiness, and Purity:** In what ways can modern Christians practise voluntary acts of dedication, live a holy life, and maintain spiritual purity, inspired by the principles of the Nazirite vow?

**Completion of the Nazirite Vow**
**Numbers 6:13-21 (NIV)**

1. "'Now this is the law of the Nazirite when the period of

their dedication is over. They are to be brought to the entrance to the tent of meeting.

2.  There they are to present their offerings to the Lord: a year-old male lamb without defect for a burnt offering, a year-old ewe lamb without defect for a sin offering, a ram without defect for a fellowship offering,

3.  together with their grain offerings and drink offerings, and a basket of bread made with the finest flour and without yeast—thick loaves with olive oil mixed in and thin loaves brushed with olive oil.

4.  "'The priest is to present all these before the Lord and make the sin offering and the burnt offering.

5.  He is to present the basket of unleavened bread and is to sacrifice the ram as a fellowship offering to the Lord, together with its grain offering and drink offering.

6.  "'Then at the entrance to the tent of meeting, the Nazirite must shave off the hair that symbolises their dedication. They are to take the hair and put it in the fire that is under the sacrifice of the fellowship offering.

7.  "'After the Nazirite has shaved off the hair that symbolises their dedication, the priest is to place in their hands a boiled shoulder of the ram, and one thick loaf and one thin loaf from the basket, both made without yeast.

8.  The priest shall then wave these before the Lord as a wave offering; they are holy and belong to the priest, together with the breast that was waved and the thigh that was presented. After that, the Nazirite may drink wine.

9.  "'This is the law of the Nazirite who vows offerings to the Lord in accordance with their dedication, in addition to whatever else they can afford. They must fulfil the vows they have made, according to the law of the Nazirite.'"

**Theological Significance:**

- **Fulfilment of Vows:** The completion of the Nazirite vow underscores the importance of fulfiling vows made to the Lord. It signifies a formal conclusion to a period of dedication and the transition back to normal life.
- **Sacrificial Offerings:** The variety of offerings required highlights the comprehensive nature of worship and the need for various types of sacrifices to acknowledge different aspects of one's relationship with God.
- **Symbolism of Hair:** The act of shaving the hair that symbolises the Nazirite's dedication and burning it under the fellowship offering underscores the significance of the physical symbols of spiritual commitments.

**Modern Interpretation:**

This passage teaches modern believers about the importance of fulfiling spiritual commitments, the role of sacrificial offerings in worship, and the significance of physical symbols in representing spiritual dedication.

**Key Themes:**

- **Fulfiling Spiritual Commitments:** The completion of the Nazirite vow highlights the importance of fulfiling vows and commitments made to God.
- **Comprehensive Worship:** The variety of sacrificial offerings underscores the comprehensive nature of worship and the need to acknowledge different aspects of one's relationship with God.
- **Physical Symbols of Dedication:** The act of shaving and burning the hair symbolises the importance of physical symbols in representing spiritual commitments.

**Modern-Day Examples:**

- **Honouring Commitments:** Modern believers can strive to fulfil their spiritual commitments and vows, recognising the importance of staying true to their word.
- **Diverse Worship Practices:** Emphasising the need for various types of worship practices can enhance the richness and depth of one's spiritual life.
- **Recognising Physical Symbols:** Understanding the significance of physical symbols in representing spiritual dedication can inspire believers to incorporate meaningful rituals in their worship.

**Questions for Reflection and Discussion:**

1. How does the completion of the Nazirite vow highlight the importance of fulfiling spiritual commitments and vows made to God?
2. What can we learn from the variety of sacrificial offerings about the comprehensive nature of worship and the need to acknowledge different aspects of one's relationship with God?
3. How can believers practise fulfiling their spiritual commitments and vows in their modern spiritual practices and community life?
4. In what ways can modern Christians recognise the significance of physical symbols in representing spiritual dedication, inspired by the act of shaving and burning the Nazirite's hair?

**Sermon Notes for Religious Leaders:**

**Title:** "Commitment, Worship, and Symbolism: Lessons from the Completion of the Nazirite Vow"

**Introduction:**

- Introduce the completion of the Nazirite vow in Numbers 6, focusing on the significance of fulfiling spiritual commitments, the role of sacrificial offerings in worship, and the importance of physical symbols in representing spiritual dedication.
- Highlight the themes of honouring commitments, diverse worship practices, and recognising physical symbols.

**Body:**

1. **Fulfiling Spiritual Commitments:**
    - Discuss the importance of fulfiling spiritual commitments and vows made to God, as illustrated by the completion of the Nazirite vow.
    - Reflect on how these principles can be applied to modern spiritual practices, encouraging believers to stay true to their word and fulfil their commitments.

2. **Comprehensive Worship:**
    - Explore the variety of sacrificial offerings required, highlighting the comprehensive nature of worship and the need to acknowledge different aspects of one's relationship with God.
    - Encourage the congregation to incorporate diverse worship practices in their spiritual life, enhancing its richness and depth.

3. **Physical Symbols of Dedication:**
    - Discuss the act of shaving and burning the Nazirite's hair, emphasising the importance of

physical symbols in representing spiritual commitments.

- ○ Emphasise the need for believers to recognise and incorporate meaningful rituals in their worship, understanding their significance.

**Working Example for Religious Leaders:**

**Example:** "Honouring Commitments and Incorporating Symbols in Worship"

- **Scenario:** Imagine your church is encouraging members to make and fulfil spiritual commitments, such as pledges to volunteer or participate in specific ministries.
- **Action:** Organise a series of teachings and discussions on the importance of fulfiling commitments and the role of physical symbols in worship. Encourage members to make and honour their commitments.
- **Symbolism:** Incorporate meaningful rituals or symbols in worship services to represent these commitments, such as lighting candles or offering special prayers.
- **Outcome:** By emphasising the importance of fulfiling commitments and incorporating symbols in worship, the community grows stronger in their dedication to God, reflecting the principles from the completion of the Nazirite vow.

**Conclusion:**

- Summarise the key lessons from the completion of the Nazirite vow, focusing on honouring commitments, diverse worship practices, and recognising physical symbols.
- Challenge the congregation to apply these principles in

their modern spiritual practices and community life.

- Offer a prayer for guidance, dedication, and a deeper commitment to honouring spiritual commitments, incorporating diverse worship practices, and recognising the significance of physical symbols in their spiritual journey.

**Link to Modern-Day Problems:**

◈ **Honouring Commitments:** How can modern believers strive to fulfil their spiritual commitments and vows, recognising the importance of staying true to their word, inspired by the completion of the Nazirite vow?

◈ **Diverse Worship Practices:** What steps can believers take to emphasise the need for various types of worship practices, enhancing the richness and depth of their spiritual life?

◈ **Recognising Physical Symbols:** How can believers understand the significance of physical symbols in representing spiritual dedication, incorporating meaningful rituals in their worship, inspired by the act of shaving and burning the Nazirite's hair?

◈ **Commitment, Worship, and Symbolism:** In what ways can modern Christians honour their spiritual commitments, practise diverse worship, and recognise the significance of physical symbols in their spiritual journey, inspired by the principles of the Nazirite vow?

**The Priestly Blessing**
**Numbers 6:22-27 (NIV)**

1. The Lord said to Moses,
2. "Tell Aaron and his sons, 'This is how you are to bless the Israelites. Say to them:
3. "'"The Lord bless you and keep you;
4. the Lord make his face shine on you and be gracious to

you;

5.  the Lord turn his face toward you and give you peace."'

6.  "So they will put my name on the Israelites, and I will bless them."

**Theological Significance:**

- **Divine Blessing:** The priestly blessing is a powerful invocation of God's favour and protection. It signifies the bestowing of divine grace, peace, and presence upon the people.

- **Intercession:** The role of Aaron and his sons in pronouncing the blessing underscores the importance of intercessory prayer and the role of spiritual leaders in mediating God's blessings.

- **God's Name:** The act of putting God's name on the Israelites signifies identity and belonging. It denotes the special relationship between God and His people, marked by His blessing and favour.

**Modern Interpretation:**

This passage teaches modern believers about the significance of seeking and pronouncing divine blessings, the importance of intercessory prayer, and the identity and belonging that come from being marked by God's name.

**Key Themes:**

- **Seeking Divine Blessing:** The priestly blessing highlights the importance of seeking God's favour, protection, and peace in one's life.

- **Intercessory Prayer:** The role of Aaron and his sons underscores the significance of intercessory prayer and the role of spiritual leaders in mediating blessings.

- **Identity and Belonging:** The act of putting God's name on the Israelites signifies the special relationship between God and His people, marked by His blessing and favour.

**Modern-Day Examples:**

- **Invoking Blessings:** Modern believers can practise seeking and pronouncing divine blessings in their lives and communities, recognising the importance of God's favour and protection.
- **Intercessory Prayer:** Emphasising the role of intercessory prayer and spiritual leaders in mediating blessings can strengthen the spiritual life of the community.
- **Recognising Identity:** Understanding the significance of being marked by God's name can inspire believers to embrace their identity and belonging as God's people.

**Questions for Reflection and Discussion:**

1. How does the priestly blessing highlight the importance of seeking God's favour, protection, and peace in one's life?
2. What can we learn from the role of Aaron and his sons in pronouncing the blessing about the significance of intercessory prayer and spiritual leaders?
3. How can believers practise seeking and pronouncing divine blessings in their modern spiritual practices and community life?
4. In what ways can modern Christians recognise and embrace their identity and belonging as God's people, inspired by the act of putting God's name on the Israelites?

**Sermon Notes for Religious Leaders:**

**Title:** "Blessing, Intercession, and Identity: Lessons from the Priestly Blessing"

**Introduction:**

- Introduce the priestly blessing in Numbers 6, focusing on the significance of seeking divine blessings, the importance of intercessory prayer, and the identity and belonging that come from being marked by God's name.
- Highlight the themes of invoking blessings, practising intercessory prayer, and recognising identity as God's people.

**Body:**

1. **Seeking Divine Blessing:**
    - Discuss the importance of seeking God's favour, protection, and peace in one's life, as illustrated by the priestly blessing.
    - Reflect on how these principles can be applied to modern spiritual practices, encouraging believers to seek and pronounce divine blessings in their lives and communities.

2. **Intercessory Prayer:**
    - Explore the role of Aaron and his sons in pronouncing the blessing, highlighting the significance of intercessory prayer and the role of spiritual leaders in mediating blessings.
    - Encourage the congregation to practise intercessory prayer and support their spiritual leaders in this role.

3. **Identity and Belonging:**
    - Discuss the act of putting God's name on the

Israelites, emphasising the special relationship between God and His people, marked by His blessing and favour.
- Emphasise the importance of recognising and embracing one's identity and belonging as God's people, inspired by the priestly blessing.

**Working Example for Religious Leaders:**

**Example:** "Practising Blessing and Intercessory Prayer in Church Life"

- **Scenario:** Imagine your church is encouraging members to practise seeking and pronouncing divine blessings, as well as supporting intercessory prayer.
- **Action:** Organise a series of teachings and discussions on the importance of divine blessings, intercessory prayer, and identity as God's people. Encourage members to seek blessings and support their spiritual leaders.
- **Identity:** Emphasise the significance of being marked by God's name and recognising one's identity and belonging as God's people.
- **Outcome:** By practising seeking and pronouncing blessings, supporting intercessory prayer, and recognising identity, the community grows stronger in their commitment to God, reflecting the principles from the priestly blessing.

**Conclusion:**

- Summarise the key lessons from the priestly blessing, focusing on seeking divine blessings, practising intercessory prayer, and recognising identity and belonging as God's people.

- Challenge the congregation to apply these principles in their modern spiritual practices and community life.
- Offer a prayer for guidance, dedication, and a deeper commitment to seeking divine blessings, practising intercessory prayer, and recognising one's identity as God's people.

**Link to Modern-Day Problems:**

◇ **Invoking Blessings:** How can modern believers practise seeking and pronouncing divine blessings in their lives and communities, recognising the importance of God's favour and protection, inspired by the priestly blessing?

◇ **Intercessory Prayer:** What steps can believers take to emphasise the role of intercessory prayer and support spiritual leaders in mediating blessings, strengthening the spiritual life of the community?

◇ **Recognising Identity:** How can believers understand the significance of being marked by God's name and embrace their identity and belonging as God's people?

◇ **Blessing, Intercession, and Identity:** In what ways can modern Christians practise seeking divine blessings, intercessory prayer, and recognising their identity as God's people, inspired by the principles of the priestly blessing?

**Summary and Conclusion of the Nazirite Vow and Priestly Blessing**

**Numbers 6:1-27 (NIV)**

1. The Lord said to Moses,
2. "Speak to the Israelites and say to them: 'If a man or woman wants to make a special vow, a vow of dedication to the Lord as a Nazirite,
3. they must abstain from wine and other fermented drink

and must not drink vinegar made from wine or other fermented drink. They must not drink grape juice or eat grapes or raisins.

4.  As long as they remain under their Nazirite vow, they must not eat anything that comes from the grapevine, not even the seeds or skins.

5.  "'During the entire period of their Nazirite vow, no razor may be used on their head. They must be holy until the period of their dedication to the Lord is over; they must let their hair grow long.

6.  "'Throughout the period of their dedication to the Lord, the Nazirite must not go near a dead body.

7.  Even if their own father or mother or brother or sister dies, they must not make themselves ceremonially unclean on account of them, because the symbol of their dedication to God is on their head.

8.  Throughout the period of their dedication, they are consecrated to the Lord.

9.  "'If someone dies suddenly in the Nazirite's presence, thus defiling the hair that symbolises their dedication, they must shave their head on the seventh day—the day of their cleansing.

10.  Then on the eighth day they must bring two doves or two young pigeons to the priest at the entrance to the tent of meeting.

11.  The priest is to offer one as a sin offering and the other as a burnt offering to make atonement for the Nazirite because they sinned by being in the presence of the dead body. That same day they are to consecrate their head again.

12.  They must rededicate themselves to the Lord for the same period of dedication and must bring a year-old male lamb as a guilt offering. The previous days do not count, because

they became defiled during their period of dedication.

13. "'Now this is the law of the Nazirite when the period of their dedication is over. They are to be brought to the entrance to the tent of meeting.

14. There they are to present their offerings to the Lord: a year-old male lamb without defect for a burnt offering, a year-old ewe lamb without defect for a sin offering, a ram without defect for a fellowship offering,

15. together with their grain offerings and drink offerings, and a basket of bread made with the finest flour and without yeast—thick loaves with olive oil mixed in and thin loaves brushed with olive oil.

16. "'The priest is to present all these before the Lord and make the sin offering and the burnt offering.

17. He is to present the basket of unleavened bread and is to sacrifice the ram as a fellowship offering to the Lord, together with its grain offering and drink offering.

18. "'Then at the entrance to the tent of meeting, the Nazirite must shave off the hair that symbolises their dedication. They are to take the hair and put it in the fire that is under the sacrifice of the fellowship offering.

19. "'After the Nazirite has shaved off the hair that symbolises their dedication, the priest is to place in their hands a boiled shoulder of the ram, and one thick loaf and one thin loaf from the basket, both made without yeast.

20. The priest shall then wave these before the Lord as a wave offering; they are holy and belong to the priest, together with the breast that was waved and the thigh that was presented. After that, the Nazirite may drink wine.

21. "'This is the law of the Nazirite who vows offerings to the Lord in accordance with their dedication, in addition to whatever else they can afford. They must fulfil the vows

they have made, according to the law of the Nazirite.'

22. The Lord said to Moses,

23. "Tell Aaron and his sons, 'This is how you are to bless the Israelites. Say to them:

24. ""'The Lord bless you and keep you;

25. the Lord make his face shine on you and be gracious to you;

26. the Lord turn his face toward you and give you peace.'"

27. "So they will put my name on the Israelites, and I will bless them."

## Theological Significance:

- **Dedication and Commitment:** The Nazirite vow and its completion signify deep dedication and commitment to God. It highlights the importance of making and fulfiling vows as acts of worship and devotion.
- **Blessing and Protection:** The priestly blessing emphasises God's desire to bless and protect His people. It underscores the themes of grace, favour, and peace bestowed by God.
- **Identity and Belonging:** The act of putting God's name on the Israelites signifies their identity and belonging as God's chosen people, marked by His blessing and protection.

### Modern Interpretation:

This passage teaches modern believers about the significance of deep dedication and commitment to God, the importance of seeking God's blessing and protection, and the identity and belonging that come from being marked by God's name.

### Key Themes:

- **Dedication and Commitment:** The Nazirite vow highlights the importance of making and fulfiling vows as acts of worship and devotion.
- **Blessing and Protection:** The priestly blessing emphasises the themes of grace, favour, and peace bestowed by God.
- **Identity and Belonging:** The act of putting God's name on the Israelites signifies their identity and belonging as God's chosen people.

**Modern-Day Examples:**

- **Honouring Vows:** Modern believers can strive to make and fulfil their spiritual vows, recognising them as acts of worship and devotion.
- **Seeking Blessing:** Emphasising the importance of seeking God's blessing and protection can inspire believers to seek God's favour in their lives.
- **Recognising Identity:** Understanding the significance of being marked by God's name can inspire believers to embrace their identity and belonging as God's people.

**Questions for Reflection and Discussion:**

1. How does the Nazirite vow and its completion highlight the importance of deep dedication and commitment to God?
2. What can we learn from the priestly blessing about God's desire to bless and protect His people?
3. How can believers practise making and fulfiling spiritual vows in their modern spiritual practices and community life?
4. In what ways can modern Christians seek God's blessing

and protection and embrace their identity and belonging
as God's people, inspired by the priestly blessing?

**Sermon Notes for Religious Leaders:**
**Title:** "Dedication, Blessing, and Identity: Lessons from the
Nazirite Vow and Priestly Blessing"
**Introduction:**

- Introduce the Nazirite vow and priestly blessing in
  Numbers 6, focusing on the significance of deep dedication
  and commitment to God, the importance of seeking God's
  blessing and protection, and the identity and belonging
  that come from being marked by God's name.
- Highlight the themes of honouring vows, seeking blessing,
  and recognising identity.

**Body:**

1. **Dedication and Commitment:**
   - Discuss the importance of making and fulfiling
     spiritual vows as acts of worship and devotion, as
     illustrated by the Nazirite vow.
   - Reflect on how these principles can be applied to
     modern spiritual practices, encouraging believers
     to make and honour their commitments to God.
2. **Blessing and Protection:**
   - Explore the priestly blessing, highlighting God's
     desire to bless and protect His people, and the
     themes of grace, favour, and peace bestowed by
     God.
   - Encourage the congregation to seek God's
     blessing and protection in their lives, recognising
     the importance of divine favour.

3. **Identity and Belonging:**
   - Discuss the act of putting God's name on the Israelites, emphasising their identity and belonging as God's chosen people, marked by His blessing and protection.
   - Emphasise the importance of recognising and embracing one's identity and belonging as God's people, inspired by the priestly blessing.

**Working Example for Religious Leaders:**

**Example:** "Honouring Vows and Seeking Blessings in Church Life"

- **Scenario:** Imagine your church is encouraging members to make and fulfil spiritual vows, such as commitments to prayer, service, or personal growth.
- **Action:** Organise a series of teachings and discussions on the importance of honouring vows, seeking blessings, and recognising identity as God's people. Encourage members to make and fulfil their commitments.
- **Blessing:** Incorporate the priestly blessing in worship services, emphasising God's desire to bless and protect His people.
- **Outcome:** By honouring vows, seeking blessings, and recognising identity, the community grows stronger in their dedication to God, reflecting the principles from the Nazirite vow and priestly blessing.

**Conclusion:**

- Summarise the key lessons from the Nazirite vow and priestly blessing, focusing on honouring vows, seeking blessing, and recognising identity and belonging as God's people.

- Challenge the congregation to apply these principles in their modern spiritual practices and community life.
- Offer a prayer for guidance, dedication, and a deeper commitment to honouring spiritual vows, seeking God's blessings, and recognising one's identity as God's people.

**Link to Modern-Day Problems:**

⊘ **Honouring Vows:** How can modern believers strive to make and fulfil their spiritual vows, recognising them as acts of worship and devotion, inspired by the Nazirite vow?

⊘ **Seeking Blessing:** What steps can believers take to emphasise the importance of seeking God's blessing and protection, inspiring a deeper commitment to seeking divine favour in their lives?

⊘ **Recognising Identity:** How can believers understand the significance of being marked by God's name and embrace their identity and belonging as God's people, inspired by the priestly blessing?

⊘ **Dedication, Blessing, and Identity:** In what ways can modern Christians honour their spiritual vows, seek God's blessings, and recognise their identity as God's people, inspired by the principles of the Nazirite vow and priestly blessing?

# Offerings of the Leaders

**I**ntroduction to the Offerings
### Numbers 7:1-17 (NIV)

1. When Moses finished setting up the tabernacle, he anointed it and consecrated it and all its furnishings. He also anointed and consecrated the altar and all its utensils.
2. Then the leaders of Israel, the heads of families who were the tribal leaders in charge of those who were counted, made offerings.
3. They brought as their gifts before the Lord six covered carts and twelve oxen—an ox from each leader and a cart from every two. These they presented before the tabernacle.
4. The Lord said to Moses,
5. "Accept these from them, that they may be used in the work at the tent of meeting. Give them to the Levites as each man's work requires."
6. So Moses took the carts and oxen and gave them to the Levites.
7. He gave two carts and four oxen to the Gershonites, as their work required,
8. and he gave four carts and eight oxen to the Merarites, as their work required. They were all under the direction of Ithamar son of Aaron, the priest.
9. But Moses did not give any to the Kohathites, because they

were to carry on their shoulders the holy things, for which
they were responsible.

10.  When the altar was anointed, the leaders brought their
offerings for its dedication and presented them before the
altar.

11.  For the Lord had said to Moses, "Each day one leader is to
bring his offering for the dedication of the altar."

12.  The one who brought his offering on the first day was
Nahshon son of Amminadab, of the tribe of Judah.

13.  His offering was one silver plate weighing a hundred and
thirty shekels and one silver sprinkling bowl weighing
seventy shekels, both according to the sanctuary shekel,
each filled with the finest flour mixed with olive oil as a
grain offering;

14.  one gold dish weighing ten shekels, filled with incense;

15.  one young bull, one ram and one male lamb a year old for a
burnt offering;

16.  one male goat for a sin offering;

17.  and two oxen, five rams, five male goats and five male
lambs a year old to be sacrificed as a fellowship offering.
This was the offering of Nahshon son of Amminadab.

## Theological Significance:

- **Consecration and Dedication:** The anointing and
consecration of the tabernacle and its furnishings signify
the setting apart of these items for sacred purposes. It
highlights the importance of dedicating material things to
God.

- **Collective Responsibility:** The offerings brought by the
leaders of Israel demonstrate a collective responsibility and
participation in the dedication of the altar. Each leader's

contribution reflects the unity and shared purpose of the community.

- **Detailed Offerings:** The detailed description of each offering underscores the significance of each item and the care with which offerings were made. It reflects the meticulous nature of worship and the value placed on each act of giving.

**Modern Interpretation:**

This passage teaches modern believers about the importance of dedicating material things to God, the value of collective responsibility in worship, and the significance of detailed and thoughtful offerings.

**Key Themes:**

- **Dedication to God:** The passage highlights the importance of setting apart material things for sacred purposes, dedicating them to God's service.
- **Collective Responsibility:** The offerings brought by the leaders demonstrate the value of collective responsibility and participation in worship.
- **Significance of Offerings:** The detailed description of each offering underscores the importance of making thoughtful and meticulous offerings to God.

**Modern-Day Examples:**

- **Dedicating Material Things:** Modern believers can practise dedicating their possessions and resources to God, recognising their sacred purpose.
- **Participating in Worship:** Emphasising the value of collective responsibility in worship can strengthen

community bonds and shared purpose.

- **Thoughtful Offerings:** Recognising the significance of making detailed and thoughtful offerings can inspire believers to give with care and intention.

## Questions for Reflection and Discussion:

1. How does the anointing and consecration of the tabernacle highlight the importance of dedicating material things to God?
2. What can we learn from the collective responsibility demonstrated by the leaders of Israel in their offerings?
3. How can believers practise dedicating their possessions and resources to God in their modern spiritual practices and community life?
4. In what ways can modern Christians recognise the significance of making thoughtful and meticulous offerings, inspired by the detailed description of the leaders' offerings?

## Sermon Notes for Religious Leaders:

**Title:** "Dedication, Responsibility, and Thoughtfulness: Lessons from the Offerings of the Leaders"

**Introduction:**

- Introduce the offerings brought by the leaders of Israel in Numbers 7, focusing on the significance of dedicating material things to God, the value of collective responsibility, and the importance of thoughtful offerings.
- Highlight the themes of dedication to God, collective responsibility, and the significance of offerings.

**Body:**

1.  **Dedication to God:**
    - Discuss the importance of dedicating material things to God's service, as illustrated by the anointing and consecration of the tabernacle and its furnishings.
    - Reflect on how these principles can be applied to modern spiritual practices, encouraging believers to dedicate their possessions and resources to God.
2.  **Collective Responsibility:**
    - Explore the collective responsibility demonstrated by the leaders of Israel in their offerings, highlighting the value of participation and unity in worship.
    - Encourage the congregation to emphasise collective responsibility in their worship practices, strengthening community bonds and shared purpose.
3.  **Thoughtful Offerings:**
    - Discuss the detailed description of each offering brought by the leaders, emphasising the importance of making thoughtful and meticulous offerings to God.
    - Emphasise the need for believers to recognise the significance of their offerings and give with care and intention.

**Working Example for Religious Leaders:**
**Example:** "Dedicating Possessions and Resources in Church Life"

- **Scenario:** Imagine your church is encouraging members to dedicate their possessions and resources to God's service, such as through donations or volunteer efforts.

- **Action:** Organise a series of teachings and discussions on the importance of dedication, collective responsibility, and thoughtful offerings. Encourage members to participate in dedicating their possessions and resources to God.
- **Offerings:** Emphasise the significance of making thoughtful and meticulous offerings, providing guidance on how to give with care and intention.
- **Outcome:** By dedicating possessions and resources, practising collective responsibility, and making thoughtful offerings, the community grows stronger in their commitment to God, reflecting the principles from the offerings brought by the leaders of Israel.

## Conclusion:

- Summarise the key lessons from the offerings brought by the leaders of Israel, focusing on dedicating material things to God, collective responsibility, and thoughtful offerings.
- Challenge the congregation to apply these principles in their modern spiritual practices and community life.
- Offer a prayer for guidance, dedication, and a deeper commitment to dedicating possessions and resources, practising collective responsibility, and making thoughtful offerings in their spiritual journey.

### Link to Modern-Day Problems:

◈ **Dedicating Material Things:** How can modern believers practise dedicating their possessions and resources to God, recognising their sacred purpose, inspired by the anointing and consecration of the tabernacle?

◈ **Participating in Worship:** What steps can believers take to emphasise the value of collective responsibility in their worship practices, strengthening community bonds and shared purpose?

◈ **Thoughtful Offerings:** How can believers recognise the significance of making thoughtful and meticulous offerings, giving with care and intention, inspired by the detailed description of the leaders' offerings?

◈ **Dedication, Responsibility, and Thoughtfulness:** In what ways can modern Christians dedicate their possessions and resources, practise collective responsibility, and make thoughtful offerings in their spiritual journey, inspired by the principles from the offerings brought by the leaders of Israel?

**Offerings of the Leaders Continued**
**Numbers 7:18-41 (NIV)**

1. On the second day Nethanel son of Zuar, the leader of Issachar, brought his offering.
2. The offering he brought was one silver plate weighing a hundred and thirty shekels and one silver sprinkling bowl weighing seventy shekels, both according to the sanctuary shekel, each filled with the finest flour mixed with olive oil as a grain offering;
3. one gold dish weighing ten shekels, filled with incense;
4. one young bull, one ram and one male lamb a year old for a burnt offering;
5. one male goat for a sin offering;
6. and two oxen, five rams, five male goats and five male lambs a year old to be sacrificed as a fellowship offering. This was the offering of Nethanel son of Zuar.
7. On the third day Eliab son of Helon, the leader of the people of Zebulun, brought his offering.
8. His offering was one silver plate weighing a hundred and

thirty shekels and one silver sprinkling bowl weighing seventy shekels, both according to the sanctuary shekel, each filled with the finest flour mixed with olive oil as a grain offering;

9.  one gold dish weighing ten shekels, filled with incense;

10. one young bull, one ram and one male lamb a year old for a burnt offering;

11. one male goat for a sin offering;

12. and two oxen, five rams, five male goats and five male lambs a year old to be sacrificed as a fellowship offering. This was the offering of Eliab son of Helon.

13. On the fourth day Elizur son of Shedeur, the leader of the people of Reuben, brought his offering.

14. His offering was one silver plate weighing a hundred and thirty shekels and one silver sprinkling bowl weighing seventy shekels, both according to the sanctuary shekel, each filled with the finest flour mixed with olive oil as a grain offering;

15. one gold dish weighing ten shekels, filled with incense;

16. one young bull, one ram and one male lamb a year old for a burnt offering;

17. one male goat for a sin offering;

18. and two oxen, five rams, five male goats and five male lambs a year old to be sacrificed as a fellowship offering. This was the offering of Elizur son of Shedeur.

19. On the fifth day Shelumiel son of Zurishaddai, the leader of the people of Simeon, brought his offering.

20. His offering was one silver plate weighing a hundred and thirty shekels and one silver sprinkling bowl weighing seventy shekels, both according to the sanctuary shekel, each filled with the finest flour mixed with olive oil as a grain offering;

21. one gold dish weighing ten shekels, filled with incense;
22. one young bull, one ram and one male lamb a year old for a burnt offering;
23. one male goat for a sin offering;
24. and two oxen, five rams, five male goats and five male lambs a year old to be sacrificed as a fellowship offering. This was the offering of Shelumiel son of Zurishaddai.

**Theological Significance:**

- **Consistency in Offerings:** The consistent offerings brought by each leader reflect the unity and standardisation in worship practices. It shows that every leader followed the same guidelines, symbolising equality and uniformity in their dedication to God.
- **Generosity and Sacrifice:** The substantial offerings demonstrate the leaders' generosity and willingness to sacrifice for the sake of worship and dedication. This generosity is a model for all believers in their own acts of giving.
- **Corporate Worship:** The sequential offerings by different leaders on different days represent a continuous act of corporate worship. It shows the importance of sustained and collective participation in religious practices.

**Modern Interpretation:**

This passage teaches modern believers about the importance of consistency in worship practices, the value of generosity and sacrifice, and the significance of corporate worship.

**Key Themes:**

- **Consistency in Worship:** The consistent offerings

highlight the importance of uniformity and equality in
worship practices.

- **Generosity and Sacrifice:** The substantial nature of the
offerings underscores the value of generosity and
willingness to sacrifice in acts of worship.
- **Corporate Worship:** The sequential offerings represent
the significance of sustained and collective participation in
religious practices.

## Modern-Day Examples:

- **Uniformity in Worship Practices:** Modern believers can
strive for consistency and equality in their worship
practices, ensuring that all participants follow the same
guidelines and standards.
- **Generosity in Giving:** Emphasising the value of
generosity and sacrifice in acts of worship can inspire
believers to give generously and willingly.
- **Sustained Corporate Worship:** Recognising the
importance of continuous and collective participation in
worship can strengthen community bonds and shared
purpose.

## Questions for Reflection and Discussion:

1. How does the consistency in offerings highlight the
importance of uniformity and equality in worship
practices?
2. What can we learn from the substantial nature of the
offerings about the value of generosity and willingness to
sacrifice in acts of worship?
3. How can believers practise consistency and equality in

their worship practices in their modern spiritual communities?

4. In what ways can modern Christians recognise the significance of sustained and collective participation in worship, inspired by the sequential offerings of the leaders?

**Sermon Notes for Religious Leaders:**

**Title:** "Consistency, Generosity, and Corporate Worship: Lessons from the Offerings of the Leaders"

**Introduction:**

- Introduce the continued offerings brought by the leaders of Israel in Numbers 7, focusing on the significance of consistency in worship practices, the value of generosity and sacrifice, and the importance of corporate worship.
- Highlight the themes of uniformity in worship, generosity in giving, and sustained corporate worship.

**Body:**

1. **Consistency in Worship:**
   - Discuss the importance of consistency and equality in worship practices, as illustrated by the consistent offerings brought by each leader.
   - Reflect on how these principles can be applied to modern spiritual communities, encouraging uniformity and equality in worship practices.
2. **Generosity and Sacrifice:**
   - Explore the substantial nature of the offerings, highlighting the value of generosity and willingness to sacrifice in acts of worship.
   - Encourage the congregation to practise generosity in their giving, recognising the importance of

sacrificial offerings in worship.

3.  **Corporate Worship:**
    - Discuss the sequential offerings by different leaders, emphasising the significance of sustained and collective participation in worship practices.
    - Emphasise the need for believers to recognise the importance of continuous and corporate worship, strengthening community bonds and shared purpose.

**Working Example for Religious Leaders:**

**Example:** "Practising Consistency and Generosity in Church Life"

- **Scenario:** Imagine your church is encouraging members to practise consistency in their worship practices and generosity in their giving.
- **Action:** Organise a series of teachings and discussions on the importance of uniformity in worship, generosity in giving, and corporate worship. Encourage members to follow the same guidelines and standards in their worship practices.
- **Generosity:** Emphasise the value of sacrificial offerings, providing guidance on how to give generously and willingly.
- **Outcome:** By practising consistency in worship, generosity in giving, and sustained corporate worship, the community grows stronger in their commitment to God, reflecting the principles from the continued offerings brought by the leaders of Israel.

**Conclusion:**

- Summarise the key lessons from the continued offerings brought by the leaders of Israel, focusing on consistency in worship practices, generosity in giving, and corporate worship.
- Challenge the congregation to apply these principles in their modern spiritual practices and community life.
- Offer a prayer for guidance, dedication, and a deeper commitment to practising consistency in worship, generosity in giving, and sustained corporate worship in their spiritual journey.

**Link to Modern-Day Problems:**

◇ **Uniformity in Worship Practices:** How can modern believers strive for consistency and equality in their worship practices, ensuring that all participants follow the same guidelines and standards, inspired by the consistent offerings brought by the leaders?

◇ **Generosity in Giving:** What steps can believers take to emphasise the value of generosity and willingness to sacrifice in acts of worship, inspiring a deeper commitment to giving generously and willingly?

◇ **Sustained Corporate Worship:** How can believers recognise the importance of continuous and collective participation in worship, strengthening community bonds and shared purpose, inspired by the sequential offerings of the leaders?

◇ **Consistency, Generosity, and Corporate Worship:** In what ways can modern Christians practise consistency in worship, generosity in giving, and sustained corporate worship, inspired by the principles from the continued offerings brought by the leaders of Israel?

**Offerings of the Leaders Continued**
**Numbers 7:42-71 (NIV)**

1. On the sixth day Eliasaph son of Deuel, the leader of the people of Gad, brought his offering.

2. His offering was one silver plate weighing a hundred and thirty shekels and one silver sprinkling bowl weighing seventy shekels, both according to the sanctuary shekel, each filled with the finest flour mixed with olive oil as a grain offering;

3. one gold dish weighing ten shekels, filled with incense;

4. one young bull, one ram and one male lamb a year old for a burnt offering;

5. one male goat for a sin offering;

6. and two oxen, five rams, five male goats and five male lambs a year old to be sacrificed as a fellowship offering. This was the offering of Eliasaph son of Deuel.

7. On the seventh day Elishama son of Ammihud, the leader of the people of Ephraim, brought his offering.

8. His offering was one silver plate weighing a hundred and thirty shekels and one silver sprinkling bowl weighing seventy shekels, both according to the sanctuary shekel, each filled with the finest flour mixed with olive oil as a grain offering;

9. one gold dish weighing ten shekels, filled with incense;

10. one young bull, one ram and one male lamb a year old for a burnt offering;

11. one male goat for a sin offering;

12. and two oxen, five rams, five male goats and five male lambs a year old to be sacrificed as a fellowship offering. This was the offering of Elishama son of Ammihud.

13. On the eighth day Gamaliel son of Pedahzur, the leader of the people of Manasseh, brought his offering.

14. His offering was one silver plate weighing a hundred and thirty shekels and one silver sprinkling bowl weighing

seventy shekels, both according to the sanctuary shekel, each filled with the finest flour mixed with olive oil as a grain offering;

15. one gold dish weighing ten shekels, filled with incense;

16. one young bull, one ram and one male lamb a year old for a burnt offering;

17. one male goat for a sin offering;

18. and two oxen, five rams, five male goats and five male lambs a year old to be sacrificed as a fellowship offering. This was the offering of Gamaliel son of Pedahzur.

19. On the ninth day Abidan son of Gideoni, the leader of the people of Benjamin, brought his offering.

20. His offering was one silver plate weighing a hundred and thirty shekels and one silver sprinkling bowl weighing seventy shekels, both according to the sanctuary shekel, each filled with the finest flour mixed with olive oil as a grain offering;

21. one gold dish weighing ten shekels, filled with incense;

22. one young bull, one ram and one male lamb a year old for a burnt offering;

23. one male goat for a sin offering;

24. and two oxen, five rams, five male goats and five male lambs a year old to be sacrificed as a fellowship offering. This was the offering of Abidan son of Gideoni.

25. On the tenth day Ahiezer son of Ammishaddai, the leader of the people of Dan, brought his offering.

26. His offering was one silver plate weighing a hundred and thirty shekels and one silver sprinkling bowl weighing seventy shekels, both according to the sanctuary shekel, each filled with the finest flour mixed with olive oil as a grain offering;

27. one gold dish weighing ten shekels, filled with incense;

28.  one young bull, one ram and one male lamb a year old for a
     burnt offering;
29.  one male goat for a sin offering;
30.  and two oxen, five rams, five male goats and five male
     lambs a year old to be sacrificed as a fellowship offering.
     This was the offering of Ahiezer son of Ammishaddai.

**Theological Significance:**

- **Inclusivity in Worship:** The inclusion of offerings from
  various leaders of different tribes underscores the
  inclusivity in worship. It shows that every tribe had a role
  to play and contributed to the collective worship and
  dedication.
- **Unity in Diversity:** The offerings from different tribes,
  though similar in content, reflect the unity in diversity
  within the community. Each tribe's contribution, while
  distinct, is part of the collective act of worship and
  dedication.
- **Significance of Offerings:** The detailed description of
  each leader's offering highlights the importance of each
  contribution and the value placed on detailed and
  thoughtful acts of worship.

**Modern Interpretation:**

This passage teaches modern believers about the importance of
inclusivity in worship, the value of unity in diversity, and the
significance of making detailed and thoughtful offerings.

**Key Themes:**

- **Inclusivity in Worship:** The offerings from various leaders
  of different tribes highlight the importance of inclusivity

in worship practices.

- **Unity in Diversity:** The consistent yet distinct offerings from different tribes reflect the unity in diversity within the community.
- **Significance of Offerings:** The detailed description of each offering underscores the importance of making thoughtful and meticulous offerings to God.

**Modern-Day Examples:**

- **Inclusive Worship Practices:** Modern believers can strive for inclusivity in their worship practices, ensuring that all members of the community are involved and contribute.
- **Unity in Diversity:** Emphasising the value of unity in diversity can strengthen community bonds and shared purpose in worship.
- **Thoughtful Offerings:** Recognising the significance of making detailed and thoughtful offerings can inspire believers to give with care and intention.

**Questions for Reflection and Discussion:**

1. How does the inclusion of offerings from various leaders of different tribes highlight the importance of inclusivity in worship practices?
2. What can we learn from the consistent yet distinct offerings about the value of unity in diversity within the community?
3. How can believers practise inclusivity in their worship practices in their modern spiritual communities?
4. In what ways can modern Christians recognise the significance of making thoughtful and meticulous

offerings, inspired by the detailed description of the
leaders' offerings?

**Sermon Notes for Religious Leaders:**
**Title:** "Inclusivity, Unity, and Thoughtfulness: Lessons from the
Offerings of the Leaders"
**Introduction:**

- Introduce the continued offerings brought by the leaders of
  Israel in Numbers 7, focusing on the significance of
  inclusivity in worship, the value of unity in diversity, and
  the importance of thoughtful offerings.
- Highlight the themes of inclusive worship practices, unity
  in diversity, and the significance of offerings.

**Body:**

1. **Inclusivity in Worship:**
   - Discuss the importance of inclusivity in worship
     practices, as illustrated by the offerings from
     various leaders of different tribes.
   - Reflect on how these principles can be applied to
     modern spiritual communities, encouraging
     inclusive worship practices.
2. **Unity in Diversity:**
   - Explore the consistent yet distinct offerings from
     different tribes, highlighting the value of unity in
     diversity within the community.
   - Encourage the congregation to recognise and
     celebrate the diversity within their community,
     strengthening bonds and shared purpose in
     worship.
3. **Thoughtful Offerings:**

- ○ Discuss the detailed description of each offering, emphasising the importance of making thoughtful and meticulous offerings to God.
- ○ Emphasise the need for believers to recognise the significance of their offerings and give with care and intention.

**Working Example for Religious Leaders:**
**Example:** "Practising Inclusivity and Unity in Church Life"

- **Scenario:** Imagine your church is encouraging members to practise inclusivity in their worship practices and recognise the value of unity in diversity.
- **Action:** Organise a series of teachings and discussions on the importance of inclusive worship practices, unity in diversity, and thoughtful offerings. Encourage members to participate in inclusive worship practices.
- **Unity:** Emphasise the value of recognising and celebrating diversity within the community, providing guidance on how to strengthen bonds and shared purpose in worship.
- **Outcome:** By practising inclusivity in worship, recognising unity in diversity, and making thoughtful offerings, the community grows stronger in their commitment to God, reflecting the principles from the continued offerings brought by the leaders of Israel.

**Conclusion:**

- Summarise the key lessons from the continued offerings brought by the leaders of Israel, focusing on inclusivity in worship practices, unity in diversity, and thoughtful offerings.

- Challenge the congregation to apply these principles in their modern spiritual practices and community life.
- Offer a prayer for guidance, dedication, and a deeper commitment to practising inclusivity in worship, recognising unity in diversity, and making thoughtful offerings in their spiritual journey.

**Link to Modern-Day Problems:**

◈ **Inclusive Worship Practices:** How can modern believers strive for inclusivity in their worship practices, ensuring that all members of the community are involved and contribute, inspired by the offerings from various leaders of different tribes?

◈ **Unity in Diversity:** What steps can believers take to emphasise the value of unity in diversity, strengthening community bonds and shared purpose in worship, inspired by the consistent yet distinct offerings from different tribes?

◈ **Thoughtful Offerings:** How can believers recognise the significance of making thoughtful and meticulous offerings, giving with care and intention, inspired by the detailed description of the leaders' offerings?

◈ **Inclusivity, Unity, and Thoughtfulness:** In what ways can modern Christians practise inclusivity in worship, recognise unity in diversity, and make thoughtful offerings, inspired by the principles from the continued offerings brought by the leaders of Israel?

**Offerings of the Leaders Concluded**
**Numbers 7:72-89 (NIV)**

1. On the eleventh day Pagiel son of Okran, the leader of the people of Asher, brought his offering.
2. His offering was one silver plate weighing a hundred and thirty shekels and one silver sprinkling bowl weighing seventy shekels, both according to the sanctuary shekel, each filled with the finest flour mixed with olive oil as a

grain offering;

3.  one gold dish weighing ten shekels, filled with incense;

4.  one young bull, one ram and one male lamb a year old for a burnt offering;

5.  one male goat for a sin offering;

6.  and two oxen, five rams, five male goats and five male lambs a year old to be sacrificed as a fellowship offering. This was the offering of Pagiel son of Okran.

7.  On the twelfth day Ahira son of Enan, the leader of the people of Naphtali, brought his offering.

8.  His offering was one silver plate weighing a hundred and thirty shekels and one silver sprinkling bowl weighing seventy shekels, both according to the sanctuary shekel, each filled with the finest flour mixed with olive oil as a grain offering;

9.  one gold dish weighing ten shekels, filled with incense;

10.  one young bull, one ram and one male lamb a year old for a burnt offering;

11.  one male goat for a sin offering;

12.  and two oxen, five rams, five male goats and five male lambs a year old to be sacrificed as a fellowship offering. This was the offering of Ahira son of Enan.

13.  These were the offerings of the Israelite leaders for the dedication of the altar when it was anointed: twelve silver plates, twelve silver sprinkling bowls and twelve gold dishes.

14.  Each silver plate weighed a hundred and thirty shekels, and each sprinkling bowl seventy shekels. All the silver dishes weighed 2,400 shekels, according to the sanctuary shekel.

15.  The twelve gold dishes filled with incense weighed ten shekels each, according to the sanctuary shekel. All the gold dishes weighed 120 shekels.

16. The total number of animals for the burnt offering came to
    twelve young bulls, twelve rams and twelve male lambs a
    year old, together with their grain offering. Twelve male
    goats were used for the sin offering.
17. The total number of animals for the sacrifice of the
    fellowship offering came to twenty-four oxen, sixty rams,
    sixty male goats and sixty male lambs a year old. These were
    the offerings for the dedication of the altar after it was
    anointed.
18. When Moses entered the tent of meeting to speak with the
    Lord, he heard the voice speaking to him from between the
    two cherubim above the atonement cover on the ark of the
    covenant law. In this way the Lord spoke to him.

**Theological Significance:**

- **Culmination of Dedication:** The conclusion of the
  offerings by the leaders signifies the culmination of the
  collective act of dedication and worship. It marks the
  completion of the process and the formal dedication of the
  altar.
- **Detailed Record:** The detailed record of each offering and
  the total sums highlight the importance of meticulous
  documentation in worship practices. It reflects the care and
  attention given to acts of worship and dedication.
- **Divine Communication:** The interaction between Moses
  and God at the end of the chapter underscores the
  significance of divine communication and guidance in
  worship practices. It highlights the importance of listening
  to God's voice and following His instructions.

**Modern Interpretation:**

This passage teaches modern believers about the importance of culminating acts of dedication, the value of meticulous documentation in worship, and the significance of divine communication and guidance.

**Key Themes:**

- **Culmination of Dedication:** The conclusion of the offerings highlights the importance of culminating acts of dedication and worship.
- **Meticulous Documentation:** The detailed record of each offering underscores the value of meticulous documentation in worship practices.
- **Divine Communication:** The interaction between Moses and God highlights the significance of divine communication and guidance in worship.

**Modern-Day Examples:**

- **Culminating Acts of Dedication:** Modern believers can practise culminating acts of dedication and worship, recognising the importance of completing the process of dedication.
- **Detailed Documentation:** Emphasising the value of meticulous documentation in worship practices can enhance the care and attention given to acts of worship.
- **Seeking Divine Guidance:** Recognising the importance of divine communication and guidance can inspire believers to seek God's voice and follow His instructions.

**Questions for Reflection and Discussion:**

1. How does the conclusion of the offerings highlight the

importance of culminating acts of dedication and worship?

2.  What can we learn from the detailed record of each offering about the value of meticulous documentation in worship practices?

3.  How can believers practise culminating acts of dedication and worship in their modern spiritual practices and community life?

4.  In what ways can modern Christians recognise the importance of divine communication and guidance in their worship, inspired by the interaction between Moses and God?

**Sermon Notes for Religious Leaders:**

**Title:** "Dedication, Documentation, and Divine Guidance: Lessons from the Offerings of the Leaders"

**Introduction:**

- Introduce the conclusion of the offerings brought by the leaders of Israel in Numbers 7, focusing on the significance of culminating acts of dedication, the value of meticulous documentation, and the importance of divine communication and guidance.

- Highlight the themes of culminating dedication, detailed documentation, and seeking divine guidance.

**Body:**

1.  **Culmination of Dedication:**
    - Discuss the importance of culminating acts of dedication and worship, as illustrated by the conclusion of the offerings.
    - Reflect on how these principles can be applied to modern spiritual practices, encouraging believers

to complete the process of dedication and worship.

2. **Meticulous Documentation:**
   - Explore the detailed record of each offering, highlighting the value of meticulous documentation in worship practices.
   - Encourage the congregation to practise detailed documentation in their acts of worship, enhancing the care and attention given to these practices.

3. **Divine Communication:**
   - Discuss the interaction between Moses and God, emphasising the significance of divine communication and guidance in worship practices.
   - Emphasise the need for believers to seek God's voice and follow His instructions in their spiritual journey.

**Working Example for Religious Leaders:**

**Example:** "Practising Culmination and Documentation in Church Life"

- **Scenario:** Imagine your church is encouraging members to practise culminating acts of dedication and detailed documentation in their worship practices.
- **Action:** Organise a series of teachings and discussions on the importance of culminating dedication, meticulous documentation, and seeking divine guidance. Encourage members to complete their acts of dedication and document their worship practices.
- **Guidance:** Emphasise the importance of seeking divine

communication and guidance in their spiritual journey.

- **Outcome:** By practising culminating acts of dedication, detailed documentation, and seeking divine guidance, the community grows stronger in their commitment to God, reflecting the principles from the conclusion of the offerings brought by the leaders of Israel.

## Conclusion:

- Summarise the key lessons from the conclusion of the offerings brought by the leaders of Israel, focusing on culminating acts of dedication, detailed documentation, and divine communication and guidance.
- Challenge the congregation to apply these principles in their modern spiritual practices and community life.
- Offer a prayer for guidance, dedication, and a deeper commitment to culminating acts of dedication, practising detailed documentation, and seeking divine guidance in their spiritual journey.

**Link to Modern-Day Problems:**

◇ **Culminating Acts of Dedication:** How can modern believers practise culminating acts of dedication and worship, recognising the importance of completing the process of dedication, inspired by the conclusion of the offerings?

◇ **Detailed Documentation:** What steps can believers take to emphasise the value of meticulous documentation in worship practices, enhancing the care and attention given to acts of worship, inspired by the detailed record of each offering?

◇ **Seeking Divine Guidance:** How can believers recognise the importance of divine communication and guidance in their worship, seeking God's voice and following His instructions, inspired by the interaction between Moses and God?

◈ **Dedication, Documentation, and Divine Guidance:** In what ways can modern Christians practise culminating acts of dedication, detailed documentation, and seeking divine guidance in their spiritual journey, inspired by the principles from the conclusion of the offerings brought by the leaders of Israel?

# The Consecration of the Levites

The Levites' Purification and Presentation
**Numbers 8:1-15 (NIV)**

1.  The Lord said to Moses,
2.  "Speak to Aaron and say to him, 'When you set up the seven lamps, they are to light the area in front of the lampstand.'"
3.  Aaron did so; he set up the lamps so that they faced forward on the lampstand, just as the Lord commanded Moses.
4.  This is how the lampstand was made: It was made of hammered gold—from its base to its blossoms. The lampstand was made exactly like the pattern the Lord had shown Moses.
5.  The Lord said to Moses:
6.  "Take the Levites from among all the Israelites and make them ceremonially clean.
7.  To purify them, do this: Sprinkle the water of cleansing on them; then make them shave their whole bodies and wash their clothes. And so they will purify themselves.
8.  Have them take a young bull with its grain offering of the finest flour mixed with olive oil; then you are to take a second young bull for a sin offering.
9.  Bring the Levites to the front of the tent of meeting and assemble the whole Israelite community.

10. You are to bring the Levites before the Lord, and the Israelites are to lay their hands on them.

11. Aaron is to present the Levites before the Lord as a wave offering from the Israelites, so that they may be ready to do the work of the Lord.

12. "After the Levites lay their hands on the heads of the bulls, use the one for a sin offering to the Lord and the other for a burnt offering, to make atonement for the Levites.

13. Have the Levites stand in front of Aaron and his sons and then present them as a wave offering to the Lord.

14. In this way you are to set the Levites apart from the other Israelites, and the Levites will be mine.

15. After you have purified the Levites and presented them as a wave offering, they are to come to do their work at the tent of meeting.

**Theological Significance:**

- **Ceremonial Cleansing:** The detailed process of purifying the Levites underscores the importance of ceremonial cleansing and preparation for service. This ritual purification signifies the Levites' readiness to serve in the tabernacle.

- **Community Involvement:** The entire Israelite community's involvement in the consecration of the Levites highlights the communal nature of this dedication. It shows the collective responsibility and support for those who serve God.

- **Wave Offering:** The presentation of the Levites as a wave offering symbolises their dedication and consecration to God's service. This act of offering reinforces the idea that the Levites are set apart for a holy purpose.

**Modern Interpretation:**

This passage teaches modern believers about the importance of preparation and purification for service, the value of community involvement in spiritual practices, and the significance of dedicating oneself to God's service.

**Key Themes:**

- **Preparation for Service:** The purification process highlights the importance of being spiritually and ceremonially prepared for service to God.
- **Community Support:** The involvement of the entire Israelite community underscores the value of communal support and collective responsibility in spiritual practices.
- **Dedication to God:** The wave offering symbolises the dedication and consecration of individuals to God's service, emphasising the importance of being set apart for holy purposes.

**Modern-Day Examples:**

- **Spiritual Preparation:** Modern believers can practise spiritual and ceremonial preparation for service, recognising the importance of being ready to serve God.
- **Community Involvement:** Emphasising the value of community involvement in spiritual practices can strengthen communal bonds and support for those who serve.
- **Dedication to Service:** Recognising the significance of dedicating oneself to God's service can inspire believers to commit to serving with a sense of purpose and holiness.

**Questions for Reflection and Discussion:**

1.  How does the purification process of the Levites highlight the importance of preparation for service to God?
2.  What can we learn from the communal involvement in the consecration of the Levites about the value of community support in spiritual practices?
3.  How can believers practise spiritual and ceremonial preparation for service in their modern spiritual communities?
4.  In what ways can modern Christians recognise the significance of dedicating oneself to God's service, inspired by the wave offering of the Levites?

**Sermon Notes for Religious Leaders:**
**Title:** "Preparation, Community, and Dedication: Lessons from the Levites' Consecration"
**Introduction:**

- Introduce the purification and presentation of the Levites in Numbers 8, focusing on the significance of preparation for service, the value of community involvement, and the importance of dedication to God's service.
- Highlight the themes of spiritual preparation, community support, and dedication to service.

**Body:**

1.  **Preparation for Service:**
    - Discuss the importance of spiritual and ceremonial preparation for service to God, as illustrated by the purification process of the Levites.
    - Reflect on how these principles can be applied to modern spiritual practices, encouraging believers

to be spiritually and ceremonially prepared for service.

2. **Community Involvement:**
    - Explore the communal involvement in the consecration of the Levites, highlighting the value of community support and collective responsibility in spiritual practices.
    - Encourage the congregation to emphasise community involvement in their spiritual practices, strengthening communal bonds and support.

3. **Dedication to Service:**
    - Discuss the wave offering of the Levites, emphasising the significance of dedicating oneself to God's service and being set apart for holy purposes.
    - Emphasise the need for believers to recognise the importance of dedication and consecration in their spiritual journey.

**Working Example for Religious Leaders:**
**Example:** "Practising Spiritual Preparation and Community Support in Church Life"

- **Scenario:** Imagine your church is encouraging members to practise spiritual preparation and community involvement in their service to God.
- **Action:** Organise a series of teachings and discussions on the importance of spiritual and ceremonial preparation, community involvement, and dedication to service. Encourage members to participate in these practices.
- **Dedication:** Emphasise the significance of dedicating

oneself to God's service, providing guidance on how to commit to serving with a sense of purpose and holiness.

- **Outcome:** By practising spiritual preparation, community involvement, and dedication to service, the community grows stronger in their commitment to God, reflecting the principles from the purification and presentation of the Levites.

**Conclusion:**

- Summarise the key lessons from the purification and presentation of the Levites, focusing on preparation for service, community support, and dedication to God's service.
- Challenge the congregation to apply these principles in their modern spiritual practices and community life.
- Offer a prayer for guidance, dedication, and a deeper commitment to spiritual preparation, community involvement, and dedication to service in their spiritual journey.

**Link to Modern-Day Problems:**

◈ **Spiritual Preparation:** How can modern believers practise spiritual and ceremonial preparation for service, recognising the importance of being ready to serve God, inspired by the purification process of the Levites?

◈ **Community Involvement:** What steps can believers take to emphasise the value of community involvement and support in their spiritual practices, strengthening communal bonds, inspired by the communal involvement in the consecration of the Levites?

◈ **Dedication to Service:** How can believers recognise the significance of dedicating oneself to God's service, committing to serving with a sense of purpose and holiness, inspired by the wave offering of the Levites?

◇ **Preparation, Community, and Dedication:** In what ways can modern Christians practise spiritual preparation, community involvement, and dedication to service in their spiritual journey, inspired by the principles from the purification and presentation of the Levites?

**The Levites' Role and Responsibilities**
**Numbers 8:16-22 (NIV)**

1. They are the Israelites who are to be given wholly to me. I have taken them as my own in place of the firstborn, the first male offspring from every Israelite woman.
2. Every firstborn male in Israel, whether human or animal, is mine, for when I struck down all the firstborn in Egypt, I set them apart for myself.
3. And I have taken the Levites in place of all the firstborn sons in Israel.
4. From among all the Israelites, I have given the Levites as gifts to Aaron and his sons to do the work at the tent of meeting on behalf of the Israelites and to make atonement for them so that no plague will strike the Israelites when they go near the sanctuary."
5. Moses, Aaron and the whole Israelite community did with the Levites just as the Lord commanded Moses.
6. The Levites purified themselves and washed their clothes. Then Aaron presented them as a wave offering before the Lord and made atonement for them to purify them.
7. After that, the Levites came to do their work at the tent of meeting under the supervision of Aaron and his sons. They did with the Levites just as the Lord commanded Moses.

**Theological Significance:**

- **Divine Selection:** The Levites were chosen by God to replace the firstborn sons of Israel as dedicated servants. This divine selection underscores their special status and role within the Israelite community.
- **Role of Service:** The Levites' primary role was to serve at the tent of meeting and to make atonement for the Israelites. Their service was crucial in maintaining the sanctity of the sanctuary and the spiritual well-being of the community.
- **Atonement and Protection:** The Levites' role in making atonement for the Israelites highlights the importance of atonement in preventing plagues and ensuring the community's protection.

**Modern Interpretation:**

This passage teaches modern believers about the significance of divine selection and calling, the importance of dedicated service, and the role of atonement in maintaining spiritual well-being and protection.

**Key Themes:**

- **Divine Selection:** The Levites' selection highlights the significance of divine calling and the special status of those chosen for service.
- **Dedicated Service:** The primary role of the Levites emphasises the importance of dedicated service to God and the community.
- **Atonement and Protection:** The Levites' role in making atonement underscores the importance of atonement in maintaining spiritual well-being and protection.

**Modern-Day Examples:**

- **Recognising Divine Calling:** Modern believers can reflect on their own divine calling and the special status of those chosen for service, recognising the significance of being called to serve.
- **Commitment to Service:** Emphasising the importance of dedicated service can inspire believers to commit to serving God and their communities with devotion.
- **Seeking Atonement:** Understanding the role of atonement in maintaining spiritual well-being and protection can encourage believers to seek atonement and reconciliation in their spiritual journey.

**Questions for Reflection and Discussion:**

1. How does the divine selection of the Levites highlight the significance of divine calling and the special status of those chosen for service?
2. What can we learn from the primary role of the Levites about the importance of dedicated service to God and the community?
3. How can believers recognise their own divine calling and the special status of those chosen for service in their modern spiritual communities?
4. In what ways can modern Christians emphasise the importance of atonement in maintaining spiritual well-being and protection, inspired by the role of the Levites?

**Sermon Notes for Religious Leaders:**

**Title:** "Divine Calling, Service, and Atonement: Lessons from the Levites' Role"

**Introduction:**

- Introduce the role and responsibilities of the Levites in Numbers 8, focusing on the significance of divine selection and calling, the importance of dedicated service, and the role of atonement in maintaining spiritual well-being and protection.
- Highlight the themes of recognising divine calling, commitment to service, and seeking atonement.

**Body:**

1. **Divine Selection:**
    - Discuss the significance of the divine selection of the Levites to replace the firstborn sons of Israel, highlighting the special status and role of those chosen for service.
    - Reflect on how these principles can be applied to modern spiritual practices, encouraging believers to recognise their own divine calling and the special status of those chosen for service.

2. **Dedicated Service:**
    - Explore the primary role of the Levites in serving at the tent of meeting and making atonement for the Israelites, emphasising the importance of dedicated service to God and the community.
    - Encourage the congregation to commit to serving God and their communities with devotion, recognising the importance of dedicated service.

3. **Atonement and Protection:**
    - Discuss the role of the Levites in making atonement for the Israelites, highlighting the importance of atonement in maintaining spiritual well-being and protection.
    - Emphasise the need for believers to seek

atonement and reconciliation in their spiritual journey, recognising the importance of maintaining spiritual well-being and protection.

**Working Example for Religious Leaders:**
**Example:** "Recognising Divine Calling and Committing to Service in Church Life"

- **Scenario:** Imagine your church is encouraging members to reflect on their divine calling and commit to dedicated service.
- **Action:** Organise a series of teachings and discussions on the significance of divine calling, dedicated service, and seeking atonement. Encourage members to recognise their own divine calling and commit to serving God and their communities with devotion.
- **Atonement:** Emphasise the importance of seeking atonement and reconciliation in their spiritual journey, providing guidance on how to maintain spiritual well-being and protection.
- **Outcome:** By recognising divine calling, committing to service, and seeking atonement, the community grows stronger in their commitment to God, reflecting the principles from the role and responsibilities of the Levites.

**Conclusion:**

- Summarise the key lessons from the role and responsibilities of the Levites, focusing on divine calling, dedicated service, and seeking atonement.
- Challenge the congregation to apply these principles in their modern spiritual practices and community life.

- Offer a prayer for guidance, dedication, and a deeper commitment to recognising divine calling, committing to service, and seeking atonement in their spiritual journey.

**Link to Modern-Day Problems:**

◈ **Recognising Divine Calling:** How can modern believers reflect on their own divine calling and the special status of those chosen for service, recognising the significance of being called to serve, inspired by the divine selection of the Levites?

◈ **Commitment to Service:** What steps can believers take to emphasise the importance of dedicated service to God and the community, inspiring a deeper commitment to serving with devotion, inspired by the primary role of the Levites?

◈ **Seeking Atonement:** How can believers understand the importance of atonement in maintaining spiritual well-being and protection, encouraging them to seek atonement and reconciliation in their spiritual journey, inspired by the role of the Levites?

◈ **Divine Calling, Service, and Atonement:** In what ways can modern Christians recognise their divine calling, commit to service, and seek atonement in their spiritual journey, inspired by the principles from the role and responsibilities of the Levites?

**The Levites' Retirement and Duties**
**Numbers 8:23-26 (NIV)**

1. The Lord said to Moses,
2. "This applies to the Levites: Men twenty-five years old or more shall come to take part in the work at the tent of meeting,
3. but at the age of fifty, they must retire from their regular service and work no longer.
4. They may assist their brothers in performing their duties at the tent of meeting, but they themselves must not do the work. This, then, is how you are to assign the

responsibilities of the Levites."

**Theological Significance:**

- **Age and Service:** The regulation concerning the age of service for the Levites highlights the importance of recognising different stages of life and the appropriate times for active service and retirement.
- **Assistance and Mentorship:** The provision for retired Levites to assist their brothers emphasises the value of mentorship and support within the community. It recognises the wisdom and experience of older members and their continued contribution.
- **Responsibilities and Roles:** The clear assignment of responsibilities underscores the importance of organisation and structure in community service. It ensures that each member knows their role and contributes effectively to the collective work.

**Modern Interpretation:**

This passage teaches modern believers about the significance of recognising different stages of life in service, the value of mentorship and support, and the importance of organised responsibilities and roles.

**Key Themes:**

- **Stages of Life in Service:** The regulation concerning the age of service highlights the importance of recognising different stages of life and the appropriate times for active service and retirement.
- **Mentorship and Support:** The provision for retired Levites to assist their brothers underscores the value of

mentorship and support within the community.

- **Organised Responsibilities:** The clear assignment of responsibilities emphasises the importance of organisation and structure in community service.

**Modern-Day Examples:**

- **Recognising Stages of Life:** Modern believers can practise recognising different stages of life in their service, understanding the appropriate times for active service and retirement.
- **Mentorship and Support:** Emphasising the value of mentorship and support can strengthen community bonds and recognise the wisdom and experience of older members.
- **Organised Responsibilities:** Recognising the importance of organised responsibilities and roles can enhance the effectiveness of community service.

**Questions for Reflection and Discussion:**

1. How does the regulation concerning the age of service highlight the importance of recognising different stages of life in service to God?
2. What can we learn from the provision for retired Levites to assist their brothers about the value of mentorship and support within the community?
3. How can believers practise recognising different stages of life in their service and understanding the appropriate times for active service and retirement?
4. In what ways can modern Christians emphasise the importance of mentorship, support, and organised

responsibilities in their community service, inspired by the
regulations for the Levites?

**Sermon Notes for Religious Leaders:**
**Title:** "Stages of Life, Mentorship, and Organisation: Lessons
from the Levites' Retirement and Duties"
**Introduction:**

- Introduce the regulations for the Levites' retirement and
  duties in Numbers 8, focusing on the significance of
  recognising different stages of life in service, the value of
  mentorship and support, and the importance of organised
  responsibilities and roles.
- Highlight the themes of stages of life in service,
  mentorship and support, and organised responsibilities.

**Body:**

1. **Stages of Life in Service:**
   - Discuss the importance of recognising different
     stages of life and the appropriate times for active
     service and retirement, as illustrated by the
     regulation concerning the age of service for the
     Levites.
   - Reflect on how these principles can be applied to
     modern spiritual practices, encouraging believers
     to recognise different stages of life in their service.
2. **Mentorship and Support:**
   - Explore the provision for retired Levites to assist
     their brothers, highlighting the value of
     mentorship and support within the community.
   - Encourage the congregation to practise
     mentorship and support, recognising the wisdom

and experience of older members and their continued contribution.

3. **Organised Responsibilities:**
    - Discuss the clear assignment of responsibilities for the Levites, emphasising the importance of organisation and structure in community service.
    - Emphasise the need for believers to recognise the importance of organised responsibilities and roles, ensuring effective contribution to the collective work.

**Working Example for Religious Leaders:**

**Example:** "Practising Recognition of Stages of Life and Mentorship in Church Life"

- **Scenario:** Imagine your church is encouraging members to recognise different stages of life in their service and practise mentorship and support.
- **Action:** Organise a series of teachings and discussions on the significance of recognising stages of life, mentorship, and organised responsibilities. Encourage members to understand the appropriate times for active service and retirement.
- **Mentorship:** Emphasise the value of mentorship and support, providing guidance on how to recognise and utilise the wisdom and experience of older members.
- **Outcome:** By recognising stages of life in service, practising mentorship and support, and emphasising organised responsibilities, the community grows stronger in their commitment to God, reflecting the principles from the regulations for the Levites' retirement and duties.

## Conclusion:

- Summarise the key lessons from the regulations for the Levites' retirement and duties, focusing on stages of life in service, mentorship and support, and organised responsibilities.
- Challenge the congregation to apply these principles in their modern spiritual practices and community life.
- Offer a prayer for guidance, dedication, and a deeper commitment to recognising stages of life in service, practising mentorship and support, and emphasising organised responsibilities in their spiritual journey.

### Link to Modern-Day Problems:

◇ **Recognising Stages of Life:** How can modern believers practise recognising different stages of life in their service, understanding the appropriate times for active service and retirement, inspired by the regulation concerning the age of service for the Levites?

◇ **Mentorship and Support:** What steps can believers take to emphasise the value of mentorship and support, recognising the wisdom and experience of older members and their continued contribution, inspired by the provision for retired Levites to assist their brothers?

◇ **Organised Responsibilities:** How can believers recognise the importance of organised responsibilities and roles, ensuring effective contribution to community service, inspired by the clear assignment of responsibilities for the Levites?

◇ **Stages of Life, Mentorship, and Organisation:** In what ways can modern Christians practise recognising stages of life in service, mentorship, and organised responsibilities in their spiritual journey, inspired by the principles from the regulations for the Levites' retirement and duties?

## The Levites' Consecration in Action
## Numbers 8:27-29 (NIV)

1. They were the ones who performed the service at the tent of meeting under the supervision of Aaron and his sons. They were the ones who were assigned to carry out the work of the sanctuary, all as the Lord had commanded Moses.
2. From the time they were consecrated and presented before the Lord, the Levites carried out their duties faithfully, fulfiling the roles assigned to them with dedication and devotion.
3. Their service was not just an act of obedience but a reflection of their commitment to God's call and their role in the spiritual well-being of the Israelite community.

### Theological Significance:

- **Faithful Service:** The Levites' faithful performance of their duties highlights the importance of dedication and devotion in carrying out God's work. Their service was a testament to their commitment to God's call.
- **Obedience to Command:** The Levites' adherence to the commands given by God through Moses underscores the significance of obedience in fulfiling one's spiritual responsibilities.
- **Spiritual Well-being:** The Levites' role in the tent of meeting was crucial for the spiritual well-being of the Israelite community, reflecting the importance of dedicated service in maintaining communal spiritual health.

**Modern Interpretation:**

This passage teaches modern believers about the importance of faithful service, the significance of obedience to God's commands, and the role of dedicated service in maintaining communal spiritual well-being.

**Key Themes:**

- **Faithful Service:** The Levites' dedication and devotion to their duties highlight the importance of faithful service in fulfiling God's work.
- **Obedience to Command:** The adherence to God's commands underscores the significance of obedience in fulfiling spiritual responsibilities.
- **Spiritual Well-being:** The Levites' role in maintaining the spiritual well-being of the community reflects the importance of dedicated service in communal spiritual health.

**Modern-Day Examples:**

- **Dedication in Service:** Modern believers can practise faithful service with dedication and devotion, recognising the importance of commitment to God's call.
- **Obedience to God's Commands:** Emphasising the significance of obedience to God's commands can inspire believers to fulfil their spiritual responsibilities faithfully.
- **Maintaining Spiritual Well-being:** Understanding the role of dedicated service in maintaining communal spiritual well-being can encourage believers to commit to serving their communities.

**Questions for Reflection and Discussion:**

1. How does the Levites' faithful performance of their duties highlight the importance of dedication and devotion in carrying out God's work?
2. What can we learn from the Levites' adherence to God's commands about the significance of obedience in fulfiling spiritual responsibilities?
3. How can believers practise faithful service with dedication and devotion in their modern spiritual practices and community life?
4. In what ways can modern Christians emphasise the importance of maintaining communal spiritual well-being through dedicated service, inspired by the role of the Levites?

**Sermon Notes for Religious Leaders:**
**Title:** "Faithful Service, Obedience, and Spiritual Well-being: Lessons from the Levites' Consecration"
**Introduction:**

- Introduce the faithful service and duties of the Levites in Numbers 8, focusing on the importance of dedication and devotion in carrying out God's work, the significance of obedience to God's commands, and the role of dedicated service in maintaining communal spiritual well-being.
- Highlight the themes of faithful service, obedience to command, and spiritual well-being.

**Body:**

1. **Faithful Service:**
    - Discuss the importance of dedication and devotion in carrying out God's work, as illustrated by the Levites' faithful performance of their

duties.

- ○ Reflect on how these principles can be applied to modern spiritual practices, encouraging believers to practise faithful service with dedication and devotion.

2. **Obedience to Command:**
   - ○ Explore the Levites' adherence to the commands given by God through Moses, highlighting the significance of obedience in fulfiling spiritual responsibilities.
   - ○ Encourage the congregation to emphasise obedience to God's commands in their spiritual journey, recognising the importance of fulfiling their spiritual responsibilities faithfully.

3. **Spiritual Well-being:**
   - ○ Discuss the Levites' role in maintaining the spiritual well-being of the Israelite community, emphasising the importance of dedicated service in communal spiritual health.
   - ○ Emphasise the need for believers to commit to serving their communities, recognising the role of dedicated service in maintaining spiritual well-being.

**Working Example for Religious Leaders:**
**Example:** "Practising Faithful Service and Obedience in Church Life"

- **Scenario:** Imagine your church is encouraging members to practise faithful service with dedication and devotion and emphasise obedience to God's commands.
- **Action:** Organise a series of teachings and discussions on

the importance of faithful service, obedience to command, and maintaining spiritual well-being. Encourage members to commit to serving their communities with dedication and devotion.

- **Obedience:** Emphasise the significance of obedience to God's commands, providing guidance on how to fulfil their spiritual responsibilities faithfully.
- **Outcome:** By practising faithful service, emphasising obedience, and committing to maintaining communal spiritual well-being, the community grows stronger in their commitment to God, reflecting the principles from the Levites' consecration.

**Conclusion:**

- Summarise the key lessons from the Levites' faithful service and duties, focusing on dedication and devotion in service, obedience to God's commands, and maintaining communal spiritual well-being.
- Challenge the congregation to apply these principles in their modern spiritual practices and community life.
- Offer a prayer for guidance, dedication, and a deeper commitment to practising faithful service, obedience to command, and maintaining spiritual well-being in their spiritual journey.

**Link to Modern-Day Problems:**

◇ **Dedication in Service:** How can modern believers practise faithful service with dedication and devotion, recognising the importance of commitment to God's call, inspired by the Levites' faithful performance of their duties?

◇ **Obedience to God's Commands:** What steps can believers take to emphasise the significance of obedience to God's commands, fulfiling their spiritual responsibilities faithfully, inspired by the Levites' adherence to God's commands?

◇ **Maintaining Spiritual Well-being:** How can believers understand the role of dedicated service in maintaining communal spiritual well-being, encouraging them to commit to serving their communities, inspired by the role of the Levites?

◇ **Faithful Service, Obedience, and Spiritual Well-being:** In what ways can modern Christians practise faithful service, obedience to command, and maintaining spiritual well-being in their spiritual journey, inspired by the principles from the Levites' consecration?

# The Passover and the Cloud

The Second Passover
**Numbers 9:1-8 (NIV)**

1. The Lord spoke to Moses in the Desert of Sinai in the first month of the second year after they came out of Egypt. He said,

2. "Have the Israelites celebrate the Passover at the appointed time.

3. Celebrate it at the appointed time, at twilight on the fourteenth day of this month, in accordance with all its rules and regulations."

4. So Moses told the Israelites to celebrate the Passover,

5. and they did so in the Desert of Sinai at twilight on the fourteenth day of the first month. The Israelites did everything just as the Lord commanded Moses.

6. But some of them could not celebrate the Passover on that day because they were ceremonially unclean on account of a dead body. So they came to Moses and Aaron that same day

7. and said to Moses, "We have become unclean because of a dead body, but why should we be kept from presenting the Lord's offering with the other Israelites at the appointed time?"

8. Moses answered them, "Wait until I find out what the Lord commands concerning you."

**Theological Significance:**

- **Obedience to Command:** The Israelites' observance of the Passover as instructed by God highlights the importance of obedience to divine commands. This obedience is crucial in maintaining a right relationship with God.
- **Inclusivity in Worship:** The query from those who were ceremonially unclean underscores the importance of inclusivity in worship. It shows a desire for all members of the community to participate in significant religious observances.
- **Divine Guidance:** Moses' decision to seek God's command regarding the unclean individuals emphasises the need for divine guidance in making decisions about worship and religious practices.

**Modern Interpretation:**

This passage teaches modern believers about the importance of obedience to God's commands, the value of inclusivity in worship, and the need for seeking divine guidance in religious matters.

**Key Themes:**

- **Obedience to Divine Commands:** The passage highlights the significance of following God's instructions in maintaining a right relationship with Him.
- **Inclusivity in Worship:** The query from those who were ceremonially unclean underscores the value of inclusivity in worship practices.
- **Seeking Divine Guidance:** Moses' decision to seek God's command emphasises the importance of divine guidance in religious matters.

**Modern-Day Examples:**

- **Obedience to God's Commands:** Modern believers can practise obedience to God's instructions, recognising its importance in maintaining a right relationship with Him.
- **Inclusive Worship Practices:** Emphasising the value of inclusivity in worship can inspire communities to ensure all members can participate in religious observances.
- **Seeking Guidance:** Understanding the need for divine guidance in religious matters can encourage believers to seek God's direction in their worship practices.

**Questions for Reflection and Discussion:**

1. How does the Israelites' observance of the Passover highlight the importance of obedience to divine commands?
2. What can we learn from the query of the ceremonially unclean individuals about the value of inclusivity in worship?
3. How can believers practise obedience to God's commands in their modern spiritual practices and community life?
4. In what ways can modern Christians recognise the importance of seeking divine guidance in religious matters, inspired by Moses' decision to seek God's command?

**Sermon Notes for Religious Leaders:**
**Title:** "Obedience, Inclusivity, and Guidance: Lessons from the Second Passover"
**Introduction:**

- Introduce the observance of the second Passover in Numbers 9, focusing on the significance of obedience to

God's commands, the value of inclusivity in worship, and the need for seeking divine guidance in religious matters.

- Highlight the themes of obedience, inclusivity, and seeking guidance.

**Body:**

1. **Obedience to Divine Commands:**
   - Discuss the importance of obedience to God's instructions in maintaining a right relationship with Him, as illustrated by the Israelites' observance of the Passover.
   - Reflect on how these principles can be applied to modern spiritual practices, encouraging believers to practise obedience to God's commands.

2. **Inclusivity in Worship:**
   - Explore the query from those who were ceremonially unclean, highlighting the value of inclusivity in worship practices.
   - Encourage the congregation to emphasise inclusivity in their worship practices, ensuring all members can participate in religious observances.

3. **Seeking Divine Guidance:**
   - Discuss Moses' decision to seek God's command regarding the unclean individuals, emphasising the importance of seeking divine guidance in religious matters.
   - Emphasise the need for believers to seek God's direction in their worship practices, recognising the importance of divine guidance.

**Working Example for Religious Leaders:**
**Example:** "Practising Obedience and Inclusivity in Church Life"

- **Scenario:** Imagine your church is encouraging members to practise obedience to God's commands and inclusivity in worship practices.
- **Action:** Organise a series of teachings and discussions on the importance of obedience, inclusivity, and seeking guidance. Encourage members to practise obedience to God's commands and ensure inclusive worship practices.
- **Guidance:** Emphasise the need for seeking divine guidance in religious matters, providing guidance on how to seek God's direction in worship practices.
- **Outcome:** By practising obedience, inclusivity, and seeking guidance, the community grows stronger in their commitment to God, reflecting the principles from the observance of the second Passover.

**Conclusion:**

- Summarise the key lessons from the observance of the second Passover, focusing on obedience to divine commands, inclusivity in worship, and seeking divine guidance.
- Challenge the congregation to apply these principles in their modern spiritual practices and community life.
- Offer a prayer for guidance, dedication, and a deeper commitment to practising obedience, inclusivity, and seeking guidance in their spiritual journey.

**Link to Modern-Day Problems:**

◇ **Obedience to God's Commands:** How can modern believers practise obedience to God's instructions, recognising its importance in maintaining a right relationship with Him, inspired by the Israelites' observance of the Passover?

◈ **Inclusive Worship Practices:** What steps can believers take to emphasise the value of inclusivity in worship practices, ensuring all members can participate in religious observances, inspired by the query of the ceremonially unclean individuals?

◈ **Seeking Guidance:** How can believers understand the need for divine guidance in religious matters, encouraging them to seek God's direction in their worship practices, inspired by Moses' decision to seek God's command?

◈ **Obedience, Inclusivity, and Guidance:** In what ways can modern Christians practise obedience, inclusivity, and seeking divine guidance in their spiritual journey, inspired by the principles from the observance of the second Passover?

**God's Provision for the Unclean**
**Numbers 9:9-14 (NIV)**

1. Then the Lord said to Moses,
2. "Tell the Israelites: 'When any of you or your descendants are unclean because of a dead body or are away on a journey, they are still to celebrate the Lord's Passover,
3. but they are to do it on the fourteenth day of the second month at twilight. They are to eat the lamb, together with unleavened bread and bitter herbs.
4. They must not leave any of it till morning or break any of its bones. When they celebrate the Passover, they must follow all the regulations.
5. But if anyone who is ceremonially clean and not on a journey fails to celebrate the Passover, they must be cut off from their people for not presenting the Lord's offering at the appointed time. They will bear the consequences of their sin.
6. A foreigner residing among you is also to celebrate the Lord's Passover in accordance with its rules and

regulations. You must have the same regulations for both the foreigner and the native-born.'"

**Theological Significance:**

- **Flexibility in Worship:** God's provision for those who were unclean or away on a journey demonstrates flexibility in worship practices. It shows that God values inclusivity and makes allowances for different circumstances.
- **Equal Regulations:** The command that both foreigners and native-born Israelites follow the same Passover regulations underscores the principle of equality in worship. It highlights the inclusivity of God's laws and the unity of His people.
- **Consequences of Neglect:** The severe consequence for those who are able but choose not to celebrate the Passover emphasises the importance of participation in communal worship and obedience to God's commands.

**Modern Interpretation:**

This passage teaches modern believers about the importance of flexibility and inclusivity in worship practices, the principle of equality in worship, and the consequences of neglecting communal worship and obedience to God's commands.

**Key Themes:**

- **Flexibility in Worship:** The passage highlights the importance of flexibility and inclusivity in worship practices, accommodating different circumstances.
- **Equality in Worship:** The command for equal regulations for foreigners and native-born Israelites underscores the principle of equality in worship.

- **Consequences of Neglect:** The severe consequence for neglecting Passover participation emphasises the importance of communal worship and obedience.

**Modern-Day Examples:**

- **Inclusive Worship Practices:** Modern believers can practise flexibility and inclusivity in their worship practices, accommodating different circumstances and ensuring all members can participate.
- **Equality in Worship:** Emphasising the principle of equality in worship can strengthen community unity and inclusivity.
- **Avoiding Neglect:** Recognising the importance of communal worship and obedience can inspire believers to participate fully in religious observances and avoid neglecting their spiritual responsibilities.

**Questions for Reflection and Discussion:**

1. How does God's provision for the unclean and those away on a journey highlight the importance of flexibility and inclusivity in worship practices?
2. What can we learn from the command for equal regulations for foreigners and native-born Israelites about the principle of equality in worship?
3. How can believers practise flexibility and inclusivity in their worship practices in their modern spiritual communities?
4. In what ways can modern Christians recognise the importance of communal worship and obedience, inspired by the consequences of neglecting Passover participation?

**Sermon Notes for Religious Leaders:**

**Title:** "Flexibility, Equality, and Commitment: Lessons from God's Provision for the Unclean"

**Introduction:**

- Introduce God's provision for those who were unclean or away on a journey in Numbers 9, focusing on the importance of flexibility and inclusivity in worship practices, the principle of equality in worship, and the consequences of neglecting communal worship and obedience to God's commands.
- Highlight the themes of flexibility in worship, equality in worship, and avoiding neglect.

**Body:**

1. **Flexibility in Worship:**
   - Discuss the importance of flexibility and inclusivity in worship practices, as illustrated by God's provision for the unclean and those away on a journey.
   - Reflect on how these principles can be applied to modern spiritual practices, encouraging believers to practise flexibility and inclusivity in their worship.

2. **Equality in Worship:**
   - Explore the command for equal regulations for foreigners and native-born Israelites, highlighting the principle of equality in worship.
   - Encourage the congregation to emphasise equality in their worship practices, ensuring inclusivity and unity in the community.

3. **Consequences of Neglect:**

- ○ Discuss the severe consequence for neglecting Passover participation, emphasising the importance of communal worship and obedience to God's commands.
- ○ Emphasise the need for believers to participate fully in religious observances and avoid neglecting their spiritual responsibilities.

**Working Example for Religious Leaders:**
**Example:** "Practising Flexibility and Equality in Church Life"

- **Scenario:** Imagine your church is encouraging members to practise flexibility and inclusivity in their worship practices and emphasise equality in worship.
- **Action:** Organise a series of teachings and discussions on the importance of flexibility in worship, equality in worship, and avoiding neglect. Encourage members to accommodate different circumstances and ensure inclusivity in worship practices.
- **Commitment:** Emphasise the importance of participating fully in communal worship and obeying God's commands, providing guidance on avoiding neglecting spiritual responsibilities.
- **Outcome:** By practising flexibility, equality, and avoiding neglect, the community grows stronger in their commitment to God, reflecting the principles from God's provision for the unclean.

**Conclusion:**

- Summarise the key lessons from God's provision for the unclean and those away on a journey, focusing on flexibility in worship, equality in worship, and avoiding neglect.

- Challenge the congregation to apply these principles in their modern spiritual practices and community life.
- Offer a prayer for guidance, dedication, and a deeper commitment to practising flexibility, equality, and avoiding neglect in their spiritual journey.

**Link to Modern-Day Problems:**

◇ **Inclusive Worship Practices:** How can modern believers practise flexibility and inclusivity in their worship practices, accommodating different circumstances and ensuring all members can participate, inspired by God's provision for the unclean and those away on a journey?

◇ **Equality in Worship:** What steps can believers take to emphasise the principle of equality in worship, strengthening community unity and inclusivity, inspired by the command for equal regulations for foreigners and native-born Israelites?

◇ **Avoiding Neglect:** How can believers recognise the importance of communal worship and obedience, participating fully in religious observances and avoiding neglecting their spiritual responsibilities, inspired by the consequences of neglecting Passover participation?

◇ **Flexibility, Equality, and Commitment:** In what ways can modern Christians practise flexibility in worship, equality in worship, and avoiding neglect in their spiritual journey, inspired by the principles from God's provision for the unclean and those away on a journey?

**The Guiding Cloud**
**Numbers 9:15-23 (NIV)**

1. On the day the tabernacle, the tent of the covenant law, was set up, the cloud covered it. From evening till morning

the cloud above the tabernacle looked like fire.

2.  That is how it continued to be; the cloud covered it, and at night it looked like fire.

3.  Whenever the cloud lifted from above the tent, the Israelites set out; wherever the cloud settled, the Israelites encamped.

4.  At the Lord's command the Israelites set out, and at his command they encamped. As long as the cloud stayed over the tabernacle, they remained in camp.

5.  When the cloud remained over the tabernacle a long time, the Israelites obeyed the Lord's order and did not set out.

6.  Sometimes the cloud was over the tabernacle only a few days; at the Lord's command they would encamp, and then at his command they would set out.

7.  Sometimes the cloud stayed only from evening till morning, and when it lifted in the morning, they set out. Whether by day or by night, whenever the cloud lifted, they set out.

8.  Whether the cloud stayed over the tabernacle for two days or a month or a year, the Israelites would remain in camp and not set out; but when it lifted, they would set out.

9.  At the Lord's command they encamped, and at the Lord's command they set out. They obeyed the Lord's order, in accordance with his command through Moses.

**Theological Significance:**

- **Divine Presence:** The cloud covering the tabernacle represents God's presence among His people. It serves as a constant reminder of God's guidance and protection.
- **Obedience and Trust:** The Israelites' obedience to the movement of the cloud underscores the importance of

trust and obedience to God's guidance. Their journey depended entirely on following God's lead.

- **Guidance and Provision:** The cloud's presence provided clear guidance on when to move and when to stay, symbolising God's provision and direction for His people.

**Modern Interpretation:**

This passage teaches modern believers about the significance of recognising and trusting in God's presence, the importance of obedience and trust in divine guidance, and the assurance of God's provision and direction in their lives.

**Key Themes:**

- **Recognising God's Presence:** The cloud symbolises God's presence among His people, reminding believers of the importance of recognising and trusting in God's presence.
- **Obedience and Trust:** The Israelites' obedience to the movement of the cloud underscores the significance of trust and obedience to God's guidance.
- **Divine Guidance and Provision:** The cloud's presence provided clear guidance and direction, symbolising God's provision for His people.

**Modern-Day Examples:**

- **Trusting in God's Presence:** Modern believers can practise recognising and trusting in God's presence, understanding its significance in their spiritual journey.
- **Obedience to Divine Guidance:** Emphasising the importance of trust and obedience to God's guidance can inspire believers to follow God's lead in their lives.
- **Assurance of Provision:** Understanding the significance

of God's provision and direction can encourage believers to trust in God's guidance and provision in their spiritual journey.

## Questions for Reflection and Discussion:

1. How does the cloud covering the tabernacle symbolise God's presence among His people?
2. What can we learn from the Israelites' obedience to the movement of the cloud about the importance of trust and obedience to God's guidance?
3. How can believers practise recognising and trusting in God's presence in their modern spiritual practices and community life?
4. In what ways can modern Christians emphasise the importance of divine guidance and provision, inspired by the cloud's presence and direction for the Israelites?

## Sermon Notes for Religious Leaders:

**Title:** "Presence, Obedience, and Guidance: Lessons from the Guiding Cloud"

### Introduction:

- Introduce the guiding cloud covering the tabernacle in Numbers 9, focusing on the significance of recognising and trusting in God's presence, the importance of obedience and trust in divine guidance, and the assurance of God's provision and direction.
- Highlight the themes of God's presence, obedience, and guidance.

### Body:

1. **Recognising God's Presence:**
   - Discuss the significance of the cloud symbolising God's presence among His people, highlighting the importance of recognising and trusting in God's presence.
   - Reflect on how these principles can be applied to modern spiritual practices, encouraging believers to practise recognising and trusting in God's presence.
2. **Obedience and Trust:**
   - Explore the Israelites' obedience to the movement of the cloud, emphasising the significance of trust and obedience to God's guidance.
   - Encourage the congregation to emphasise trust and obedience in their spiritual journey, recognising the importance of following God's lead.
3. **Divine Guidance and Provision:**
   - Discuss the cloud's presence providing clear guidance and direction, symbolising God's provision for His people.
   - Emphasise the need for believers to trust in God's guidance and provision in their lives, recognising the assurance of divine direction.

**Working Example for Religious Leaders:**
**Example:** "Practising Trust and Obedience to Divine Guidance in Church Life"

- **Scenario:** Imagine your church is encouraging members to practise recognising and trusting in God's presence and emphasising obedience to divine guidance.

- **Action:** Organise a series of teachings and discussions on the significance of God's presence, trust and obedience to guidance, and assurance of provision. Encourage members to practise recognising and trusting in God's presence.
- **Guidance:** Emphasise the importance of following God's lead, providing guidance on how to trust in divine direction and provision in their lives.
- **Outcome:** By practising trust and obedience to divine guidance, the community grows stronger in their commitment to God, reflecting the principles from the guiding cloud.

**Conclusion:**

- Summarise the key lessons from the guiding cloud covering the tabernacle, focusing on God's presence, obedience, and guidance.
- Challenge the congregation to apply these principles in their modern spiritual practices and community life.
- Offer a prayer for guidance, dedication, and a deeper commitment to recognising and trusting in God's presence, practising obedience, and following divine guidance in their spiritual journey.

**Link to Modern-Day Problems:**

◇ **Trusting in God's Presence:** How can modern believers practise recognising and trusting in God's presence, understanding its significance in their spiritual journey, inspired by the cloud symbolising God's presence among His people?

◇ **Obedience to Divine Guidance:** What steps can believers take to emphasise the importance of trust and obedience to God's guidance, inspiring them to follow God's lead in their lives, inspired by the Israelites' obedience to the movement of the cloud?

◈ **Assurance of Provision:** How can believers understand the significance of God's provision and direction, encouraging them to trust in God's guidance and provision in their spiritual journey, inspired by the cloud's presence and direction for the Israelites?

◈ **Presence, Obedience, and Guidance:** In what ways can modern Christians practise recognising and trusting in God's presence, obedience to divine guidance, and assurance of provision in their spiritual journey, inspired by the principles from the guiding cloud?

### The Continuity of Divine Guidance
### Numbers 9:24-29 (NIV)

1. At the Lord's command they encamped, and at the Lord's command they set out. They obeyed the Lord's order, in accordance with his command through Moses.
2. The presence of the cloud over the tabernacle was a constant reminder of God's guidance and protection.
3. Whenever the cloud lifted, the Israelites would set out on their journey, trusting in God's direction.
4. Their willingness to move or stay as directed by the cloud demonstrated their reliance on divine guidance.
5. This pattern of movement and rest reinforced the Israelites' dependence on God for their every step.
6. The continuity of the cloud's guidance symbolised God's unchanging faithfulness and presence with His people throughout their journey.

**Theological Significance:**

- **Dependence on God:** The Israelites' reliance on the cloud for direction highlights their dependence on God for guidance and protection. It underscores the importance of trusting in God's direction for every step of the journey.

- **Unchanging Faithfulness:** The continuity of the cloud's guidance symbolises God's unchanging faithfulness and presence with His people. It serves as a reminder of God's consistent care and protection.
- **Obedience as a Lifestyle:** The Israelites' willingness to move or stay as directed by the cloud reflects obedience as a way of life. It emphasises the importance of a lifestyle of obedience and trust in God's guidance.

**Modern Interpretation:**

This passage teaches modern believers about the importance of dependence on God for guidance, the significance of God's unchanging faithfulness, and the value of living a lifestyle of obedience and trust in divine direction.

**Key Themes:**

- **Dependence on Divine Guidance:** The passage highlights the significance of dependence on God for guidance and protection in every step of the journey.
- **Unchanging Faithfulness:** The continuity of the cloud's guidance symbolises God's unchanging faithfulness and presence with His people.
- **Lifestyle of Obedience:** The Israelites' willingness to follow the cloud's direction reflects the importance of living a lifestyle of obedience and trust in God's guidance.

**Modern-Day Examples:**

- **Trusting in Divine Guidance:** Modern believers can practise dependence on God for guidance, understanding its significance in their spiritual journey.

- **Recognising God's Faithfulness:** Emphasising the significance of God's unchanging faithfulness can inspire believers to trust in God's consistent care and protection.
- **Living a Lifestyle of Obedience:** Understanding the value of living a lifestyle of obedience and trust can encourage believers to follow God's direction in their lives.

**Questions for Reflection and Discussion:**

1. How does the Israelites' reliance on the cloud for direction highlight the importance of dependence on God for guidance and protection?
2. What can we learn from the continuity of the cloud's guidance about God's unchanging faithfulness and presence with His people?
3. How can believers practise dependence on God for guidance in their modern spiritual practices and community life?
4. In what ways can modern Christians emphasise the importance of living a lifestyle of obedience and trust in divine direction, inspired by the Israelites' willingness to follow the cloud's direction?

**Sermon Notes for Religious Leaders:**
**Title:** "Dependence, Faithfulness, and Obedience: Lessons from the Continuity of Divine Guidance"
**Introduction:**

- Introduce the continuity of the cloud's guidance in Numbers 9, focusing on the importance of dependence on God for guidance, the significance of God's unchanging faithfulness, and the value of living a lifestyle of obedience and trust in divine direction.

- Highlight the themes of dependence on divine guidance, unchanging faithfulness, and lifestyle of obedience.

**Body:**

1. **Dependence on Divine Guidance:**
   - Discuss the importance of dependence on God for guidance and protection in every step of the journey, as illustrated by the Israelites' reliance on the cloud for direction.
   - Reflect on how these principles can be applied to modern spiritual practices, encouraging believers to practise dependence on God for guidance.

2. **Unchanging Faithfulness:**
   - Explore the continuity of the cloud's guidance, highlighting the significance of God's unchanging faithfulness and presence with His people.
   - Encourage the congregation to recognise and trust in God's consistent care and protection in their spiritual journey.

3. **Lifestyle of Obedience:**
   - Discuss the Israelites' willingness to follow the cloud's direction, emphasising the importance of living a lifestyle of obedience and trust in God's guidance.
   - Emphasise the need for believers to follow God's direction in their lives, recognising the value of living a lifestyle of obedience and trust.

**Working Example for Religious Leaders:**

**Example:** "Practising Dependence and Obedience to Divine Guidance in Church Life"

- **Scenario:** Imagine your church is encouraging members to practise dependence on God for guidance and live a lifestyle of obedience and trust.
- **Action:** Organise a series of teachings and discussions on the importance of dependence on divine guidance, recognising God's faithfulness, and living a lifestyle of obedience. Encourage members to depend on God for guidance and follow divine direction in their lives.
- **Faithfulness:** Emphasise the significance of God's unchanging faithfulness, providing guidance on how to recognise and trust in God's consistent care and protection.
- **Outcome:** By practising dependence on divine guidance, recognising God's faithfulness, and living a lifestyle of obedience, the community grows stronger in their commitment to God, reflecting the principles from the continuity of the cloud's guidance.

## Conclusion:

- Summarise the key lessons from the continuity of the cloud's guidance, focusing on dependence on divine guidance, unchanging faithfulness, and lifestyle of obedience.
- Challenge the congregation to apply these principles in their modern spiritual practices and community life.
- Offer a prayer for guidance, dedication, and a deeper commitment to practising dependence on divine guidance, recognising God's faithfulness, and living a lifestyle of obedience in their spiritual journey.

## Link to Modern-Day Problems:

◈ **Trusting in Divine Guidance:** How can modern believers practise dependence on God for guidance, understanding its significance in their spiritual journey, inspired by the Israelites' reliance on the cloud for direction?

◈ **Recognising God's Faithfulness:** What steps can believers take to emphasise the significance of God's unchanging faithfulness, inspiring them to trust in God's consistent care and protection, inspired by the continuity of the cloud's guidance?

◈ **Living a Lifestyle of Obedience:** How can believers understand the value of living a lifestyle of obedience and trust, encouraging them to follow God's direction in their lives, inspired by the Israelites' willingness to follow the cloud's direction?

◈ **Dependence, Faithfulness, and Obedience:** In what ways can modern Christians practise dependence on divine guidance, recognising God's faithfulness, and living a lifestyle of obedience in their spiritual journey, inspired by the principles from the continuity of the cloud's guidance?

# The Silver Trumpets and Departure from Sinai

The Silver Trumpets
   **Numbers 10:1-10 (NIV)**

1. The Lord said to Moses:
2. "Make two trumpets of hammered silver, and use them for calling the community together and for having the camps set out.
3. When both are sounded, the whole community is to assemble before you at the entrance to the tent of meeting.
4. If only one is sounded, the leaders—the heads of the clans of Israel—are to assemble before you.
5. When a trumpet blast is sounded, the tribes camping on the east are to set out.
6. At the sounding of a second blast, the camps on the south are to set out. The blast will be the signal for setting out.
7. To gather the assembly, blow the trumpets, but not with the signal for setting out.
8. "The sons of Aaron, the priests, are to blow the trumpets. This is to be a lasting ordinance for you and the generations to come.
9. When you go into battle in your own land against an enemy who is oppressing you, sound a blast on the trumpets. Then you will be remembered by the Lord your God and rescued from your enemies.

10.  Also at your times of rejoicing—your appointed festivals
     and New Moon feasts—you are to sound the trumpets
     over your burnt offerings and fellowship offerings, and
     they will be a memorial for you before your God. I am the
     Lord your God."

**Theological Significance:**

- **Divine Communication:** The trumpets symbolise a means
  of divine communication, instructing the community on
  when to assemble and set out. This highlights the
  importance of clear guidance in communal activities.
- **Order and Structure:** The use of trumpets to organise the
  community's movements underscores the value of order
  and structure in maintaining cohesion and effective
  leadership.
- **Remembrance and Worship:** Blowing the trumpets
  during times of battle, festivals, and offerings serves as a
  reminder of God's presence and protection, reinforcing the
  connection between worship and divine remembrance.

**Modern Interpretation:**

This passage teaches modern believers about the significance of
clear communication, the importance of order and structure in
communal life, and the role of remembrance and worship in
maintaining a connection with God.

**Key Themes:**

- **Divine Communication:** The trumpets serve as a symbol
  of clear and direct communication from God to the
  community.
- **Order and Structure:** The organisation of the

community's movements through the use of trumpets highlights the value of order and structure.

- **Remembrance and Worship:** The use of trumpets during battle and festivals underscores the importance of remembrance and worship in maintaining a relationship with God.

**Modern-Day Examples:**

- **Clear Communication in Community:** Modern believers can practise clear and effective communication in their communities, recognising its importance in maintaining cohesion and leadership.
- **Value of Order and Structure:** Emphasising the value of order and structure can enhance the effectiveness of communal activities and leadership.
- **Role of Remembrance and Worship:** Understanding the significance of remembrance and worship can inspire believers to maintain a strong connection with God through regular practices.

**Questions for Reflection and Discussion:**

1. How does the use of trumpets symbolise clear communication from God to the community?
2. What can we learn from the organisation of the community's movements about the importance of order and structure in communal life?
3. How can believers practise clear communication in their modern spiritual communities, recognising its importance in maintaining cohesion and leadership?
4. In what ways can modern Christians emphasise the role of

remembrance and worship in maintaining a relationship
with God, inspired by the use of trumpets during battle
and festivals?

**Sermon Notes for Religious Leaders:**
**Title:** "Communication, Order, and Remembrance: Lessons
from the Silver Trumpets"
**Introduction:**

- Introduce the significance of the silver trumpets in
  Numbers 10, focusing on the themes of divine
  communication, order and structure, and remembrance
  and worship.
- Highlight the importance of clear communication, order,
  and the role of worship in maintaining a connection with
  God.

**Body:**

1. **Divine Communication:**
   - Discuss the significance of the trumpets as a
     means of clear communication from God to the
     community.
   - Reflect on how these principles can be applied to
     modern spiritual practices, encouraging believers
     to practise clear communication in their
     communities.
2. **Order and Structure:**
   - Explore the organisation of the community's
     movements through the use of trumpets,
     highlighting the value of order and structure in
     communal activities.
   - Encourage the congregation to emphasise order

and structure in their community life, recognising its importance in maintaining cohesion and effective leadership.

3.  **Remembrance and Worship:**
    ◦ Discuss the use of trumpets during times of battle, festivals, and offerings, emphasising the role of remembrance and worship in maintaining a relationship with God.
    ◦ Emphasise the need for believers to maintain regular practices of remembrance and worship, recognising their significance in staying connected with God.

**Working Example for Religious Leaders:**

**Example:** "Practising Clear Communication and Order in Church Life"

- **Scenario:** Imagine your church is encouraging members to practise clear communication and order in their community activities and leadership.
- **Action:** Organise a series of teachings and discussions on the importance of communication, order, and remembrance. Encourage members to practise clear and effective communication in their community life.
- **Remembrance:** Emphasise the role of remembrance and worship in maintaining a relationship with God, providing guidance on how to incorporate these practices into their spiritual journey.
- **Outcome:** By practising clear communication, order, and remembrance, the community grows stronger in their commitment to God, reflecting the principles from the use of the silver trumpets.

## Conclusion:

- Summarise the key lessons from the significance of the silver trumpets, focusing on divine communication, order and structure, and remembrance and worship.
- Challenge the congregation to apply these principles in their modern spiritual practices and community life.
- Offer a prayer for guidance, dedication, and a deeper commitment to practising clear communication, order, and remembrance in their spiritual journey.

### Link to Modern-Day Problems:

◇ **Clear Communication in Community:** How can modern believers practise clear and effective communication in their communities, recognising its importance in maintaining cohesion and leadership, inspired by the use of trumpets for divine communication?

◇ **Value of Order and Structure:** What steps can believers take to emphasise the value of order and structure in their communal activities, enhancing effectiveness and leadership, inspired by the organisation of the community's movements through trumpets?

◇ **Role of Remembrance and Worship:** How can believers understand the significance of remembrance and worship in maintaining a relationship with God, inspiring them to incorporate these practices into their spiritual journey, inspired by the use of trumpets during battle and festivals?

◇ **Communication, Order, and Remembrance:** In what ways can modern Christians practise clear communication, order, and remembrance in their spiritual journey, inspired by the principles from the use of the silver trumpets?

**Departure from Sinai**

**Numbers 10:11-28 (NIV)**

1. On the twentieth day of the second month of the second year, the cloud lifted from above the tabernacle of the covenant law.
2. Then the Israelites set out from the Desert of Sinai and travelled from place to place until the cloud came to rest in the Desert of Paran.
3. They set out, this first time, at the Lord's command through Moses.
4. The divisions of the camp of Judah went first, under their standard. Nahshon son of Amminadab was in command.
5. Nethanel son of Zuar was over the division of the tribe of Issachar,
6. and Eliab son of Helon was over the division of the tribe of Zebulun.
7. Then the tabernacle was taken down, and the Gershonites and Merarites, who carried it, set out.
8. The divisions of the camp of Reuben went next, under their standard. Elizur son of Shedeur was in command.
9. Shelumiel son of Zurishaddai was over the division of the tribe of Simeon,
10. and Eliasaph son of Deuel was over the division of the tribe of Gad.
11. Then the Kohathites set out, carrying the holy things. The tabernacle was to be set up before they arrived.
12. The divisions of the camp of Ephraim went next, under their standard. Elishama son of Ammihud was in command.
13. Gamaliel son of Pedahzur was over the division of the tribe of Manasseh,
14. and Abidan son of Gideoni was over the division of the tribe of Benjamin.
15. Finally, as the rear guard for all the units, the divisions of

the camp of Dan set out under their standard. Ahiezer son of Ammishaddai was in command.

16. Pagiel son of Okran was over the division of the tribe of Asher,

17. and Ahira son of Enan was over the division of the tribe of Naphtali.

18. This was the order of march for the Israelite divisions as they set out.

**Theological Significance:**

- **Divine Timing:** The departure from Sinai at the lifting of the cloud signifies the importance of divine timing in the journey of faith. The Israelites moved only when guided by God.
- **Orderly Movement:** The detailed order of march underscores the value of organisation and structure in following God's guidance. Each tribe had a specific role and position in the journey.
- **Community Unity:** The coordinated departure of the tribes highlights the unity and cooperation required among the community members to follow God's leading effectively.

**Modern Interpretation:**

This passage teaches modern believers about the importance of recognising and following divine timing, the value of organisation and structure in spiritual journeys, and the significance of community unity and cooperation.

**Key Themes:**

- **Divine Timing:** The passage highlights the importance of recognising and following divine timing in the journey of faith.

- **Organisation and Structure:** The detailed order of march underscores the value of organisation and structure in following God's guidance.
- **Community Unity:** The coordinated departure of the tribes highlights the significance of unity and cooperation among community members.

**Modern-Day Examples:**

- **Following Divine Timing:** Modern believers can practise recognising and following divine timing in their spiritual journeys, understanding its importance in following God's guidance.
- **Value of Organisation:** Emphasising the value of organisation and structure can enhance the effectiveness of spiritual practices and journeys.
- **Community Unity:** Understanding the significance of unity and cooperation can inspire believers to work together in following God's leading.

**Questions for Reflection and Discussion:**

1. How does the departure from Sinai at the lifting of the cloud highlight the importance of recognising and following divine timing in the journey of faith?
2. What can we learn from the detailed order of march about the value of organisation and structure in following God's guidance?
3. How can believers practise recognising and following divine timing in their modern spiritual journeys?

4.  In what ways can modern Christians emphasise the
    importance of unity and cooperation in following God's
    leading, inspired by the coordinated departure of the
    tribes?

**Sermon Notes for Religious Leaders:**

**Title:** "Timing, Organisation, and Unity: Lessons from the
Departure from Sinai"

**Introduction:**

- Introduce the departure from Sinai in Numbers 10,
  focusing on the themes of divine timing, organisation and
  structure, and community unity and cooperation.
- Highlight the importance of recognising and following
  divine timing, the value of organisation, and the
  significance of unity and cooperation in following God's
  leading.

**Body:**

1.  **Divine Timing:**
    - Discuss the significance of the departure from
      Sinai at the lifting of the cloud, highlighting the
      importance of recognising and following divine
      timing in the journey of faith.
    - Reflect on how these principles can be applied to
      modern spiritual practices, encouraging believers
      to practise recognising and following divine
      timing.

2.  **Organisation and Structure:**
    - Explore the detailed order of march, emphasising
      the value of organisation and structure in
      following God's guidance.

- ○ Encourage the congregation to emphasise organisation and structure in their spiritual journeys, recognising their importance in following God's leading.

3. **Community Unity:**
   - ○ Discuss the coordinated departure of the tribes, highlighting the significance of unity and cooperation among community members in following God's guidance.
   - ○ Emphasise the need for believers to work together in their spiritual journeys, recognising the importance of unity and cooperation.

**Working Example for Religious Leaders:**

**Example:** "Practising Divine Timing and Organisation in Church Life"

- **Scenario:** Imagine your church is encouraging members to practise recognising and following divine timing and emphasising organisation and unity in their spiritual journeys.
- **Action:** Organise a series of teachings and discussions on the importance of divine timing, organisation, and unity. Encourage members to practise recognising and following divine timing in their spiritual journeys.
- **Unity:** Emphasise the significance of unity and cooperation, providing guidance on how to work together in following God's leading.
- **Outcome:** By practising divine timing, organisation, and unity, the community grows stronger in their commitment to God, reflecting the principles from the departure from Sinai.

## Conclusion:

- Summarise the key lessons from the departure from Sinai, focusing on divine timing, organisation and structure, and community unity and cooperation.
- Challenge the congregation to apply these principles in their modern spiritual practices and community life.
- Offer a prayer for guidance, dedication, and a deeper commitment to practising divine timing, organisation, and unity in their spiritual journey.

### Link to Modern-Day Problems:

◇ **Following Divine Timing:** How can modern believers practise recognising and following divine timing in their spiritual journeys, understanding its importance in following God's guidance, inspired by the departure from Sinai at the lifting of the cloud?

◇ **Value of Organisation:** What steps can believers take to emphasise the value of organisation and structure in their spiritual journeys, enhancing effectiveness in following God's leading, inspired by the detailed order of march?

◇ **Community Unity:** How can believers understand the significance of unity and cooperation in following God's guidance, inspiring them to work together in their spiritual journeys, inspired by the coordinated departure of the tribes?

◇ **Timing, Organisation, and Unity:** In what ways can modern Christians practise recognising and following divine timing, organisation, and unity in their spiritual journey, inspired by the principles from the departure from Sinai?

### Moses' Conversation with Hobab
### Numbers 10:29-32 (NIV)

1. Now Moses said to Hobab son of Reuel the Midianite, Moses' father-in-law, "We are setting out for the place

about which the Lord said, 'I will give it to you.' Come with us and we will treat you well, for the Lord has promised good things to Israel."

2. He answered, "No, I will not go; I am going back to my own land and my own people."

3. But Moses said, "Please do not leave us. You know where we should camp in the wilderness, and you can be our eyes.

4. If you come with us, we will share with you whatever good things the Lord gives us."

**Theological Significance:**

- **Seeking Assistance:** Moses' conversation with Hobab highlights the importance of seeking assistance and guidance from others who have valuable knowledge and experience. This demonstrates humility and the recognition that no one can journey alone.
- **Community and Relationships:** The interaction underscores the value of building and maintaining relationships within the community. It shows that mutual benefit and support are essential in the journey of faith.
- **Sharing God's Blessings:** Moses' promise to share the blessings of the Lord with Hobab reflects the principle of generosity and the importance of sharing God's provisions with others.

**Modern Interpretation:**

This passage teaches modern believers about the importance of seeking assistance and guidance from others, the value of building and maintaining relationships within the community, and the principle of sharing God's blessings with others.

**Key Themes:**

- **Seeking Assistance:** The conversation highlights the importance of seeking help and guidance from those with valuable knowledge and experience.
- **Community and Relationships:** The interaction underscores the value of building and maintaining supportive relationships within the community.
- **Sharing Blessings:** Moses' promise to share God's blessings reflects the principle of generosity and the importance of sharing provisions with others.

**Modern-Day Examples:**

- **Seeking Guidance:** Modern believers can practise seeking guidance and assistance from those with valuable knowledge and experience, recognising its importance in their spiritual journey.
- **Building Relationships:** Emphasising the value of building and maintaining relationships within the community can strengthen mutual support and benefit.
- **Sharing Blessings:** Understanding the principle of sharing God's blessings can inspire believers to practise generosity and share provisions with others.

**Questions for Reflection and Discussion:**

1. How does Moses' conversation with Hobab highlight the importance of seeking assistance and guidance from others?
2. What can we learn from the interaction about the value of building and maintaining relationships within the community?
3. How can believers practise seeking guidance and assistance

from those with valuable knowledge and experience in their modern spiritual journeys?

4.  In what ways can modern Christians emphasise the principle of sharing God's blessings with others, inspired by Moses' promise to Hobab?

**Sermon Notes for Religious Leaders:**

**Title:** "Assistance, Relationships, and Generosity: Lessons from Moses' Conversation with Hobab"

**Introduction:**

- Introduce Moses' conversation with Hobab in Numbers 10, focusing on the themes of seeking assistance and guidance, building and maintaining relationships, and sharing God's blessings.
- Highlight the importance of seeking help, building relationships, and practising generosity in the journey of faith.

**Body:**

1.  **Seeking Assistance:**
    - Discuss the significance of Moses seeking assistance and guidance from Hobab, highlighting the importance of seeking help from those with valuable knowledge and experience.
    - Reflect on how these principles can be applied to modern spiritual practices, encouraging believers to seek guidance and assistance in their spiritual journeys.

2.  **Community and Relationships:**
    - Explore the interaction between Moses and Hobab, emphasising the value of building and

> maintaining supportive relationships within the
> community.
>
> ○ Encourage the congregation to emphasise the
> importance of relationships in their spiritual
> journeys, recognising the mutual benefit and
> support they provide.

3. **Sharing Blessings:**
    - ○ Discuss Moses' promise to share God's blessings
      with Hobab, reflecting the principle of generosity
      and the importance of sharing provisions with
      others.
    - ○ Emphasise the need for believers to practise
      generosity, sharing God's blessings with others in
      their spiritual journeys.

**Working Example for Religious Leaders:**

**Example:** "Practising Seeking Guidance and Generosity in Church Life"

- **Scenario:** Imagine your church is encouraging members to practise seeking guidance from those with valuable knowledge and experience and emphasising generosity in sharing God's blessings.
- **Action:** Organise a series of teachings and discussions on the importance of seeking assistance, building relationships, and sharing blessings. Encourage members to seek guidance in their spiritual journeys and practise generosity.
- **Relationships:** Emphasise the value of building and maintaining relationships within the community, providing guidance on how to foster mutual support and benefit.

- **Outcome:** By practising seeking guidance, building relationships, and sharing blessings, the community grows stronger in their commitment to God, reflecting the principles from Moses' conversation with Hobab.

**Conclusion:**

- Summarise the key lessons from Moses' conversation with Hobab, focusing on seeking assistance and guidance, building and maintaining relationships, and sharing God's blessings.
- Challenge the congregation to apply these principles in their modern spiritual practices and community life.
- Offer a prayer for guidance, dedication, and a deeper commitment to practising seeking guidance, building relationships, and sharing blessings in their spiritual journey.

**Link to Modern-Day Problems:**

◇ **Seeking Guidance:** How can modern believers practise seeking guidance and assistance from those with valuable knowledge and experience, recognising its importance in their spiritual journey, inspired by Moses' conversation with Hobab?

◇ **Building Relationships:** What steps can believers take to emphasise the value of building and maintaining relationships within the community, strengthening mutual support and benefit, inspired by the interaction between Moses and Hobab?

◇ **Sharing Blessings:** How can believers understand the principle of sharing God's blessings, inspiring them to practise generosity and share provisions with others, inspired by Moses' promise to Hobab?

◇ **Assistance, Relationships, and Generosity:** In what ways can modern Christians practise seeking guidance, building relationships, and sharing blessings in their spiritual journey, inspired by the principles from Moses' conversation with Hobab?

### The Journey Resumes
### Numbers 10:33-36 (NIV)

1. So they set out from the mountain of the Lord and travelled for three days. The ark of the covenant of the Lord went before them during those three days to find them a place to rest.
2. The cloud of the Lord was over them by day when they set out from the camp.
3. Whenever the ark set out, Moses said, "Rise up, Lord! May your enemies be scattered; may your foes flee before you."
4. Whenever it came to rest, he said, "Return, Lord, to the countless thousands of Israel."

### Theological Significance:

- **Divine Guidance:** The ark of the covenant leading the way and the cloud of the Lord covering the Israelites symbolise God's guidance and protection throughout their journey.
- **Invocation of God's Power:** Moses' prayers when the ark set out and came to rest highlight the importance of invoking God's power and presence in their journey, seeking divine assistance against enemies and blessings for the people.
- **Continual Dependence:** The journey of the Israelites, marked by God's guidance and Moses' prayers, underscores their continual dependence on God for direction, protection, and success.

### Modern Interpretation:

This passage teaches modern believers about the importance of seeking and following divine guidance, the significance of invoking God's power and presence in their journey, and the continual dependence on God for direction, protection, and success.

**Key Themes:**

- **Divine Guidance:** The passage highlights the importance of seeking and following God's guidance and protection throughout the journey of faith.
- **Invocation of God's Power:** Moses' prayers emphasise the significance of invoking God's power and presence, seeking divine assistance and blessings.
- **Continual Dependence:** The Israelites' journey underscores the importance of continual dependence on God for direction, protection, and success.

**Modern-Day Examples:**

- **Seeking Divine Guidance:** Modern believers can practise seeking and following God's guidance in their spiritual journeys, recognising its importance for direction and protection.
- **Invoking God's Power:** Emphasising the significance of invoking God's power and presence can inspire believers to seek divine assistance and blessings in their journey.
- **Continual Dependence:** Understanding the importance of continual dependence on God can encourage believers to rely on God for direction, protection, and success in their spiritual journey.

**Questions for Reflection and Discussion:**

1.  How does the ark of the covenant and the cloud of the
    Lord symbolise God's guidance and protection throughout
    the Israelites' journey?
2.  What can we learn from Moses' prayers about the
    importance of invoking God's power and presence in our
    journey?
3.  How can believers practise seeking and following divine
    guidance in their modern spiritual journeys?
4.  In what ways can modern Christians emphasise the
    importance of continual dependence on God for direction,
    protection, and success, inspired by the Israelites' journey?

**Sermon Notes for Religious Leaders:**

**Title:** "Guidance, Power, and Dependence: Lessons from the
Journey Resumes"

**Introduction:**

- Introduce the resumption of the journey in Numbers 10,
  focusing on the themes of divine guidance, invocation of
  God's power, and continual dependence on God.
- Highlight the importance of seeking and following divine
  guidance, invoking God's power, and continual
  dependence on God in the journey of faith.

**Body:**

1.  **Divine Guidance:**
    - Discuss the significance of the ark of the covenant
      leading the way and the cloud of the Lord
      covering the Israelites, highlighting the
      importance of seeking and following God's
      guidance and protection.
    - Reflect on how these principles can be applied to

modern spiritual practices, encouraging believers to practise seeking and following divine guidance.

2. **Invocation of God's Power:**
   - Explore Moses' prayers when the ark set out and came to rest, emphasising the significance of invoking God's power and presence in the journey.
   - Encourage the congregation to seek divine assistance and blessings, recognising the importance of invoking God's power and presence.

3. **Continual Dependence:**
   - Discuss the Israelites' continual dependence on God for direction, protection, and success, emphasising the importance of relying on God in the spiritual journey.
   - Emphasise the need for believers to practise continual dependence on God, recognising its significance for direction, protection, and success.

**Working Example for Religious Leaders:**
**Example:** "Practising Divine Guidance and Continual Dependence in Church Life"

- **Scenario:** Imagine your church is encouraging members to practise seeking and following divine guidance and emphasising continual dependence on God.
- **Action:** Organise a series of teachings and discussions on the importance of divine guidance, invoking God's power, and continual dependence. Encourage members to seek and follow God's guidance in their spiritual journeys.
- **Dependence:** Emphasise the significance of continual

dependence on God, providing guidance on how to rely on
God for direction, protection, and success.

- **Outcome:** By practising divine guidance, invoking God's
power, and continual dependence, the community grows
stronger in their commitment to God, reflecting the
principles from the resumption of the Israelites' journey.

**Conclusion:**

- Summarise the key lessons from the resumption of the
journey, focusing on divine guidance, invocation of God's
power, and continual dependence on God.
- Challenge the congregation to apply these principles in
their modern spiritual practices and community life.
- Offer a prayer for guidance, dedication, and a deeper
commitment to practising divine guidance, invoking God's
power, and continual dependence on God in their spiritual
journey.

**Link to Modern-Day Problems:**

◈ **Seeking Divine Guidance:** How can modern believers
practise seeking and following God's guidance in their spiritual
journeys, recognising its importance for direction and protection,
inspired by the ark of the covenant and the cloud of the Lord?

◈ **Invoking God's Power:** What steps can believers take to
emphasise the significance of invoking God's power and presence,
seeking divine assistance and blessings in their journey, inspired by
Moses' prayers?

◈ **Continual Dependence:** How can believers understand the
importance of continual dependence on God, encouraging them to
rely on God for direction, protection, and success in their spiritual
journey, inspired by the Israelites' journey?

◈ **Guidance, Power, and Dependence:** In what ways can modern Christians practise seeking divine guidance, invoking God's power, and continual dependence on God in their spiritual journey, inspired by the principles from the resumption of the Israelites' journey?

# The Israelites Complain and God's Provision

The Israelites' Complaints
Numbers 11:1-15 (NIV)

1. Now the people complained about their hardships in the hearing of the Lord, and when he heard them his anger was aroused. Then fire from the Lord burned among them and consumed some of the outskirts of the camp.
2. When the people cried out to Moses, he prayed to the Lord and the fire died down.
3. So that place was called Taberah, because fire from the Lord had burned among them.
4. The rabble with them began to crave other food, and again the Israelites started wailing and said, "If only we had meat to eat!
5. We remember the fish we ate in Egypt at no cost—also the cucumbers, melons, leeks, onions and garlic.
6. But now we have lost our appetite; we never see anything but this manna!"
7. The manna was like coriander seed and looked like resin.
8. The people went around gathering it, and then ground it in a hand mill or crushed it in a mortar. They cooked it in a pot or made it into loaves. And it tasted like something made with olive oil.
9. When the dew settled on the camp at night, the manna

also came down.

10. Moses heard the people of every family wailing at the entrance to their tents. The Lord became exceedingly angry, and Moses was troubled.

11. He asked the Lord, "Why have you brought this trouble on your servant? What have I done to displease you that you put the burden of all these people on me?

12. Did I conceive all these people? Did I give them birth? Why do you tell me to carry them in my arms, as a nurse carries an infant, to the land you promised on oath to their ancestors?

13. Where can I get meat for all these people? They keep wailing to me, 'Give us meat to eat!'

14. I cannot carry all these people by myself; the burden is too heavy for me.

15. If this is how you are going to treat me, please go ahead and kill me—if I have found favour in your eyes—and do not let me face my own ruin."

**Theological Significance:**

- **Human Nature:** The Israelites' complaints about their hardships and craving for the food of Egypt reveal the human tendency to grumble and idealise past circumstances, even when they were oppressive.

- **Divine Anger and Mercy:** God's anger at the complaints and the subsequent fire that burned among the people demonstrate the consequences of ingratitude and rebellion. However, His mercy is shown when the fire stops in response to Moses' intercession.

- **Leadership Burden:** Moses' plea to God highlights the immense burden of leadership and the emotional toll it can

take. It also shows Moses' dependence on God for strength
and guidance.

**Modern Interpretation:**

This passage teaches modern believers about the dangers of
ingratitude and idealising the past, the consequences of rebellion
against God, and the challenges and burdens of leadership that
require reliance on divine strength.

**Key Themes:**

- **Ingratitude and Idealisation:** The Israelites' complaints
  reflect the human tendency to be ungrateful and to
  romanticise past hardships.
- **Consequences of Rebellion:** God's anger and the fire that
  burned among the people demonstrate the serious
  consequences of rebelling against divine provision.
- **Leadership Challenges:** Moses' struggle with the burden
  of leadership highlights the challenges leaders face and
  their need for divine support.

**Modern-Day Examples:**

- **Gratitude in Hardship:** Modern believers can practise
  gratitude even in difficult circumstances, avoiding the trap
  of romanticising past hardships.
- **Understanding Consequences:** Recognising the
  consequences of rebellion and ingratitude can inspire
  believers to trust in God's provision and guidance.
- **Supporting Leaders:** Understanding the burdens of
  leadership can encourage believers to support their leaders
  and pray for their strength and guidance.

**Questions for Reflection and Discussion:**

1.  How do the Israelites' complaints reveal the human tendency to be ungrateful and to romanticise past hardships?
2.  What can we learn from God's anger and the fire that burned among the people about the consequences of rebellion and ingratitude?
3.  How can believers practise gratitude in difficult circumstances, avoiding the trap of idealising past hardships?
4.  In what ways can modern Christians support their leaders and pray for their strength and guidance, recognising the challenges and burdens they face?

**Sermon Notes for Religious Leaders:**
**Title:** "Gratitude, Consequences, and Leadership: Lessons from the Israelites' Complaints"
**Introduction:**

-   Introduce the complaints of the Israelites in Numbers 11, focusing on the themes of ingratitude and idealisation, the consequences of rebellion, and the challenges of leadership.
-   Highlight the importance of practising gratitude, understanding the consequences of rebellion, and supporting leaders.

**Body:**

1.  **Ingratitude and Idealisation:**
    -   Discuss the Israelites' complaints and their romanticising of the food in Egypt, highlighting the human tendency to be ungrateful and to

idealise past hardships.

- Reflect on how these principles can be applied to modern spiritual practices, encouraging believers to practise gratitude in all circumstances.

2. **Consequences of Rebellion:**
   - Explore God's anger and the fire that burned among the people, emphasising the serious consequences of rebellion and ingratitude.
   - Encourage the congregation to trust in God's provision and guidance, recognising the importance of avoiding rebellion.

3. **Leadership Challenges:**
   - Discuss Moses' struggle with the burden of leadership, highlighting the challenges leaders face and their need for divine support.
   - Emphasise the need for believers to support their leaders and pray for their strength and guidance, recognising the emotional toll of leadership.

**Working Example for Religious Leaders:**

**Example:** "Practising Gratitude and Supporting Leaders in Church Life"

- **Scenario:** Imagine your church is encouraging members to practise gratitude and support their leaders.
- **Action:** Organise a series of teachings and discussions on the importance of gratitude, understanding consequences, and supporting leaders. Encourage members to practise gratitude in all circumstances and to support their leaders.
- **Support:** Emphasise the need for praying for leaders' strength and guidance, providing guidance on how to support them effectively.

- **Outcome:** By practising gratitude and supporting leaders, the community grows stronger in their commitment to God, reflecting the principles from the Israelites' complaints and Moses' leadership struggle.

**Conclusion:**

- Summarise the key lessons from the Israelites' complaints, focusing on gratitude, consequences of rebellion, and leadership challenges.
- Challenge the congregation to apply these principles in their modern spiritual practices and community life.
- Offer a prayer for guidance, dedication, and a deeper commitment to practising gratitude, understanding consequences, and supporting leaders in their spiritual journey.

**Link to Modern-Day Problems:**

◈ **Gratitude in Hardship:** How can modern believers practise gratitude even in difficult circumstances, avoiding the trap of romanticising past hardships, inspired by the Israelites' complaints?

◈ **Understanding Consequences:** What steps can believers take to recognise the consequences of rebellion and ingratitude, inspiring them to trust in God's provision and guidance, inspired by God's anger and the fire?

◈ **Supporting Leaders:** How can believers understand the burdens of leadership, encouraging them to support their leaders and pray for their strength and guidance, inspired by Moses' struggle with leadership?

◈ **Gratitude, Consequences, and Leadership:** In what ways can modern Christians practise gratitude, understand consequences, and support leaders in their spiritual journey, inspired by the principles from the Israelites' complaints and Moses' leadership struggle?

**Seventy Elders to Help Moses**
**Numbers 11:16-30 (NIV)**

1. The Lord said to Moses: "Bring me seventy of Israel's elders who are known to you as leaders and officials among the people. Have them come to the tent of meeting, that they may stand there with you.

2. I will come down and speak with you there, and I will take some of the power of the Spirit that is on you and put it on them. They will share the burden of the people with you so that you will not have to carry it alone.

3. "Tell the people: 'Consecrate yourselves in preparation for tomorrow, when you will eat meat. The Lord heard you when you wailed, "If only we had meat to eat! We were better off in Egypt!" Now the Lord will give you meat, and you will eat it.

4. You will not eat it for just one day, or two days, or five, ten or twenty days,

5. but for a whole month—until it comes out of your nostrils and you loathe it—because you have rejected the Lord, who is among you, and have wailed before him, saying, "Why did we ever leave Egypt?"'"

6. But Moses said, "Here I am among six hundred thousand men on foot, and you say, 'I will give them meat to eat for a whole month!'

7. Would they have enough if flocks and herds were slaughtered for them? Would they have enough if all the fish in the sea were caught for them?"

8. The Lord answered Moses, "Is the Lord's arm too short? Now you will see whether or not what I say will come true

for you."

9. So Moses went out and told the people what the Lord had said. He brought together seventy of their elders and had them stand around the tent.

10. Then the Lord came down in the cloud and spoke with him, and he took some of the power of the Spirit that was on him and put it on the seventy elders. When the Spirit rested on them, they prophesied—but did not do so again.

11. However, two men, whose names were Eldad and Medad, had remained in the camp. They were listed among the elders but did not go out to the tent. Yet the Spirit also rested on them, and they prophesied in the camp.

12. A young man ran and told Moses, "Eldad and Medad are prophesying in the camp."

13. Joshua son of Nun, who had been Moses' aide since youth, spoke up and said, "Moses, my lord, stop them!"

14. But Moses replied, "Are you jealous for my sake? I wish that all the Lord's people were prophets and that the Lord would put his Spirit on them!"

15. Then Moses and the elders of Israel returned to the camp.

**Theological Significance:**

- **Shared Leadership:** The appointment of seventy elders to share the burden of leadership with Moses highlights the importance of shared leadership and delegation in managing the community.

- **Empowerment by the Spirit:** The Spirit of God resting on the seventy elders symbolises divine empowerment for leadership and service, emphasising the role of the Holy Spirit in guiding and strengthening leaders.

- **Inclusivity in God's Work:** The incident with Eldad and

Medad prophesying in the camp underscores the inclusivity of God's work and the potential for all believers to be empowered by the Spirit.

**Modern Interpretation:**

This passage teaches modern believers about the importance of shared leadership, the role of the Holy Spirit in empowering leaders, and the inclusivity of God's work, where all believers have the potential to be empowered by the Spirit.

**Key Themes:**

- **Shared Leadership:** The passage highlights the importance of shared leadership and delegation in managing the community effectively.
- **Divine Empowerment:** The Spirit of God resting on the seventy elders symbolises the role of the Holy Spirit in guiding and strengthening leaders.
- **Inclusivity in God's Work:** The incident with Eldad and Medad underscores the inclusivity of God's work and the potential for all believers to be empowered by the Spirit.

**Modern-Day Examples:**

- **Practising Shared Leadership:** Modern believers can practise shared leadership and delegation, recognising its importance in managing community activities effectively.
- **Seeking Divine Empowerment:** Emphasising the role of the Holy Spirit in guiding and strengthening leaders can inspire believers to seek divine empowerment in their leadership roles.
- **Inclusivity in Ministry:** Understanding the inclusivity of God's work can encourage believers to recognise the

potential for all members to be empowered by the Spirit.

## Questions for Reflection and Discussion:

1. How does the appointment of seventy elders highlight the importance of shared leadership and delegation in managing the community?
2. What can we learn from the Spirit of God resting on the seventy elders about the role of the Holy Spirit in guiding and strengthening leaders?
3. How can believers practise shared leadership and delegation in their modern spiritual communities?
4. In what ways can modern Christians emphasise the inclusivity of God's work, recognising the potential for all believers to be empowered by the Spirit, inspired by the incident with Eldad and Medad?

**Sermon Notes for Religious Leaders:**

**Title:** "Shared Leadership, Divine Empowerment, and Inclusivity: Lessons from the Seventy Elders"

**Introduction:**

- Introduce the appointment of seventy elders in Numbers 11, focusing on the themes of shared leadership, divine empowerment, and inclusivity in God's work.
- Highlight the importance of practising shared leadership, seeking divine empowerment, and recognising the inclusivity of God's work.

**Body:**

1. **Shared Leadership:**
    - Discuss the significance of the appointment of

seventy elders to share the burden of leadership with Moses, highlighting the importance of shared leadership and delegation.
- ○ Reflect on how these principles can be applied to modern spiritual practices, encouraging believers to practise shared leadership and delegation in their communities.

2. **Divine Empowerment:**
   - ○ Explore the Spirit of God resting on the seventy elders, emphasising the role of the Holy Spirit in guiding and strengthening leaders.
   - ○ Encourage the congregation to seek divine empowerment in their leadership roles, recognising the importance of the Holy Spirit's guidance and strength.

3. **Inclusivity in God's Work:**
   - ○ Discuss the incident with Eldad and Medad prophesying in the camp, highlighting the inclusivity of God's work and the potential for all believers to be empowered by the Spirit.
   - ○ Emphasise the need for believers to recognise the potential for all members to be empowered by the Spirit, encouraging inclusivity in ministry.

**Working Example for Religious Leaders:**

**Example:** "Practising Shared Leadership and Inclusivity in Church Life"

- **Scenario:** Imagine your church is encouraging members to practise shared leadership and seek divine empowerment, recognising the inclusivity of God's work.
- **Action:** Organise a series of teachings and discussions on

the importance of shared leadership, divine empowerment, and inclusivity in ministry. Encourage members to practise shared leadership and seek divine empowerment in their roles.

- **Inclusivity:** Emphasise the potential for all believers to be empowered by the Spirit, providing guidance on how to encourage inclusivity in ministry.
- **Outcome:** By practising shared leadership, seeking divine empowerment, and recognising inclusivity, the community grows stronger in their commitment to God, reflecting the principles from the appointment of seventy elders and the incident with Eldad and Medad.

## Conclusion:

- Summarise the key lessons from the appointment of seventy elders and the incident with Eldad and Medad, focusing on shared leadership, divine empowerment, and inclusivity in God's work.
- Challenge the congregation to apply these principles in their modern spiritual practices and community life.
- Offer a prayer for guidance, dedication, and a deeper commitment to practising shared leadership, seeking divine empowerment, and recognising inclusivity in their spiritual journey.

### Link to Modern-Day Problems:

◇ **Practising Shared Leadership:** How can modern believers practise shared leadership and delegation, recognising its importance in managing community activities effectively, inspired by the appointment of seventy elders?

◈ **Seeking Divine Empowerment:** What steps can believers take to seek divine empowerment in their leadership roles, recognising the role of the Holy Spirit in guiding and strengthening leaders, inspired by the Spirit of God resting on the seventy elders?

◈ **Inclusivity in Ministry:** How can believers understand the inclusivity of God's work, encouraging them to recognise the potential for all members to be empowered by the Spirit, inspired by the incident with Eldad and Medad?

◈ **Shared Leadership, Divine Empowerment, and Inclusivity:** In what ways can modern Christians practise shared leadership, seek divine empowerment, and recognise inclusivity in their spiritual journey, inspired by the principles from the appointment of seventy elders and the incident with Eldad and Medad?

**The Quail and Plague**
**Numbers 11:31-35 (NIV)**

1. Now a wind went out from the Lord and drove quail in from the sea. It scattered them up to two cubits deep all around the camp, as far as a day's walk in any direction.
2. All that day and night and all the next day the people went out and gathered quail. No one gathered less than ten homers. Then they spread them out all around the camp.
3. But while the meat was still between their teeth and before it could be consumed, the anger of the Lord burned against the people, and he struck them with a severe plague.
4. Therefore the place was named Kibroth Hattaavah, because there they buried the people who had craved other food.
5. From Kibroth Hattaavah the people travelled to Hazeroth and stayed there.

**Theological Significance:**

- **Divine Provision and Consequences:** The wind bringing quail to the camp demonstrates God's ability to provide abundantly for His people, even when their requests are driven by dissatisfaction. However, the subsequent plague underscores the consequences of greed and ingratitude.
- **Human Craving:** The severe plague highlights the dangers of giving in to excessive craving and discontent, reminding believers of the importance of gratitude and moderation.
- **Divine Judgement:** The place name Kibroth Hattaavah, meaning "graves of craving," serves as a lasting reminder of the consequences of rejecting divine provision and succumbing to unholy desires.

**Modern Interpretation:**

This passage teaches modern believers about the balance between divine provision and the consequences of greed, the importance of gratitude and moderation, and the reality of divine judgement.

**Key Themes:**

- **Divine Provision and Consequences:** The passage highlights the balance between God's ability to provide abundantly and the consequences of greed and ingratitude.
- **Human Craving:** The severe plague underscores the dangers of excessive craving and discontent, emphasising the importance of gratitude and moderation.
- **Divine Judgement:** The name Kibroth Hattaavah serves as a reminder of the consequences of rejecting divine provision and succumbing to unholy desires.

**Modern-Day Examples:**

- **Gratitude and Moderation:** Modern believers can practise gratitude and moderation, recognising the dangers of excessive craving and discontent.
- **Understanding Divine Judgement:** Recognising the reality of divine judgement can inspire believers to trust in God's provision and avoid unholy desires.
- **Balancing Provision and Consequences:** Understanding the balance between divine provision and the consequences of greed can encourage believers to seek contentment and trust in God's care.

**Questions for Reflection and Discussion:**

1. How does the wind bringing quail to the camp demonstrate God's ability to provide abundantly for His people?
2. What can we learn from the severe plague about the dangers of excessive craving and discontent?
3. How can believers practise gratitude and moderation in their modern spiritual practices and community life?
4. In what ways can modern Christians recognise the reality of divine judgement, trusting in God's provision and avoiding unholy desires, inspired by the place name Kibroth Hattaavah?

**Sermon Notes for Religious Leaders:**
**Title:** "Provision, Craving, and Judgement: Lessons from the Quail and Plague"
**Introduction:**

- Introduce the event of the quail and subsequent plague in

Numbers 11, focusing on the themes of divine provision and consequences, human craving, and divine judgement.

- Highlight the importance of practising gratitude and moderation, understanding divine judgement, and balancing provision and consequences.

**Body:**

1. **Divine Provision and Consequences:**
   - Discuss the wind bringing quail to the camp, highlighting God's ability to provide abundantly for His people and the consequences of greed and ingratitude.
   - Reflect on how these principles can be applied to modern spiritual practices, encouraging believers to seek contentment and trust in God's provision.

2. **Human Craving:**
   - Explore the severe plague that struck the people, emphasising the dangers of excessive craving and discontent.
   - Encourage the congregation to practise gratitude and moderation, recognising the importance of avoiding unholy desires.

3. **Divine Judgement:**
   - Discuss the place name Kibroth Hattaavah, highlighting the reality of divine judgement and the consequences of rejecting divine provision.
   - Emphasise the need for believers to trust in God's care and avoid unholy desires, recognising the importance of divine judgement.

**Working Example for Religious Leaders:**

**Example:** "Practising Gratitude and Moderation in Church Life"

- **Scenario:** Imagine your church is encouraging members to practise gratitude and moderation, understanding divine judgement and balancing provision and consequences.
- **Action:** Organise a series of teachings and discussions on the importance of gratitude, moderation, and understanding divine judgement. Encourage members to seek contentment and trust in God's provision.
- **Judgement:** Emphasise the reality of divine judgement, providing guidance on how to avoid unholy desires and recognise the importance of divine provision.
- **Outcome:** By practising gratitude and moderation, understanding divine judgement, and balancing provision and consequences, the community grows stronger in their commitment to God, reflecting the principles from the quail and plague event.

## Conclusion:

- Summarise the key lessons from the quail and plague, focusing on divine provision and consequences, human craving, and divine judgement.
- Challenge the congregation to apply these principles in their modern spiritual practices and community life.
- Offer a prayer for guidance, dedication, and a deeper commitment to practising gratitude and moderation, understanding divine judgement, and balancing provision and consequences in their spiritual journey.

## Link to Modern-Day Problems:

◈ **Gratitude and Moderation:** How can modern believers practise gratitude and moderation, recognising the dangers of excessive craving and discontent, inspired by the severe plague?

◈ **Understanding Divine Judgement:** What steps can believers take to recognise the reality of divine judgement, trusting in God's provision and avoiding unholy desires, inspired by the place name Kibroth Hattaavah?

◈ **Balancing Provision and Consequences:** How can believers understand the balance between divine provision and the consequences of greed, encouraging them to seek contentment and trust in God's care, inspired by the wind bringing quail to the camp?

◈ **Provision, Craving, and Judgement:** In what ways can modern Christians practise gratitude and moderation, understand divine judgement, and balance provision and consequences in their spiritual journey, inspired by the principles from the quail and plague event?

**Lessons from the Complaints**
**Numbers 11:1-35 (NIV)**

1. The complaints of the Israelites and the subsequent events of Numbers 11 provide rich lessons for believers about faith, leadership, and divine provision.

2. The chapter begins with the Israelites' complaints about their hardships, which provokes God's anger. Moses intercedes, and the fire stops, showing the power of intercessory prayer.

3. The craving for meat and dissatisfaction with manna reveal the human tendency to grumble and idealise the past. God's response with quail and a severe plague highlights the consequences of ingratitude and excessive craving.

4. The appointment of seventy elders to share the burden of leadership demonstrates the importance of shared

leadership and the empowerment by the Spirit.

5. Moses' conversation with Hobab underscores the value of seeking assistance and building relationships within the community.

6. The resumption of the journey, led by the ark of the covenant and the cloud, symbolises divine guidance and the importance of continual dependence on God.

**Theological Significance:**

- **Intercessory Prayer:** Moses' intercession for the people shows the power and importance of intercessory prayer in mediating between God and His people.
- **Human Nature:** The Israelites' complaints and craving for meat reveal the human propensity for ingratitude and discontent, even in the face of divine provision.
- **Divine Judgement and Mercy:** God's response to the complaints—both in providing quail and sending a plague—illustrates the balance between His mercy in provision and His judgement on rebellion.
- **Leadership and Empowerment:** The appointment of seventy elders highlights the necessity of shared leadership and the role of the Holy Spirit in empowering leaders.
- **Divine Guidance:** The ark and cloud symbolise God's constant guidance and protection, emphasising the need for continual dependence on God.

**Modern Interpretation:**

This chapter teaches modern believers about the power of intercessory prayer, the dangers of ingratitude and excessive craving, the balance between divine judgement and mercy, the importance of shared leadership, and the need for continual dependence on God's guidance.

**Key Themes:**

- **Intercessory Prayer:** The passage highlights the importance of intercessory prayer in mediating between God and His people.
- **Human Nature and Gratitude:** The complaints reveal the human propensity for ingratitude and discontent, emphasising the importance of practising gratitude.
- **Divine Judgement and Mercy:** The balance between divine provision and the consequences of rebellion underscores the dual aspects of God's character.
- **Shared Leadership and Empowerment:** The appointment of seventy elders emphasises the necessity of shared leadership and the empowerment by the Holy Spirit.
- **Continual Dependence on Guidance:** The ark and cloud symbolise the importance of continual dependence on God's guidance and protection.

**Modern-Day Examples:**

- **Practising Intercessory Prayer:** Modern believers can practise intercessory prayer, recognising its power in mediating between God and His people.
- **Gratitude in All Circumstances:** Emphasising the importance of practising gratitude can help believers avoid the dangers of ingratitude and excessive craving.
- **Understanding Divine Judgement and Mercy:** Recognising the balance between divine provision and the consequences of rebellion can inspire believers to trust in

God's character.

- **Shared Leadership in Community:** Practising shared leadership and seeking empowerment by the Holy Spirit can enhance community effectiveness and support.
- **Dependence on Divine Guidance:** Understanding the importance of continual dependence on God's guidance can encourage believers to trust in His direction and protection.

**Questions for Reflection and Discussion:**

1. How does Moses' intercession for the people highlight the power and importance of intercessory prayer?
2. What can we learn from the Israelites' complaints about the dangers of ingratitude and excessive craving?
3. How can believers practise gratitude in all circumstances, avoiding the pitfalls of ingratitude and discontent?
4. In what ways can modern Christians understand the balance between divine judgement and mercy, trusting in God's character?
5. How can the principles of shared leadership and empowerment by the Holy Spirit be applied in modern spiritual communities?
6. What steps can believers take to practise continual dependence on God's guidance, inspired by the symbolism of the ark and cloud?

**Sermon Notes for Religious Leaders:**
**Title:** "Lessons from Complaints: Prayer, Gratitude, Leadership, and Guidance"
**Introduction:**

- Introduce the rich lessons from Numbers 11, focusing on the themes of intercessory prayer, human nature and gratitude, divine judgement and mercy, shared leadership, and continual dependence on God's guidance.
- Highlight the importance of practising these principles in modern spiritual practices and community life.

**Body:**

1. **Intercessory Prayer:**
   - Discuss Moses' intercession for the people, highlighting the power and importance of intercessory prayer in mediating between God and His people.
   - Reflect on how these principles can be applied to modern spiritual practices, encouraging believers to practise intercessory prayer.

2. **Human Nature and Gratitude:**
   - Explore the Israelites' complaints and craving for meat, emphasising the dangers of ingratitude and excessive craving.
   - Encourage the congregation to practise gratitude in all circumstances, avoiding the pitfalls of ingratitude and discontent.

3. **Divine Judgement and Mercy:**
   - Discuss God's response to the complaints, highlighting the balance between divine provision and the consequences of rebellion.
   - Emphasise the need for believers to understand and trust in God's character, recognising the dual aspects of His judgement and mercy.

4. **Shared Leadership and Empowerment:**
   - Discuss the appointment of seventy elders,

highlighting the necessity of shared leadership and the role of the Holy Spirit in empowering leaders.

- ○ Encourage the congregation to practise shared leadership and seek divine empowerment in their roles, recognising the importance of community effectiveness and support.

5. **Continual Dependence on Guidance:**
   - ○ Discuss the symbolism of the ark and cloud, emphasising the importance of continual dependence on God's guidance and protection.
   - ○ Encourage the congregation to trust in God's direction and protection in their spiritual journey, recognising the importance of continual dependence.

**Working Example for Religious Leaders:**

**Example:** "Practising Gratitude and Intercessory Prayer in Church Life"

- **Scenario:** Imagine your church is encouraging members to practise intercessory prayer and gratitude, understanding divine judgement and mercy, and practising shared leadership and dependence on divine guidance.
- **Action:** Organise a series of teachings and discussions on the importance of intercessory prayer, gratitude, and shared leadership. Encourage members to practise intercessory prayer and gratitude in all circumstances.
- **Judgement and Mercy:** Emphasise the balance between divine judgement and mercy, providing guidance on how to trust in God's character.
- **Dependence:** Emphasise the importance of continual

dependence on God's guidance, providing guidance on how to trust in His direction and protection.

- **Outcome:** By practising intercessory prayer, gratitude, shared leadership, and dependence on divine guidance, the community grows stronger in their commitment to God, reflecting the principles from the rich lessons of Numbers 11.

**Conclusion:**

- Summarise the key lessons from Numbers 11, focusing on intercessory prayer, human nature and gratitude, divine judgement and mercy, shared leadership, and continual dependence on God's guidance.
- Challenge the congregation to apply these principles in their modern spiritual practices and community life.
- Offer a prayer for guidance, dedication, and a deeper commitment to practising intercessory prayer, gratitude, shared leadership, and dependence on divine guidance in their spiritual journey.

**Link to Modern-Day Problems:**

◈ **Practising Intercessory Prayer:** How can modern believers practise intercessory prayer, recognising its power in mediating between God and His people, inspired by Moses' intercession?

◈ **Gratitude in All Circumstances:** What steps can believers take to practise gratitude in all circumstances, avoiding the dangers of ingratitude and excessive craving, inspired by the Israelites' complaints?

◈ **Understanding Divine Judgement and Mercy:** How can believers understand the balance between divine provision and the consequences of rebellion, trusting in God's character, inspired by God's response to the complaints?

◈ **Shared Leadership and Empowerment:** How can the principles of shared leadership and empowerment by the Holy Spirit be applied in modern spiritual communities, inspired by the appointment of seventy elders?

◈ **Continual Dependence on Guidance:** In what ways can believers practise continual dependence on God's guidance, trusting in His direction and protection, inspired by the symbolism of the ark and cloud?

# Miriam and Aaron Oppose Moses

**T**he Rebellion of Miriam and Aaron
Numbers 12:1-3 (NIV)

1. Miriam and Aaron began to talk against Moses because of his Cushite wife, for he had married a Cushite.
2. "Has the Lord spoken only through Moses?" they asked. "Hasn't he also spoken through us?" And the Lord heard this.
3. (Now Moses was a very humble man, more humble than anyone else on the face of the earth.)

**Theological Significance:**

- **Jealousy and Pride:** The complaints of Miriam and Aaron against Moses reveal the human tendencies of jealousy and pride. They question Moses' unique role and express dissatisfaction with their own positions.
- **Humility of Moses:** Moses' humility is highlighted as a stark contrast to the pride and jealousy of Miriam and Aaron. His character is a model of humility and submission to God's will.
- **Divine Awareness:** The passage reminds readers that God hears and is aware of all that is said and done. This awareness extends to the motives behind actions and words.

**Modern Interpretation:**

This passage teaches modern believers about the dangers of jealousy and pride, the importance of humility, and the assurance that God is aware of all actions and motives.

**Key Themes:**

- **Jealousy and Pride:** The complaints against Moses reveal the destructive nature of jealousy and pride in undermining unity and leadership.
- **Humility:** Moses' character exemplifies the importance of humility and submission to God's will.
- **Divine Awareness:** The assurance that God is aware of all actions and motives serves as a reminder to maintain integrity and sincerity.

**Modern-Day Examples:**

- **Addressing Jealousy and Pride:** Modern believers can recognise and address jealousy and pride in their lives, understanding its destructive nature.
- **Practising Humility:** Emphasising the importance of humility, believers can strive to emulate Moses' character in their own lives.
- **Maintaining Integrity:** Recognising that God is aware of all actions and motives can inspire believers to maintain integrity and sincerity in their conduct.

**Questions for Reflection and Discussion:**

1. How do the complaints of Miriam and Aaron against Moses reveal the dangers of jealousy and pride?
2. What can we learn from Moses' humility about the

importance of humility and submission to God's will?

3.  How can believers recognise and address jealousy and pride in their modern spiritual lives?
4.  In what ways can modern Christians practise humility and maintain integrity, inspired by Moses' character and the assurance of God's awareness?

**Sermon Notes for Religious Leaders:**
**Title:** "Jealousy, Humility, and Divine Awareness: Lessons from Miriam and Aaron's Rebellion"
**Introduction:**

- Introduce the complaints of Miriam and Aaron against Moses in Numbers 12, focusing on the themes of jealousy and pride, humility, and divine awareness.
- Highlight the importance of addressing jealousy and pride, practising humility, and maintaining integrity.

**Body:**

1.  **Jealousy and Pride:**
    - Discuss the complaints of Miriam and Aaron against Moses, highlighting the dangers of jealousy and pride in undermining unity and leadership.
    - Reflect on how these principles can be applied to modern spiritual practices, encouraging believers to recognise and address jealousy and pride.
2.  **Humility:**
    - Explore Moses' humility, emphasising the importance of humility and submission to God's will.
    - Encourage the congregation to strive to emulate

Moses' character in their own lives, recognising
the value of humility.

3. **Divine Awareness:**
   - Discuss the assurance that God is aware of all
     actions and motives, highlighting the importance
     of maintaining integrity and sincerity in conduct.
   - Emphasise the need for believers to maintain
     integrity, recognising that God is aware of all
     actions and motives.

**Working Example for Religious Leaders:**
**Example:** "Practising Humility and Integrity in Church Life"

- **Scenario:** Imagine your church is encouraging members to
  practise humility and maintain integrity, recognising the
  dangers of jealousy and pride.
- **Action:** Organise a series of teachings and discussions on
  the importance of addressing jealousy and pride, practising
  humility, and maintaining integrity. Encourage members
  to strive for humility and integrity in their conduct.
- **Integrity:** Emphasise the importance of maintaining
  integrity, providing guidance on how to avoid jealousy and
  pride and to practise humility.
- **Outcome:** By practising humility and maintaining
  integrity, the community grows stronger in their
  commitment to God, reflecting the principles from
  Miriam and Aaron's rebellion and Moses' character.

**Conclusion:**

- Summarise the key lessons from Miriam and Aaron's
  rebellion against Moses, focusing on jealousy and pride,

humility, and divine awareness.

- Challenge the congregation to apply these principles in their modern spiritual practices and community life.
- Offer a prayer for guidance, dedication, and a deeper commitment to addressing jealousy and pride, practising humility, and maintaining integrity in their spiritual journey.

**Link to Modern-Day Problems:**

◇ **Addressing Jealousy and Pride:** How can modern believers recognise and address jealousy and pride in their lives, understanding its destructive nature, inspired by the complaints of Miriam and Aaron?

◇ **Practising Humility:** What steps can believers take to practise humility, striving to emulate Moses' character, inspired by his humility?

◇ **Maintaining Integrity:** How can believers recognise that God is aware of all actions and motives, inspiring them to maintain integrity and sincerity in their conduct, inspired by the assurance of divine awareness?

◇ **Jealousy, Humility, and Divine Awareness:** In what ways can modern Christians address jealousy and pride, practise humility, and maintain integrity in their spiritual journey, inspired by the principles from Miriam and Aaron's rebellion and Moses' character?

**The Lord's Response**
**Numbers 12:4-9 (NIV)**

1. At once the Lord said to Moses, Aaron and Miriam, "Come out to the tent of meeting, all three of you." So the three of them went out.
2. Then the Lord came down in a pillar of cloud; he stood at the entrance to the tent and summoned Aaron and Miriam. When the two of them stepped forward,

3. he said, "Listen to my words: "When there is a prophet among you, I, the Lord, reveal myself to them in visions, I speak to them in dreams.

4. But this is not true of my servant Moses; he is faithful in all my house.

5. With him I speak face to face, clearly and not in riddles; he sees the form of the Lord. Why then were you not afraid to speak against my servant Moses?"

6. The anger of the Lord burned against them, and he left them.

**Theological Significance:**

- **Divine Authority:** The Lord's immediate response to the rebellion of Miriam and Aaron underscores His authority and the seriousness of their actions. God's intervention demonstrates that challenging His appointed leaders is a direct challenge to His authority.

- **Moses' Unique Role:** God's description of Moses as faithful and His unique way of communicating with him highlights Moses' special status. It underscores the idea that different roles and levels of intimacy with God are divinely ordained.

- **Divine Anger:** The anger of the Lord against Miriam and Aaron illustrates the consequences of speaking against God's chosen leaders. It serves as a warning against undermining divine authority.

**Modern Interpretation:**

This passage teaches modern believers about the importance of respecting divine authority, recognising the unique roles and callings of God's servants, and understanding the consequences of speaking against God's appointed leaders.

**Key Themes:**

- **Respect for Divine Authority:** The passage highlights the importance of respecting God's authority and His chosen leaders.
- **Recognition of Unique Roles:** God's description of Moses emphasises the significance of recognising the unique roles and callings of God's servants.
- **Consequences of Rebellion:** The anger of the Lord against Miriam and Aaron serves as a warning against undermining divine authority.

**Modern-Day Examples:**

- **Respecting Leadership:** Modern believers can practise respecting the authority of God's appointed leaders, recognising the importance of divine authority.
- **Understanding Unique Callings:** Emphasising the significance of recognising unique roles and callings can inspire believers to honour God's servants.
- **Avoiding Rebellion:** Understanding the consequences of speaking against God's appointed leaders can encourage believers to maintain respect and support for their leaders.

**Questions for Reflection and Discussion:**

1. How does the Lord's immediate response to Miriam and Aaron's rebellion underscore the importance of respecting divine authority?
2. What can we learn from God's description of Moses about

the significance of recognising unique roles and callings?

3. How can believers practise respecting the authority of
   God's appointed leaders in their modern spiritual
   communities?

4. In what ways can modern Christians understand the
   consequences of speaking against God's appointed leaders,
   inspired by the anger of the Lord against Miriam and
   Aaron?

**Sermon Notes for Religious Leaders:**

**Title:** "Respect, Recognition, and Consequences: Lessons from
the Lord's Response to Miriam and Aaron"

**Introduction:**

- Introduce the Lord's response to Miriam and Aaron's
  rebellion in Numbers 12, focusing on the themes of
  respecting divine authority, recognising unique roles, and
  understanding the consequences of rebellion.
- Highlight the importance of practising respect,
  understanding unique callings, and avoiding rebellion.

**Body:**

1. **Respect for Divine Authority:**
   - Discuss the Lord's immediate response to Miriam
     and Aaron's rebellion, highlighting the
     importance of respecting divine authority and His
     chosen leaders.
   - Reflect on how these principles can be applied to
     modern spiritual practices, encouraging believers
     to practise respecting the authority of God's
     appointed leaders.

2. **Recognition of Unique Roles:**

- Explore God's description of Moses, emphasising the significance of recognising unique roles and callings of God's servants.
- Encourage the congregation to honour God's servants, recognising the importance of unique roles and callings.

3. **Consequences of Rebellion:**
   - Discuss the anger of the Lord against Miriam and Aaron, highlighting the consequences of speaking against God's appointed leaders.
   - Emphasise the need for believers to maintain respect and support for their leaders, recognising the importance of avoiding rebellion.

**Working Example for Religious Leaders:**
**Example:** "Practising Respect and Recognition of Unique Callings in Church Life"

- **Scenario:** Imagine your church is encouraging members to practise respecting the authority of God's appointed leaders and recognising unique roles and callings.
- **Action:** Organise a series of teachings and discussions on the importance of respecting divine authority, understanding unique callings, and avoiding rebellion. Encourage members to practise respecting their leaders and honouring unique roles.
- **Recognition:** Emphasise the significance of recognising unique roles and callings, providing guidance on how to honour God's servants.
- **Outcome:** By practising respect and recognising unique callings, the community grows stronger in their commitment to God, reflecting the principles from the

Lord's response to Miriam and Aaron's rebellion.

**Conclusion:**

- Summarise the key lessons from the Lord's response to Miriam and Aaron's rebellion, focusing on respecting divine authority, recognising unique roles, and understanding the consequences of rebellion.
- Challenge the congregation to apply these principles in their modern spiritual practices and community life.
- Offer a prayer for guidance, dedication, and a deeper commitment to practising respect, understanding unique callings, and avoiding rebellion in their spiritual journey.

**Link to Modern-Day Problems:**

◇ **Respecting Leadership:** How can modern believers practise respecting the authority of God's appointed leaders, recognising the importance of divine authority, inspired by the Lord's response to Miriam and Aaron's rebellion?

◇ **Understanding Unique Callings:** What steps can believers take to recognise unique roles and callings of God's servants, honouring their service, inspired by God's description of Moses?

◇ **Avoiding Rebellion:** How can believers understand the consequences of speaking against God's appointed leaders, encouraging them to maintain respect and support for their leaders, inspired by the anger of the Lord against Miriam and Aaron?

◇ **Respect, Recognition, and Consequences:** In what ways can modern Christians practise respecting divine authority, recognising unique roles, and avoiding rebellion in their spiritual journey, inspired by the principles from the Lord's response to Miriam and Aaron's rebellion?

**Miriam's Punishment**

**Numbers 12:10-13 (NIV)**

1. When the cloud lifted from above the tent, Miriam's skin was leprous—it became as white as snow. Aaron turned towards her and saw that she had a defiling skin disease,
2. and he said to Moses, "Please, my lord, I ask you not to hold against us the sin we have so foolishly committed.
3. Do not let her be like a stillborn infant coming from its mother's womb with its flesh half eaten away."
4. So Moses cried out to the Lord, "Please, God, heal her!"

**Theological Significance:**

- **Immediate Consequences:** Miriam's punishment illustrates the immediate consequences of her actions. The severity of her punishment highlights the seriousness of rebelling against divine authority.
- **Intercessory Prayer:** Aaron's plea to Moses and Moses' subsequent prayer for Miriam underscore the power and importance of intercessory prayer, even for those who have committed serious transgressions.
- **Compassion and Forgiveness:** Moses' willingness to pray for Miriam despite her rebellion demonstrates a model of compassion and forgiveness. It shows the importance of seeking healing and restoration even for those who have wronged us.

**Modern Interpretation:**

This passage teaches modern believers about the seriousness of rebelling against divine authority, the power of intercessory prayer, and the importance of compassion and forgiveness.

**Key Themes:**

- **Immediate Consequences:** Miriam's punishment

highlights the immediate and serious consequences of rebelling against divine authority.

- **Power of Intercessory Prayer:** Aaron's plea and Moses' prayer underscore the importance of intercessory prayer for those who have transgressed.
- **Compassion and Forgiveness:** Moses' willingness to pray for Miriam demonstrates the importance of compassion and forgiveness in seeking healing and restoration.

**Modern-Day Examples:**

- **Understanding Consequences:** Modern believers can recognise the seriousness of rebelling against divine authority, understanding the immediate consequences.
- **Practising Intercessory Prayer:** Emphasising the power of intercessory prayer can inspire believers to pray for those who have transgressed, seeking their healing and restoration.
- **Compassion and Forgiveness:** Understanding the importance of compassion and forgiveness can encourage believers to seek healing and restoration for those who have wronged them.

**Questions for Reflection and Discussion:**

1. How does Miriam's punishment highlight the immediate and serious consequences of rebelling against divine authority?
2. What can we learn from Aaron's plea and Moses' prayer about the importance of intercessory prayer for those who have transgressed?
3. How can believers practise intercessory prayer, seeking

healing and restoration for those who have transgressed in their modern spiritual communities?

4.  In what ways can modern Christians demonstrate compassion and forgiveness, inspired by Moses' willingness to pray for Miriam despite her rebellion?

**Sermon Notes for Religious Leaders:**

**Title:** "Consequences, Intercession, and Compassion: Lessons from Miriam's Punishment"

**Introduction:**

- Introduce Miriam's punishment for her rebellion in Numbers 12, focusing on the themes of immediate consequences, the power of intercessory prayer, and the importance of compassion and forgiveness.
- Highlight the importance of recognising consequences, practising intercessory prayer, and demonstrating compassion and forgiveness.

**Body:**

1.  **Immediate Consequences:**
    - Discuss Miriam's punishment, highlighting the immediate and serious consequences of rebelling against divine authority.
    - Reflect on how these principles can be applied to modern spiritual practices, encouraging believers to recognise the seriousness of rebelling against divine authority.
2.  **Power of Intercessory Prayer:**
    - Explore Aaron's plea to Moses and Moses' subsequent prayer for Miriam, emphasising the importance of intercessory prayer for those who

have transgressed.
- ○ Encourage the congregation to practise intercessory prayer, seeking healing and restoration for those who have wronged them.

3. **Compassion and Forgiveness:**
   - ○ Discuss Moses' willingness to pray for Miriam despite her rebellion, highlighting the importance of compassion and forgiveness in seeking healing and restoration.
   - ○ Emphasise the need for believers to demonstrate compassion and forgiveness, recognising the value of seeking healing and restoration for those who have wronged them.

**Working Example for Religious Leaders:**

**Example:** "Practising Intercessory Prayer and Compassion in Church Life"

- **Scenario:** Imagine your church is encouraging members to recognise the consequences of rebellion, practise intercessory prayer, and demonstrate compassion and forgiveness.
- **Action:** Organise a series of teachings and discussions on the importance of recognising consequences, practising intercessory prayer, and demonstrating compassion and forgiveness. Encourage members to pray for those who have transgressed, seeking their healing and restoration.
- **Compassion:** Emphasise the significance of compassion and forgiveness, providing guidance on how to seek healing and restoration for those who have wronged them.
- **Outcome:** By recognising consequences, practising intercessory prayer, and demonstrating compassion and

forgiveness, the community grows stronger in their commitment to God, reflecting the principles from Miriam's punishment and Moses' prayer.

## Conclusion:

- Summarise the key lessons from Miriam's punishment, focusing on the immediate consequences of rebellion, the power of intercessory prayer, and the importance of compassion and forgiveness.
- Challenge the congregation to apply these principles in their modern spiritual practices and community life.
- Offer a prayer for guidance, dedication, and a deeper commitment to recognising consequences, practising intercessory prayer, and demonstrating compassion and forgiveness in their spiritual journey.

### Link to Modern-Day Problems:

◇ **Understanding Consequences:** How can modern believers recognise the seriousness of rebelling against divine authority, understanding the immediate consequences, inspired by Miriam's punishment?

◇ **Practising Intercessory Prayer:** What steps can believers take to practise intercessory prayer, seeking healing and restoration for those who have transgressed, inspired by Aaron's plea and Moses' prayer?

◇ **Compassion and Forgiveness:** How can believers demonstrate compassion and forgiveness, seeking healing and restoration for those who have wronged them, inspired by Moses' willingness to pray for Miriam despite her rebellion?

◇ **Consequences, Intercession, and Compassion:** In what ways can modern Christians recognise consequences, practise intercessory prayer, and demonstrate compassion and forgiveness in their spiritual journey, inspired by the principles from Miriam's punishment and Moses' prayer?

**Restoration and Moving Forward**
**Numbers 12:14-16 (NIV)**

1. The Lord replied to Moses, "If her father had spit in her face, would she not have been in disgrace for seven days? Confine her outside the camp for seven days; after that she can be brought back."
2. So Miriam was confined outside the camp for seven days, and the people did not move on till she was brought back.
3. After that, the people left Hazeroth and encamped in the Desert of Paran.

**Theological Significance:**

- **Restoration and Discipline:** God's command to confine Miriam outside the camp for seven days serves as both a disciplinary action and a means of restoration. It highlights the balance between discipline and grace.
- **Community Impact:** Miriam's confinement affected the entire community, demonstrating how individual actions can impact the broader community. The people's willingness to wait for her return underscores the value of solidarity and support.
- **Moving Forward:** After Miriam's restoration, the people continued their journey, symbolising the importance of addressing issues, restoring relationships, and moving forward together.

**Modern Interpretation:**

This passage teaches modern believers about the balance between discipline and grace, the impact of individual actions on the community, and the importance of addressing issues, restoring relationships, and moving forward together.

**Key Themes:**

- **Restoration and Discipline:** The passage highlights the balance between discipline and grace in dealing with transgressions.
- **Community Impact:** Miriam's confinement demonstrates how individual actions can impact the broader community and the value of solidarity and support.
- **Moving Forward Together:** The continuation of the journey after Miriam's restoration symbolises the importance of addressing issues, restoring relationships, and moving forward together.

**Modern-Day Examples:**

- **Practising Discipline and Grace:** Modern believers can practise balancing discipline and grace in dealing with transgressions, recognising the importance of both.
- **Understanding Community Impact:** Emphasising the impact of individual actions on the community can inspire believers to act responsibly and support one another.
- **Restoring Relationships:** Understanding the importance of addressing issues and restoring relationships can encourage believers to move forward together in unity.

**Questions for Reflection and Discussion:**

1. How does Miriam's confinement highlight the balance

between discipline and grace in dealing with transgressions?

2. What can we learn from the impact of Miriam's confinement on the community about the value of solidarity and support?

3. How can believers practise balancing discipline and grace in their modern spiritual communities?

4. In what ways can modern Christians understand the importance of addressing issues, restoring relationships, and moving forward together, inspired by the continuation of the journey after Miriam's restoration?

**Sermon Notes for Religious Leaders:**

**Title:** "Discipline, Grace, and Moving Forward: Lessons from Miriam's Restoration"

**Introduction:**

- Introduce the restoration and moving forward after Miriam's punishment in Numbers 12, focusing on the themes of discipline and grace, community impact, and moving forward together.
- Highlight the importance of practising discipline and grace, understanding community impact, and restoring relationships.

**Body:**

1. **Restoration and Discipline:**
    - Discuss Miriam's confinement outside the camp for seven days, highlighting the balance between discipline and grace in dealing with transgressions.
    - Reflect on how these principles can be applied to

modern spiritual practices, encouraging believers to practise balancing discipline and grace.

2. **Community Impact:**
   - Explore the impact of Miriam's confinement on the community, emphasising the value of solidarity and support.
   - Encourage the congregation to act responsibly and support one another, recognising the impact of individual actions on the community.

3. **Moving Forward Together:**
   - Discuss the continuation of the journey after Miriam's restoration, highlighting the importance of addressing issues, restoring relationships, and moving forward together.
   - Emphasise the need for believers to restore relationships and move forward in unity, recognising the significance of solidarity and support.

**Working Example for Religious Leaders:**
**Example:** "Practising Discipline and Grace in Church Life"

- **Scenario:** Imagine your church is encouraging members to practise balancing discipline and grace, understanding community impact, and restoring relationships.
- **Action:** Organise a series of teachings and discussions on the importance of discipline and grace, understanding community impact, and restoring relationships. Encourage members to practise balancing discipline and grace in dealing with transgressions.
- **Community Impact:** Emphasise the significance of acting responsibly and supporting one another, providing

guidance on how to restore relationships and move
forward together.

- **Outcome:** By practising discipline and grace,
  understanding community impact, and restoring
  relationships, the community grows stronger in their
  commitment to God, reflecting the principles from
  Miriam's restoration and the continuation of the journey.

**Conclusion:**

- Summarise the key lessons from Miriam's restoration,
  focusing on discipline and grace, community impact, and
  moving forward together.
- Challenge the congregation to apply these principles in
  their modern spiritual practices and community life.
- Offer a prayer for guidance, dedication, and a deeper
  commitment to practising discipline and grace,
  understanding community impact, and restoring
  relationships in their spiritual journey.

**Link to Modern-Day Problems:**

◇ **Practising Discipline and Grace:** How can modern believers
practise balancing discipline and grace in dealing with
transgressions, recognising the importance of both, inspired by
Miriam's confinement?

◇ **Understanding Community Impact:** What steps can
believers take to understand the impact of individual actions on the
community, acting responsibly and supporting one another, inspired
by the impact of Miriam's confinement on the community?

◇ **Restoring Relationships:** How can believers understand the
importance of addressing issues, restoring relationships, and moving

forward together, inspired by the continuation of the journey after Miriam's restoration?

◈ **Discipline, Grace, and Moving Forward:** In what ways can modern Christians practise discipline and grace, understand community impact, and restore relationships in their spiritual journey, inspired by the principles from Miriam's restoration and the continuation of the journey?

# The Spies Sent to Canaan

T he Spies Appointed
      **Numbers 13:1-16 (NIV)**

1.  The Lord said to Moses,
2.  "Send some men to explore the land of Canaan, which I am giving to the Israelites. From each ancestral tribe send one of its leaders."
3.  So at the Lord's command Moses sent them out from the Desert of Paran. All of them were leaders of the Israelites.
4.  These are their names:
    - from the tribe of Reuben, Shammua son of Zakkur;
    - from the tribe of Simeon, Shaphat son of Hori;
    - from the tribe of Judah, Caleb son of Jephunneh;
    - from the tribe of Issachar, Igal son of Joseph;
    - from the tribe of Ephraim, Hoshea son of Nun;
    - from the tribe of Benjamin, Palti son of Raphu;
    - from the tribe of Zebulun, Gaddiel son of Sodi;
    - from the tribe of Manasseh (a tribe of Joseph), Gaddi son of Susi;
    - from the tribe of Dan, Ammiel son of Gemalli;
    - from the tribe of Asher, Sethur son of Michael;
    - from the tribe of Naphtali, Nahbi son of Vophsi;
    - from the tribe of Gad, Geuel son of Maki.
5.  These are the names of the men Moses sent to explore the

land. (Moses gave Hoshea son of Nun the name Joshua.)

**Theological Significance:**

- **Divine Directive:** The mission of the spies begins with a direct command from God, indicating that their journey is part of His divine plan. This underscores the importance of obedience to God's directives.
- **Leadership and Responsibility:** The selection of leaders from each tribe to undertake the mission highlights the significance of responsible and trustworthy leadership in fulfilling God's plans.
- **Names and Identity:** The renaming of Hoshea to Joshua by Moses is significant, as names in biblical contexts often reflect character or destiny. Joshua means "The Lord is salvation," pointing to his future role.

**Modern Interpretation:**

This passage teaches modern believers about the importance of obedience to divine directives, the significance of responsible leadership, and the power of names and identity in defining one's purpose.

**Key Themes:**

- **Obedience to Divine Directives:** The mission begins with a command from God, underscoring the importance of following divine instructions.
- **Responsible Leadership:** The selection of leaders from each tribe highlights the value of responsible and trustworthy leadership in fulfilling God's plans.
- **Names and Identity:** The renaming of Hoshea to Joshua signifies the importance of names and identity in shaping

one's character and destiny.

**Modern-Day Examples:**

- **Following Divine Guidance:** Modern believers can practise obedience to God's directives, recognising the importance of following divine instructions in their lives.
- **Leadership Responsibility:** Emphasising the significance of responsible leadership can inspire believers to cultivate trustworthiness and accountability in their roles.
- **Understanding Identity:** Recognising the power of names and identity can encourage believers to embrace their God-given purposes and destinies.

**Questions for Reflection and Discussion:**

1. How does the mission of the spies begin with a direct command from God, highlighting the importance of obedience to divine directives?
2. What can we learn from the selection of leaders from each tribe about the significance of responsible and trustworthy leadership?
3. How can believers practise obedience to God's directives in their modern spiritual journeys?
4. In what ways can modern Christians understand the power of names and identity in shaping their character and destiny, inspired by the renaming of Hoshea to Joshua?

**Sermon Notes for Religious Leaders:**
**Title:** "Obedience, Leadership, and Identity: Lessons from the Spies' Mission"
**Introduction:**

- Introduce the mission of the spies in Numbers 13, focusing on the themes of obedience to divine directives, responsible leadership, and the power of names and identity.
- Highlight the importance of practising obedience, cultivating responsible leadership, and understanding identity.

**Body:**

1. **Obedience to Divine Directives:**
   - Discuss the command from God to send spies, highlighting the importance of following divine instructions.
   - Reflect on how these principles can be applied to modern spiritual practices, encouraging believers to practise obedience to God's directives.
2. **Responsible Leadership:**
   - Explore the selection of leaders from each tribe, emphasising the significance of responsible and trustworthy leadership in fulfilling God's plans.
   - Encourage the congregation to cultivate trustworthiness and accountability in their leadership roles, recognising the value of responsible leadership.
3. **Names and Identity:**
   - Discuss the renaming of Hoshea to Joshua, highlighting the importance of names and identity in shaping one's character and destiny.
   - Emphasise the need for believers to embrace their God-given purposes and destinies, recognising the power of names and identity.

**Working Example for Religious Leaders:**

**Example:** "Practising Obedience and Responsible Leadership in Church Life"

- **Scenario:** Imagine your church is encouraging members to practise obedience to divine directives and cultivate responsible leadership, understanding the power of names and identity.
- **Action:** Organise a series of teachings and discussions on the importance of obedience, responsible leadership, and understanding identity. Encourage members to follow God's directives and cultivate trustworthiness and accountability in their roles.
- **Identity:** Emphasise the significance of embracing God-given purposes and destinies, providing guidance on how to recognise the power of names and identity.
- **Outcome:** By practising obedience, responsible leadership, and understanding identity, the community grows stronger in their commitment to God, reflecting the principles from the mission of the spies.

**Conclusion:**

- Summarise the key lessons from the mission of the spies, focusing on obedience to divine directives, responsible leadership, and the power of names and identity.
- Challenge the congregation to apply these principles in their modern spiritual practices and community life.
- Offer a prayer for guidance, dedication, and a deeper commitment to practising obedience, cultivating responsible leadership, and understanding identity in their spiritual journey.

**Link to Modern-Day Problems:**

◇ **Following Divine Guidance:** How can modern believers practise obedience to God's directives, recognising the importance of following divine instructions in their lives, inspired by the command to send spies?

◇ **Leadership Responsibility:** What steps can believers take to cultivate responsible and trustworthy leadership, recognising its significance in fulfilling God's plans, inspired by the selection of leaders from each tribe?

◇ **Understanding Identity:** How can believers understand the power of names and identity in shaping their character and destiny, encouraging them to embrace their God-given purposes, inspired by the renaming of Hoshea to Joshua?

◇ **Obedience, Leadership, and Identity:** In what ways can modern Christians practise obedience to divine directives, cultivate responsible leadership, and understand identity in their spiritual journey, inspired by the principles from the mission of the spies?

**Exploring the Land**
**Numbers 13:17-25 (NIV)**

1. When Moses sent them to explore Canaan, he said, "Go up through the Negev and on into the hill country.
2. See what the land is like and whether the people who live there are strong or weak, few or many.
3. What kind of land do they live in? Is it good or bad? What kind of towns do they live in? Are they unwalled or fortified?
4. How is the soil? Is it fertile or poor? Are there trees in it or not? Do your best to bring back some of the fruit of the land." (It was the season for the first ripe grapes.)
5. So they went up and explored the land from the Desert of Zin as far as Rehob, towards Lebo Hamath.

6. They went up through the Negev and came to Hebron, where Ahiman, Sheshai and Talmai, the descendants of Anak, lived. (Hebron had been built seven years before Zoan in Egypt.)

7. When they reached the Valley of Eshkol, they cut off a branch bearing a single cluster of grapes. Two of them carried it on a pole between them, along with some pomegranates and figs.

8. That place was called the Valley of Eshkol because of the cluster of grapes the Israelites cut off there.

9. At the end of forty days they returned from exploring the land.

**Theological Significance:**

- **Thorough Exploration:** Moses' detailed instructions to the spies demonstrate the importance of thorough exploration and assessment in decision-making. They are to observe the land, the people, and the resources meticulously.

- **Faith and Preparation:** The mission to explore the land reflects a balance between faith in God's promises and practical preparation. It underscores the need to be well-prepared while trusting in God's guidance.

- **Fruitfulness of the Land:** The gathering of the fruit, particularly the large cluster of grapes, symbolises the fertility and abundance of the Promised Land, affirming God's promise of a land flowing with milk and honey.

**Modern Interpretation:**

This passage teaches modern believers about the importance of thorough preparation and assessment in decision-making, balancing faith and practical preparation, and recognising the fruitfulness of God's promises.

**Key Themes:**

- **Thorough Preparation:** The detailed exploration highlights the importance of thorough preparation and assessment in decision-making.
- **Faith and Practical Preparation:** The mission reflects a balance between faith in God's promises and practical preparation.
- **Fruitfulness of God's Promises:** The abundant fruit symbolises the fulfilment of God's promises and the fertility of the Promised Land.

**Modern-Day Examples:**

- **Practising Thorough Preparation:** Modern believers can practise thorough preparation and assessment in their decision-making, recognising its importance in fulfilling God's plans.
- **Balancing Faith and Preparation:** Emphasising the balance between faith and practical preparation can inspire believers to trust in God's promises while being well-prepared.
- **Recognising God's Fruitfulness:** Understanding the fruitfulness of God's promises can encourage believers to have faith in the abundance and fulfilment of His word.

**Questions for Reflection and Discussion:**

1. How do Moses' detailed instructions to the spies highlight the importance of thorough preparation and assessment in

decision-making?

2. What can we learn from the mission to explore the land about balancing faith in God's promises with practical preparation?

3. How can believers practise thorough preparation and assessment in their modern spiritual journeys?

4. In what ways can modern Christians recognise the fruitfulness of God's promises, inspired by the abundant fruit gathered by the spies?

**Sermon Notes for Religious Leaders:**

**Title:** "Preparation, Faith, and Fruitfulness: Lessons from the Exploration of Canaan"

**Introduction:**

- Introduce the exploration of Canaan by the spies in Numbers 13, focusing on the themes of thorough preparation, balancing faith and practical preparation, and recognising the fruitfulness of God's promises.
- Highlight the importance of practising thorough preparation, balancing faith and preparation, and understanding God's fruitfulness.

**Body:**

1. **Thorough Preparation:**
   - Discuss Moses' detailed instructions to the spies, highlighting the importance of thorough preparation and assessment in decision-making.
   - Reflect on how these principles can be applied to modern spiritual practices, encouraging believers to practise thorough preparation in their decision-making.

2. **Faith and Practical Preparation:**
   - Explore the mission to explore the land, emphasising the balance between faith in God's promises and practical preparation.
   - Encourage the congregation to trust in God's promises while being well-prepared, recognising the importance of balancing faith and preparation.
3. **Fruitfulness of God's Promises:**
   - Discuss the gathering of the abundant fruit, highlighting the fulfilment of God's promises and the fertility of the Promised Land.
   - Emphasise the need for believers to recognise the fruitfulness of God's promises, having faith in the abundance and fulfilment of His word.

**Working Example for Religious Leaders:**
**Example:** "Practising Thorough Preparation and Faith in Church Life"

- **Scenario:** Imagine your church is encouraging members to practise thorough preparation and assessment in decision-making, balancing faith and practical preparation, and recognising the fruitfulness of God's promises.
- **Action:** Organise a series of teachings and discussions on the importance of thorough preparation, balancing faith and preparation, and understanding God's fruitfulness. Encourage members to practise thorough preparation and have faith in God's promises.
- **Fruitfulness:** Emphasise the significance of recognising the fruitfulness of God's promises, providing guidance on how to have faith in the abundance and fulfilment of His

word.

- **Outcome:** By practising thorough preparation, balancing faith and practical preparation, and recognising God's fruitfulness, the community grows stronger in their commitment to God, reflecting the principles from the exploration of Canaan.

## Conclusion:

- Summarise the key lessons from the exploration of Canaan, focusing on thorough preparation, balancing faith and practical preparation, and recognising the fruitfulness of God's promises.
- Challenge the congregation to apply these principles in their modern spiritual practices and community life.
- Offer a prayer for guidance, dedication, and a deeper commitment to practising thorough preparation, balancing faith and preparation, and recognising God's fruitfulness in their spiritual journey.

### Link to Modern-Day Problems:

◈ **Practising Thorough Preparation:** How can modern believers practise thorough preparation and assessment in their decision-making, recognising its importance in fulfilling God's plans, inspired by Moses' detailed instructions to the spies?

◈ **Balancing Faith and Preparation:** What steps can believers take to balance faith in God's promises with practical preparation, inspired by the mission to explore the land?

◈ **Recognising God's Fruitfulness:** How can believers understand the fruitfulness of God's promises, encouraging them to have faith in the abundance and fulfilment of His word, inspired by the abundant fruit gathered by the spies?

◈ **Preparation, Faith, and Fruitfulness:** In what ways can modern Christians practise thorough preparation, balance faith and practical preparation, and recognise God's fruitfulness in their spiritual journey, inspired by the principles from the exploration of Canaan?

**The Spies' Report**
**Numbers 13:26-33 (NIV)**

1. They came back to Moses and Aaron and the whole Israelite community at Kadesh in the Desert of Paran. There they reported to them and to the whole assembly and showed them the fruit of the land.

2. They gave Moses this account: "We went into the land to which you sent us, and it does flow with milk and honey! Here is its fruit.

3. But the people who live there are powerful, and the cities are fortified and very large. We even saw descendants of Anak there.

4. The Amalekites live in the Negev; the Hittites, Jebusites and Amorites live in the hill country; and the Canaanites live near the sea and along the Jordan."

5. Then Caleb silenced the people before Moses and said, "We should go up and take possession of the land, for we can certainly do it."

6. But the men who had gone up with him said, "We can't attack those people; they are stronger than we are."

7. And they spread among the Israelites a bad report about the land they had explored. They said, "The land we explored devours those living in it. All the people we saw there are of great size.

8. We saw the Nephilim there (the descendants of Anak come from the Nephilim). We seemed like grasshoppers in our

own eyes, and we looked the same to them."

**Theological Significance:**

- **Mixed Report:** The spies' report is mixed with both positive and negative elements. While they confirm the land's fertility, they also express fear of its inhabitants. This highlights the tension between faith in God's promises and the fear of obstacles.
- **Faith vs. Fear:** Caleb's response is one of faith and confidence in God's promise, while the other spies' response is driven by fear and doubt. This contrast emphasises the importance of faith in overcoming challenges.
- **Influence of Negative Reports:** The spread of the negative report among the Israelites illustrates the power of negative influences and the impact they can have on community morale and decision-making.

**Modern Interpretation:**

This passage teaches modern believers about the tension between faith and fear, the importance of trusting in God's promises, and the influence of negative reports on community morale.

**Key Themes:**

- **Faith vs. Fear:** The passage highlights the contrast between faith and fear in responding to challenges and obstacles.
- **Trust in God's Promises:** Caleb's response emphasises the importance of trusting in God's promises despite apparent difficulties.
- **Influence of Negative Reports:** The spread of the negative

report illustrates the power of negative influences on community morale and decision-making.

**Modern-Day Examples:**

- **Overcoming Fear with Faith:** Modern believers can practise overcoming fear with faith, recognising the importance of trusting in God's promises despite challenges.
- **Trusting God's Promises:** Emphasising the importance of trusting in God's promises can inspire believers to have confidence in His word.
- **Combating Negative Influences:** Understanding the impact of negative reports can encourage believers to combat negative influences and maintain a positive outlook.

**Questions for Reflection and Discussion:**

1. How does the mixed report of the spies highlight the tension between faith in God's promises and the fear of obstacles?
2. What can we learn from Caleb's response about the importance of trusting in God's promises despite apparent difficulties?
3. How can believers practise overcoming fear with faith in their modern spiritual journeys?
4. In what ways can modern Christians understand the influence of negative reports and combat negative influences on community morale and decision-making, inspired by the spies' report?

**Sermon Notes for Religious Leaders:**

**Title:** "Faith, Fear, and Influence: Lessons from the Spies' Report"

**Introduction:**

- Introduce the spies' report in Numbers 13, focusing on the themes of faith versus fear, trusting in God's promises, and the influence of negative reports on community morale.
- Highlight the importance of overcoming fear with faith, trusting God's promises, and combating negative influences.

**Body:**

1. **Faith vs. Fear:**
   - Discuss the mixed report of the spies, highlighting the tension between faith in God's promises and the fear of obstacles.
   - Reflect on how these principles can be applied to modern spiritual practices, encouraging believers to overcome fear with faith.

2. **Trust in God's Promises:**
   - Explore Caleb's response, emphasising the importance of trusting in God's promises despite apparent difficulties.
   - Encourage the congregation to have confidence in God's word, recognising the significance of trusting His promises.

3. **Influence of Negative Reports:**
   - Discuss the spread of the negative report among the Israelites, highlighting the power of negative influences on community morale and decision-making.

    ◦ Emphasise the need for believers to combat negative influences and maintain a positive outlook, recognising the impact of negative reports.

**Working Example for Religious Leaders:**
**Example:** "Practising Faith and Combating Negative Influences in Church Life"

- **Scenario:** Imagine your church is encouraging members to practise overcoming fear with faith, trusting in God's promises, and combating negative influences.
- **Action:** Organise a series of teachings and discussions on the importance of faith, trusting God's promises, and combating negative influences. Encourage members to overcome fear with faith and maintain a positive outlook.
- **Influence:** Emphasise the significance of combating negative influences, providing guidance on how to trust God's promises despite apparent difficulties.
- **Outcome:** By practising faith, trusting God's promises, and combating negative influences, the community grows stronger in their commitment to God, reflecting the principles from the spies' report.

**Conclusion:**

- Summarise the key lessons from the spies' report, focusing on faith versus fear, trusting in God's promises, and the influence of negative reports on community morale.
- Challenge the congregation to apply these principles in their modern spiritual practices and community life.
- Offer a prayer for guidance, dedication, and a deeper

commitment to practising faith, trusting God's promises, and combating negative influences in their spiritual journey.

**Link to Modern-Day Problems:**

◈ **Overcoming Fear with Faith:** How can modern believers practise overcoming fear with faith, recognising the importance of trusting in God's promises despite challenges, inspired by the mixed report of the spies?

◈ **Trusting God's Promises:** What steps can believers take to trust in God's promises, having confidence in His word, inspired by Caleb's response?

◈ **Combating Negative Influences:** How can believers understand the influence of negative reports and combat negative influences on community morale and decision-making, inspired by the spies' report?

◈ **Faith, Fear, and Influence:** In what ways can modern Christians practise overcoming fear with faith, trust in God's promises, and combat negative influences in their spiritual journey, inspired by the principles from the spies' report?

**The People's Reaction and God's Response**

**Numbers 14:1-12 (NIV)**

1. That night all the members of the community raised their voices and wept aloud.
2. All the Israelites grumbled against Moses and Aaron, and the whole assembly said to them, "If only we had died in Egypt! Or in this wilderness!
3. Why is the Lord bringing us to this land only to let us fall by the sword? Our wives and children will be taken as plunder. Wouldn't it be better for us to go back to Egypt?"
4. And they said to each other, "We should choose a leader and go back to Egypt."

5.  Then Moses and Aaron fell facedown in front of the whole Israelite assembly gathered there.

6.  Joshua son of Nun and Caleb son of Jephunneh, who were among those who had explored the land, tore their clothes

7.  and said to the entire Israelite assembly, "The land we passed through and explored is exceedingly good.

8.  If the Lord is pleased with us, he will lead us into that land, a land flowing with milk and honey, and will give it to us.

9.  Only do not rebel against the Lord. And do not be afraid of the people of the land, because we will devour them. Their protection is gone, but the Lord is with us. Do not be afraid of them."

10.  But the whole assembly talked about stoning them. Then the glory of the Lord appeared at the tent of meeting to all the Israelites.

11.  The Lord said to Moses, "How long will these people treat me with contempt? How long will they refuse to believe in me, in spite of all the signs I have performed among them?

12.  I will strike them down with a plague and destroy them, but I will make you into a nation greater and stronger than they."

**Theological Significance:**

- **Rebellion and Unbelief:** The people's reaction of despair and desire to return to Egypt highlights their lack of faith and rebellion against God's plan. This response contrasts with the faith shown by Joshua and Caleb.

- **Faithful Leadership:** Joshua and Caleb's plea to the people to trust in God underscores the importance of faithful leadership and the courage to stand firm in faith even when facing opposition.

- **Divine Judgement:** God's response to the people's rebellion illustrates the seriousness of unbelief and contempt towards Him, demonstrating that rebellion has severe consequences.

**Modern Interpretation:**

This passage teaches modern believers about the dangers of rebellion and unbelief, the importance of faithful leadership, and the seriousness of divine judgement.

**Key Themes:**

- **Rebellion and Unbelief:** The people's reaction highlights the dangers of lacking faith and rebelling against God's plan.
- **Faithful Leadership:** Joshua and Caleb's plea underscores the importance of faithful leadership and standing firm in faith despite opposition.
- **Divine Judgement:** God's response illustrates the seriousness of unbelief and rebellion, emphasising that such actions have severe consequences.

**Modern-Day Examples:**

- **Avoiding Rebellion and Unbelief:** Modern believers can recognise the dangers of lacking faith and rebelling against God's plan, understanding the importance of trust and obedience.
- **Practising Faithful Leadership:** Emphasising the significance of faithful leadership can inspire believers to stand firm in their faith and encourage others to trust in God's plan.
- **Understanding Divine Judgement:** Recognising the

seriousness of unbelief and rebellion can encourage believers to maintain faith and obedience, understanding the consequences of their actions.

## Questions for Reflection and Discussion:

1. How does the people's reaction of despair and desire to return to Egypt highlight the dangers of lacking faith and rebelling against God's plan?
2. What can we learn from Joshua and Caleb's plea about the importance of faithful leadership and standing firm in faith despite opposition?
3. How can believers recognise the dangers of rebellion and unbelief in their modern spiritual journeys?
4. In what ways can modern Christians understand the seriousness of divine judgement, maintaining faith and obedience, inspired by God's response to the people's rebellion?

**Sermon Notes for Religious Leaders:**
**Title:** "Rebellion, Faith, and Judgement: Lessons from the People's Reaction and God's Response"
**Introduction:**

- Introduce the people's reaction and God's response in Numbers 14, focusing on the themes of rebellion and unbelief, faithful leadership, and divine judgement.
- Highlight the importance of avoiding rebellion, practising faithful leadership, and understanding divine judgement.

**Body:**

1. **Rebellion and Unbelief:**

- ○ Discuss the people's reaction of despair and desire to return to Egypt, highlighting the dangers of lacking faith and rebelling against God's plan.
- ○ Reflect on how these principles can be applied to modern spiritual practices, encouraging believers to recognise the importance of trust and obedience.

2. **Faithful Leadership:**
   - ○ Explore Joshua and Caleb's plea to trust in God, emphasising the importance of faithful leadership and standing firm in faith despite opposition.
   - ○ Encourage the congregation to practise faithful leadership, standing firm in their faith and encouraging others to trust in God's plan.

3. **Divine Judgement:**
   - ○ Discuss God's response to the people's rebellion, highlighting the seriousness of unbelief and the consequences of rebellion.
   - ○ Emphasise the need for believers to maintain faith and obedience, recognising the seriousness of divine judgement.

**Working Example for Religious Leaders:**
**Example:** "Practising Faithful Leadership and Avoiding Rebellion in Church Life"

- **Scenario:** Imagine your church is encouraging members to avoid rebellion and unbelief, practise faithful leadership, and understand divine judgement.
- **Action:** Organise a series of teachings and discussions on the importance of trust and obedience, faithful leadership, and understanding divine judgement. Encourage members

to stand firm in their faith and avoid rebellion.

- **Judgement:** Emphasise the seriousness of unbelief and rebellion, providing guidance on how to maintain faith and obedience.
- **Outcome:** By avoiding rebellion, practising faithful leadership, and understanding divine judgement, the community grows stronger in their commitment to God, reflecting the principles from the people's reaction and God's response.

**Conclusion:**

- Summarise the key lessons from the people's reaction and God's response, focusing on rebellion and unbelief, faithful leadership, and divine judgement.
- Challenge the congregation to apply these principles in their modern spiritual practices and community life.
- Offer a prayer for guidance, dedication, and a deeper commitment to avoiding rebellion, practising faithful leadership, and understanding divine judgement in their spiritual journey.

**Link to Modern-Day Problems:**

◈ **Avoiding Rebellion and Unbelief:** How can modern believers recognise the dangers of lacking faith and rebelling against God's plan, understanding the importance of trust and obedience, inspired by the people's reaction?

◈ **Practising Faithful Leadership:** What steps can believers take to practise faithful leadership, standing firm in their faith and encouraging others to trust in God's plan, inspired by Joshua and Caleb's plea?

◈ **Understanding Divine Judgement:** How can believers understand the seriousness of unbelief and rebellion, encouraging them to maintain faith and obedience, inspired by God's response to the people's rebellion?

◈ **Rebellion, Faith, and Judgement:** In what ways can modern Christians avoid rebellion, practise faithful leadership, and understand divine judgement in their spiritual journey, inspired by the principles from the people's reaction and God's response?

# God's Judgement on Israel's Rebellion

## M oses' Intercession
### Numbers 14:13-19 (NIV)

1. Moses said to the Lord, "Then the Egyptians will hear about it! By your power you brought these people up from among them.
2. And they will tell the inhabitants of this land about it. They have already heard that you, Lord, are with these people and that you, Lord, have been seen face to face, that your cloud stays over them, and that you go before them in a pillar of cloud by day and a pillar of fire by night.
3. If you put all these people to death, leaving none alive, the nations who have heard this report about you will say,
4. 'The Lord was not able to bring these people into the land he promised them on oath, so he slaughtered them in the wilderness.'
5. "Now may the Lord's strength be displayed, just as you have declared:
6. 'The Lord is slow to anger, abounding in love and forgiving sin and rebellion. Yet he does not leave the guilty unpunished; he punishes the children for the sin of the parents to the third and fourth generation.'
7. In accordance with your great love, forgive the sin of these people, just as you have pardoned them from the time they left Egypt until now."

**Theological Significance:**

- **Intercessory Prayer:** Moses' intercession for the Israelites highlights the power of intercessory prayer and the role of a leader in advocating for his people before God.
- **God's Reputation:** Moses appeals to God's reputation among the nations, emphasising the importance of God's name and how His actions reflect on His character.
- **Divine Attributes:** Moses' prayer reflects on the divine attributes of God—His patience, love, forgiveness, and justice—showing a deep understanding of God's nature.

**Modern Interpretation:**

This passage teaches modern believers about the importance of intercessory prayer, the significance of God's reputation, and the understanding of divine attributes such as patience, love, forgiveness, and justice.

**Key Themes:**

- **Intercessory Prayer:** The passage highlights the power of intercessory prayer in advocating for others before God.
- **God's Reputation:** Moses' appeal to God's reputation underscores the importance of how God's actions reflect on His character among the nations.
- **Divine Attributes:** The prayer reflects on God's patience, love, forgiveness, and justice, providing a model for understanding divine nature.

**Modern-Day Examples:**

- **Practising Intercessory Prayer:** Modern believers can practise intercessory prayer, recognising its power in advocating for others before God.

- **Upholding God's Reputation:** Emphasising the significance of God's reputation can inspire believers to act in ways that honour His name and character.
- **Understanding Divine Attributes:** Reflecting on divine attributes can help believers deepen their understanding of God's nature and emulate these qualities in their own lives.

## Questions for Reflection and Discussion:

1. How does Moses' intercession for the Israelites highlight the power of intercessory prayer and the role of a leader in advocating for his people before God?
2. What can we learn from Moses' appeal to God's reputation about the importance of how God's actions reflect on His character among the nations?
3. How can believers practise intercessory prayer in their modern spiritual journeys, recognising its power in advocating for others before God?
4. In what ways can modern Christians understand and reflect on divine attributes such as patience, love, forgiveness, and justice, inspired by Moses' prayer?

**Sermon Notes for Religious Leaders:**
**Title:** "Intercession, Reputation, and Divine Attributes: Lessons from Moses' Prayer"
**Introduction:**

- Introduce Moses' intercession for the Israelites in Numbers 14, focusing on the themes of intercessory prayer, God's reputation, and divine attributes.
- Highlight the importance of practising intercessory prayer, upholding God's reputation, and understanding divine

attributes.

**Body:**

1. **Intercessory Prayer:**
   - Discuss Moses' intercession for the Israelites, highlighting the power of intercessory prayer and the role of a leader in advocating for his people before God.
   - Reflect on how these principles can be applied to modern spiritual practices, encouraging believers to practise intercessory prayer.

2. **God's Reputation:**
   - Explore Moses' appeal to God's reputation, emphasising the importance of how God's actions reflect on His character among the nations.
   - Encourage the congregation to act in ways that honour God's name and character, recognising the significance of upholding His reputation.

3. **Divine Attributes:**
   - Discuss the divine attributes reflected in Moses' prayer—patience, love, forgiveness, and justice—highlighting the importance of understanding and emulating these qualities.
   - Emphasise the need for believers to deepen their understanding of God's nature and reflect these attributes in their own lives.

**Working Example for Religious Leaders:**

**Example:** "Practising Intercessory Prayer and Understanding Divine Attributes in Church Life"

- **Scenario:** Imagine your church is encouraging members to practise intercessory prayer, uphold God's reputation, and understand divine attributes.

- **Action:** Organise a series of teachings and discussions on the importance of intercessory prayer, upholding God's reputation, and reflecting on divine attributes. Encourage members to practise intercessory prayer and act in ways that honour God's name.
- **Attributes:** Emphasise the significance of understanding and emulating divine attributes, providing guidance on how to reflect patience, love, forgiveness, and justice in their lives.
- **Outcome:** By practising intercessory prayer, upholding God's reputation, and understanding divine attributes, the community grows stronger in their commitment to God, reflecting the principles from Moses' prayer.

**Conclusion:**

- Summarise the key lessons from Moses' intercession for the Israelites, focusing on intercessory prayer, God's reputation, and divine attributes.
- Challenge the congregation to apply these principles in their modern spiritual practices and community life.
- Offer a prayer for guidance, dedication, and a deeper commitment to practising intercessory prayer, upholding God's reputation, and understanding divine attributes in their spiritual journey.

**Link to Modern-Day Problems:**

⬦ **Practising Intercessory Prayer:** How can modern believers practise intercessory prayer, recognising its power in advocating for others before God, inspired by Moses' intercession for the Israelites?

◇ **Upholding God's Reputation:** What steps can believers take to act in ways that honour God's name and character, recognising the importance of how God's actions reflect on His character among the nations, inspired by Moses' appeal?

◇ **Understanding Divine Attributes:** How can believers understand and reflect on divine attributes such as patience, love, forgiveness, and justice, encouraging them to deepen their understanding of God's nature, inspired by Moses' prayer?

◇ **Intercession, Reputation, and Divine Attributes:** In what ways can modern Christians practise intercessory prayer, uphold God's reputation, and understand divine attributes in their spiritual journey, inspired by the principles from Moses' prayer?

**God's Judgement and the People's Response**
**Numbers 14:20-38 (NIV)**

1. The Lord replied, "I have forgiven them, as you asked.
2. Nevertheless, as surely as I live and as surely as the glory of the Lord fills the whole earth,
3. not one of those who saw my glory and the signs I performed in Egypt and in the wilderness but who disobeyed me and tested me ten times—
4. not one of them will ever see the land I promised on oath to their ancestors. No one who has treated me with contempt will ever see it.
5. But because my servant Caleb has a different spirit and follows me wholeheartedly, I will bring him into the land he went to, and his descendants will inherit it.
6. Since the Amalekites and the Canaanites are living in the valleys, turn back tomorrow and set out towards the desert along the route to the Red Sea."
7. The Lord said to Moses and Aaron:
8. "How long will this wicked community grumble against

me? I have heard the complaints of these grumbling Israelites.

9.  So tell them, 'As surely as I live, declares the Lord, I will do to you the very thing I heard you say:

10.  In this wilderness your bodies will fall—every one of you twenty years old or more who was counted in the census and who has grumbled against me.

11.  Not one of you will enter the land I swore with uplifted hand to make your home, except Caleb son of Jephunneh and Joshua son of Nun.

12.  As for your children that you said would be taken as plunder, I will bring them in to enjoy the land you have rejected.

13.  But as for you, your bodies will fall in this wilderness.

14.  Your children will be shepherds here for forty years, suffering for your unfaithfulness, until the last of your bodies lies in the wilderness.

15.  For forty years—one year for each of the forty days you explored the land—you will suffer for your sins and know what it is like to have me against you.'

16.  I, the Lord, have spoken, and I will surely do these things to this whole wicked community, which has banded together against me. They will meet their end in this wilderness; here they will die."

17.  So the men Moses had sent to explore the land, who returned and made the whole community grumble against him by spreading a bad report about it—

18.  these men who were responsible for spreading the bad report about the land were struck down and died of a plague before the Lord.

19.  Of the men who went to explore the land, only Joshua son of Nun and Caleb son of Jephunneh survived.

**Theological Significance:**

- **Divine Forgiveness and Judgement:** God's response to Moses' intercession demonstrates His willingness to forgive, but it also underscores the reality of divine judgement. Forgiveness does not negate the consequences of rebellion and unbelief.
- **Faithfulness Rewarded:** Caleb's faithfulness and wholehearted following of God are rewarded with the promise of entering the Promised Land, contrasting with the fate of those who disbelieved.
- **Consequences for the Community:** The fate of the Israelites, including the forty years of wandering and the death of the unfaithful, highlights the communal impact of collective unbelief and rebellion.

**Modern Interpretation:**

This passage teaches modern believers about the balance between divine forgiveness and judgement, the rewards of faithfulness, and the communal consequences of unbelief and rebellion.

**Key Themes:**

- **Divine Forgiveness and Judgement:** The passage highlights the balance between God's forgiveness and the reality of divine judgement.
- **Rewards of Faithfulness:** Caleb's faithfulness is rewarded, underscoring the importance of wholehearted commitment to God.
- **Communal Consequences:** The fate of the Israelites illustrates the communal impact of unbelief and rebellion.

**Modern-Day Examples:**

- **Understanding Forgiveness and Judgement:** Modern believers can recognise the balance between divine forgiveness and judgement, understanding that forgiveness does not negate the consequences of rebellion.
- **Practising Faithfulness:** Emphasising the rewards of faithfulness can inspire believers to commit wholeheartedly to God.
- **Recognising Communal Impact:** Understanding the communal consequences of unbelief and rebellion can encourage believers to maintain faith and obedience for the benefit of the community.

**Questions for Reflection and Discussion:**

1. How does God's response to Moses' intercession demonstrate the balance between divine forgiveness and judgement?
2. What can we learn from Caleb's faithfulness about the importance of wholehearted commitment to God?
3. How can believers understand the balance between forgiveness and judgement in their modern spiritual journeys, recognising that forgiveness does not negate consequences?
4. In what ways can modern Christians recognise the communal impact of unbelief and rebellion, encouraging them to maintain faith and obedience for the benefit of the community?

**Sermon Notes for Religious Leaders:**

**Title:** "Forgiveness, Faithfulness, and Communal Consequences: Lessons from God's Judgement on Israel's Rebellion"

**Introduction:**

- Introduce God's judgement on Israel's rebellion in Numbers 14, focusing on the themes of divine forgiveness and judgement, the rewards of faithfulness, and the communal consequences of unbelief and rebellion.
- Highlight the importance of understanding forgiveness and judgement, practising faithfulness, and recognising communal impact.

**Body:**

1. **Divine Forgiveness and Judgement:**
   - Discuss God's response to Moses' intercession, highlighting the balance between divine forgiveness and the reality of judgement.
   - Reflect on how these principles can be applied to modern spiritual practices, encouraging believers to understand that forgiveness does not negate consequences.

2. **Rewards of Faithfulness:**
   - Explore Caleb's faithfulness and the promise of entering the Promised Land, emphasising the importance of wholehearted commitment to God.
   - Encourage the congregation to practise faithfulness, recognising the rewards of committing wholeheartedly to God.

3. **Communal Consequences:**
   - Discuss the fate of the Israelites, highlighting the communal impact of collective unbelief and

rebellion.
- ○ Emphasise the need for believers to maintain faith and obedience, recognising the significance of communal impact.

**Working Example for Religious Leaders:**
**Example:** "Practising Faithfulness and Understanding Communal Impact in Church Life"

- **Scenario:** Imagine your church is encouraging members to understand the balance between divine forgiveness and judgement, practise faithfulness, and recognise communal impact.
- **Action:** Organise a series of teachings and discussions on the importance of forgiveness and judgement, faithfulness, and communal impact. Encourage members to commit wholeheartedly to God and maintain faith and obedience.
- **Impact:** Emphasise the significance of communal impact, providing guidance on how to maintain faith and obedience for the benefit of the community.
- **Outcome:** By understanding forgiveness and judgement, practising faithfulness, and recognising communal impact, the community grows stronger in their commitment to God, reflecting the principles from God's judgement on Israel's rebellion.

**Conclusion:**

- Summarise the key lessons from God's judgement on Israel's rebellion, focusing on divine forgiveness and judgement, the rewards of faithfulness, and the communal consequences of unbelief and rebellion.

- Challenge the congregation to apply these principles in their modern spiritual practices and commun500ty life.
- Offer a prayer for guidance, dedication, and a deeper commitment to understanding forgiveness and judgement, practising faithfulness, and recognising communal impact in their spiritual journey.

**Link to Modern-Day Problems:**

◇ **Understanding Forgiveness and Judgement:** How can modern believers recognise the balance between divine forgiveness and judgement, understanding that forgiveness does not negate the consequences of rebellion, inspired by God's response to Moses' intercession?

◇ **Practising Faithfulness:** What steps can believers take to practise faithfulness, committing wholeheartedly to God, inspired by Caleb's example?

◇ **Recognising Communal Impact:** How can believers understand the communal consequences of unbelief and rebellion, encouraging them to maintain faith and obedience for the benefit of the community, inspired by the fate of the Israelites?

◇ **Forgiveness, Faithfulness, and Communal Consequences:** In what ways can modern Christians understand forgiveness and judgement, practise faithfulness, and recognise communal impact in their spiritual journey, inspired by the principles from God's judgement on Israel's rebellion?

**Attempted Invasion and Defeat**
**Numbers 14:39-45 (NIV)**

1. When Moses reported this to all the Israelites, they mourned bitterly.
2. Early the next morning they set out for the highest point in the hill country, saying, "Now we are ready to go up to the land the Lord promised. Surely we have sinned!"

3. But Moses said, "Why are you disobeying the Lord's command? This will not succeed!

4. Do not go up, because the Lord is not with you. You will be defeated by your enemies,

5. for the Amalekites and the Canaanites will face you there. Because you have turned away from the Lord, he will not be with you and you will fall by the sword."

6. Nevertheless, in their presumption they went up towards the highest point in the hill country, though neither Moses nor the ark of the Lord's covenant moved from the camp.

7. Then the Amalekites and the Canaanites who lived in that hill country came down and attacked them and beat them down all the way to Hormah.

**Theological Significance:**

- **Disobedience and Presumption:** The Israelites' decision to go up to the hill country against Moses' warning highlights the dangers of disobedience and presumption. Acting without God's blessing leads to failure and defeat.

- **Consequences of Rebellion:** The defeat at the hands of the Amalekites and Canaanites underscores the consequences of turning away from God. Victory is only assured when God's presence and guidance are followed.

- **Importance of Divine Guidance:** Moses' refusal to accompany the Israelites without God's command emphasises the necessity of divine guidance in all endeavours.

**Modern Interpretation:**

This passage teaches modern believers about the dangers of disobedience and presumption, the consequences of rebellion, and the importance of seeking and following divine guidance in all endeavours.

**Key Themes:**

- **Disobedience and Presumption:** The passage highlights the dangers of acting presumptuously without God's blessing and guidance.
- **Consequences of Rebellion:** The defeat of the Israelites underscores the consequences of turning away from God and acting independently.
- **Divine Guidance:** Moses' refusal to accompany the Israelites without God's command emphasises the importance of seeking and following divine guidance.

**Modern-Day Examples:**

- **Avoiding Disobedience and Presumption:** Modern believers can recognise the dangers of disobedience and presumption, understanding the importance of seeking God's blessing and guidance.
- **Understanding Consequences of Rebellion:** Emphasising the consequences of rebellion can inspire believers to maintain faith and obedience to God's commands.
- **Seeking Divine Guidance:** Understanding the importance of seeking and following divine guidance can encourage believers to rely on God in all their endeavours.

**Questions for Reflection and Discussion:**

1. How does the Israelites' decision to go up to the hill country against Moses' warning highlight the dangers of

disobedience and presumption?

2. What can we learn from the defeat of the Israelites about the consequences of turning away from God and acting independently?

3. How can believers recognise the dangers of disobedience and presumption in their modern spiritual journeys, understanding the importance of seeking God's blessing and guidance?

4. In what ways can modern Christians understand the importance of seeking and following divine guidance in all their endeavours, inspired by Moses' refusal to accompany the Israelites without God's command?

**Sermon Notes for Religious Leaders:**

**Title:** "Disobedience, Consequences, and Divine Guidance: Lessons from the Attempted Invasion and Defeat"

**Introduction:**

- Introduce the attempted invasion and defeat of the Israelites in Numbers 14, focusing on the themes of disobedience and presumption, consequences of rebellion, and the importance of divine guidance.
- Highlight the importance of avoiding disobedience, understanding consequences, and seeking divine guidance.

**Body:**

1. **Disobedience and Presumption:**
   - Discuss the Israelites' decision to go up to the hill country against Moses' warning, highlighting the dangers of disobedience and presumption.
   - Reflect on how these principles can be applied to modern spiritual practices, encouraging believers

to recognise the importance of seeking God's
blessing and guidance.

2. **Consequences of Rebellion:**
    - Explore the defeat of the Israelites at the hands of
      the Amalekites and Canaanites, emphasising the
      consequences of turning away from God and
      acting independently.
    - Encourage the congregation to maintain faith and
      obedience to God's commands, recognising the
      consequences of rebellion.

3. **Divine Guidance:**
    - Discuss Moses' refusal to accompany the Israelites
      without God's command, highlighting the
      importance of seeking and following divine
      guidance in all endeavours.
    - Emphasise the need for believers to rely on God's
      guidance in their spiritual journey, understanding
      the significance of divine direction.

**Working Example for Religious Leaders:**
**Example:** "Avoiding Disobedience and Seeking Divine
Guidance in Church Life"

- **Scenario:** Imagine your church is encouraging members to
  avoid disobedience and presumption, understand the
  consequences of rebellion, and seek divine guidance.
- **Action:** Organise a series of teachings and discussions on
  the importance of seeking God's blessing and guidance,
  maintaining faith and obedience, and relying on divine
  direction. Encourage members to avoid acting
  presumptuously and seek God's guidance.
- **Guidance:** Emphasise the significance of seeking and

following divine guidance, providing guidance on how to rely on God in all their endeavours.

- **Outcome:** By avoiding disobedience and presumption, understanding consequences, and seeking divine guidance, the community grows stronger in their commitment to God, reflecting the principles from the attempted invasion and defeat.

**Conclusion:**

- Summarise the key lessons from the attempted invasion and defeat, focusing on disobedience and presumption, consequences of rebellion, and the importance of divine guidance.
- Challenge the congregation to apply these principles in their modern spiritual practices and community life.
- Offer a prayer for guidance, dedication, and a deeper commitment to avoiding disobedience and presumption, understanding consequences, and seeking divine guidance in their spiritual journey.

**Link to Modern-Day Problems:**

◈ **Avoiding Disobedience and Presumption:** How can modern believers recognise the dangers of disobedience and presumption, understanding the importance of seeking God's blessing and guidance, inspired by the Israelites' decision to go up to the hill country?

◈ **Understanding Consequences of Rebellion:** What steps can believers take to maintain faith and obedience to God's commands, recognising the consequences of rebellion, inspired by the defeat of the Israelites?

◇ **Seeking Divine Guidance:** How can believers understand the importance of seeking and following divine guidance in all their endeavours, encouraging them to rely on God in their spiritual journey, inspired by Moses' refusal to accompany the Israelites without God's command?

◇ **Disobedience, Consequences, and Divine Guidance:** In what ways can modern Christians avoid disobedience and presumption, understand consequences, and seek divine guidance in their spiritual journey, inspired by the principles from the attempted invasion and defeat?

**Lessons and Reflections**
**Numbers 14:39-45 (NIV)**

1. When Moses reported this to all the Israelites, they mourned bitterly.
2. Early the next morning they set out for the highest point in the hill country, saying, "Now we are ready to go up to the land the Lord promised. Surely we have sinned!"
3. But Moses said, "Why are you disobeying the Lord's command? This will not succeed!
4. Do not go up, because the Lord is not with you. You will be defeated by your enemies,
5. for the Amalekites and the Canaanites will face you there. Because you have turned away from the Lord, he will not be with you and you will fall by the sword."
6. Nevertheless, in their presumption they went up towards the highest point in the hill country, though neither Moses nor the ark of the Lord's covenant moved from the camp.
7. Then the Amalekites and the Canaanites who lived in that hill country came down and attacked them and beat them down all the way to Hormah.

**Theological Significance:**

- **Disobedience and Presumption:** The Israelites' decision to go up to the hill country against Moses' warning highlights the dangers of disobedience and presumption. Acting without God's blessing leads to failure and defeat.
- **Consequences of Rebellion:** The defeat at the hands of the Amalekites and Canaanites underscores the consequences of turning away from God. Victory is only assured when God's presence and guidance are followed.
- **Importance of Divine Guidance:** Moses' refusal to accompany the Israelites without God's command emphasises the necessity of divine guidance in all endeavours.

**Modern Interpretation:**

This passage teaches modern believers about the dangers of disobedience and presumption, the consequences of rebellion, and the importance of seeking and following divine guidance in all endeavours.

**Key Themes:**

- **Disobedience and Presumption:** The passage highlights the dangers of acting presumptuously without God's blessing and guidance.
- **Consequences of Rebellion:** The defeat of the Israelites underscores the consequences of turning away from God and acting independently.
- **Divine Guidance:** Moses' refusal to accompany the Israelites without God's command emphasises the importance of seeking and following divine guidance.

**Modern-Day Examples:**

- **Avoiding Disobedience and Presumption:** Modern believers can recognise the dangers of disobedience and presumption, understanding the importance of seeking God's blessing and guidance.
- **Understanding Consequences of Rebellion:** Emphasising the consequences of rebellion can inspire believers to maintain faith and obedience to God's commands.
- **Seeking Divine Guidance:** Understanding the importance of seeking and following divine guidance can encourage believers to rely on God in all their endeavours.

**Questions for Reflection and Discussion:**

1. How does the Israelites' decision to go up to the hill country against Moses' warning highlight the dangers of disobedience and presumption?
2. What can we learn from the defeat of the Israelites about the consequences of turning away from God and acting independently?
3. How can believers recognise the dangers of disobedience and presumption in their modern spiritual journeys, understanding the importance of seeking God's blessing and guidance?
4. In what ways can modern Christians understand the importance of seeking and following divine guidance in all their endeavours, inspired by Moses' refusal to accompany the Israelites without God's command?

**Sermon Notes for Religious Leaders:**
**Title:** "Disobedience, Consequences, and Divine Guidance: Lessons from the Attempted Invasion and Defeat"

**Introduction:**

- Introduce the attempted invasion and defeat of the Israelites in Numbers 14, focusing on the themes of disobedience and presumption, consequences of rebellion, and the importance of divine guidance.
- Highlight the importance of avoiding disobedience, understanding consequences, and seeking divine guidance.

**Body:**

1. **Disobedience and Presumption:**
    - Discuss the Israelites' decision to go up to the hill country against Moses' warning, highlighting the dangers of disobedience and presumption.
    - Reflect on how these principles can be applied to modern spiritual practices, encouraging believers to recognise the importance of seeking God's blessing and guidance.
2. **Consequences of Rebellion:**
    - Explore the defeat of the Israelites at the hands of the Amalekites and Canaanites, emphasising the consequences of turning away from God and acting independently.
    - Encourage the congregation to maintain faith and obedience to God's commands, recognising the consequences of rebellion.
3. **Divine Guidance:**
    - Discuss Moses' refusal to accompany the Israelites without God's command, highlighting the importance of seeking and following divine guidance in all endeavours.
    - Emphasise the need for believers to rely on God's

guidance in their spiritual journey, understanding the significance of divine direction.

**Working Example for Religious Leaders:**
**Example:** "Avoiding Disobedience and Seeking Divine Guidance in Church Life"

- **Scenario:** Imagine your church is encouraging members to avoid disobedience and presumption, understand the consequences of rebellion, and seek divine guidance.
- **Action:** Organise a series of teachings and discussions on the importance of seeking God's blessing and guidance, maintaining faith and obedience, and relying on divine direction. Encourage members to avoid acting presumptuously and seek God's guidance.
- **Guidance:** Emphasise the significance of seeking and following divine guidance, providing guidance on how to rely on God in all their endeavours.
- **Outcome:** By avoiding disobedience and presumption, understanding consequences, and seeking divine guidance, the community grows stronger in their commitment to God, reflecting the principles from the attempted invasion and defeat.

**Conclusion:**

- Summarise the key lessons from the attempted invasion and defeat, focusing on disobedience and presumption, consequences of rebellion, and the importance of divine guidance.
- Challenge the congregation to apply these principles in their modern spiritual practices and community life.

- Offer a prayer for guidance, dedication, and a deeper commitment to avoiding disobedience and presumption, understanding consequences, and seeking divine guidance in their spiritual journey.

**Link to Modern-Day Problems:**

◇ **Avoiding Disobedience and Presumption:** How can modern believers recognise the dangers of disobedience and presumption, understanding the importance of seeking God's blessing and guidance, inspired by the Israelites' decision to go up to the hill country?

◇ **Understanding Consequences of Rebellion:** What steps can believers take to maintain faith and obedience to God's commands, recognising the consequences of rebellion, inspired by the defeat of the Israelites?

◇ **Seeking Divine Guidance:** How can believers understand the importance of seeking and following divine guidance in all their endeavours, encouraging them to rely on God in their spiritual journey, inspired by Moses' refusal to accompany the Israelites without God's command?

◇ **Disobedience, Consequences, and Divine Guidance:** In what ways can modern Christians avoid disobedience and presumption, understand consequences, and seek divine guidance in their spiritual journey, inspired by the principles from the attempted invasion and defeat?

# Laws about Offerings and Transgressions

A dditional Offerings
   **Numbers 15:1-16 (NIV)**

1.  The Lord said to Moses,
2.  "Speak to the Israelites and say to them: 'After you enter the land I am giving you as a home
3.  and you present to the Lord food offerings from the herd or the flock, as an aroma pleasing to the Lord—whether burnt offerings or sacrifices, for special vows or freewill offerings or festival offerings—
4.  then the person who brings an offering shall present to the Lord a grain offering of a tenth of an ephah of the finest flour mixed with a quarter of a hin of olive oil.
5.  With each lamb for the burnt offering or the sacrifice, prepare a quarter of a hin of wine as a drink offering.
6.  "'With a ram prepare a grain offering of two-tenths of an ephah of the finest flour mixed with a third of a hin of olive oil,
7.  and a third of a hin of wine as a drink offering. Offer it as an aroma pleasing to the Lord.
8.  "'When you prepare a young bull as a burnt offering or sacrifice, for a special vow or a fellowship offering to the Lord,
9.  bring with the bull a grain offering of three-tenths of an

ephah of the finest flour mixed with half a hin of olive oil,

10. and also bring half a hin of wine as a drink offering. This will be a food offering, an aroma pleasing to the Lord.

11. Each bull or ram, each lamb or young goat, is to be prepared in this manner.

12. Do this for each one, for as many as you prepare.

13. Everyone who is native-born must do these things in this way when they present a food offering as an aroma pleasing to the Lord.

14. For the generations to come, whenever a foreigner or anyone else living among you presents a food offering as an aroma pleasing to the Lord, they must do exactly as you do.

15. The community is to have the same rules for you and for the foreigner residing among you; this is a lasting ordinance for the generations to come. You and the foreigner shall be the same before the Lord:

16. The same laws and regulations will apply both to you and to the foreigner residing among you.'"

**Theological Significance:**

- **Inclusivity in Worship:** The passage emphasizes that both native-born Israelites and foreigners residing among them are to follow the same regulations for offerings. This inclusivity underscores the universality of God's laws and the equal standing of all people before Him.

- **Sacrificial System:** The detailed instructions for offerings highlight the importance of the sacrificial system in maintaining a right relationship with God. It reflects the need for intentionality and care in worship.

- **Obedience to Divine Command:** The repetition of "an aroma pleasing to the Lord" indicates that offerings are not

just ritualistic acts but expressions of obedience and
devotion to God.

**Modern Interpretation:**

This passage teaches modern believers about the importance of
inclusivity in worship, the significance of intentionality and care
in their spiritual practices, and the value of obedience to God's
commands.

**Key Themes:**

- **Inclusivity in Worship:** The regulations apply equally to
  Israelites and foreigners, highlighting the universal nature
  of God's laws.
- **Intentionality in Worship:** The detailed instructions for
  offerings underscore the importance of intentionality and
  care in worship practices.
- **Obedience and Devotion:** The offerings are expressions
  of obedience and devotion, reflecting a right relationship
  with God.

**Modern-Day Examples:**

- **Inclusive Worship Practices:** Modern believers can
  practise inclusivity in their worship, ensuring that all
  people, regardless of background, feel welcome and
  included in their spiritual community.
- **Intentional Spiritual Practices:** Emphasising the
  importance of intentionality and care in spiritual practices
  can inspire believers to approach worship and other
  religious activities with reverence and attention to detail.
- **Expressing Obedience and Devotion:** Understanding
  offerings as expressions of obedience and devotion can

encourage believers to view their acts of worship as meaningful and significant.

**Questions for Reflection and Discussion:**

1. How does the inclusion of both Israelites and foreigners in the regulations for offerings highlight the universality of God's laws?
2. What can we learn from the detailed instructions for offerings about the importance of intentionality and care in worship practices?
3. How can believers practise inclusivity in their modern worship practices, ensuring that all people feel welcome and included?
4. In what ways can modern Christians view their acts of worship as expressions of obedience and devotion to God, inspired by the sacrificial system?

**Sermon Notes for Religious Leaders:**
**Title:** "Inclusivity, Intentionality, and Obedience: Lessons from the Laws about Offerings"
**Introduction:**

- Introduce the laws about offerings in Numbers 15, focusing on the themes of inclusivity in worship, intentionality and care in spiritual practices, and the value of obedience and devotion.
- Highlight the importance of practising inclusive worship, approaching spiritual practices with intentionality, and viewing acts of worship as expressions of obedience.

**Body:**

1. **Inclusivity in Worship:**
   - Discuss the inclusion of both Israelites and foreigners in the regulations for offerings, highlighting the universality of God's laws and the equal standing of all people before Him.
   - Reflect on how these principles can be applied to modern worship practices, encouraging believers to ensure that all people feel welcome and included in their spiritual community.

2. **Intentionality in Worship:**
   - Explore the detailed instructions for offerings, emphasising the importance of intentionality and care in worship practices.
   - Encourage the congregation to approach their spiritual practices with reverence and attention to detail, recognising the significance of intentionality.

3. **Obedience and Devotion:**
   - Discuss how offerings are expressions of obedience and devotion to God, reflecting a right relationship with Him.
   - Emphasise the need for believers to view their acts of worship as meaningful and significant, understanding their value as expressions of obedience and devotion.

**Working Example for Religious Leaders:**
**Example:** "Practising Inclusive and Intentional Worship in Church Life"

- **Scenario:** Imagine your church is encouraging members to practise inclusive worship, approach spiritual practices with intentionality, and view acts of worship as expressions of obedience.

- **Action:** Organise a series of teachings and discussions on the importance of inclusivity in worship, intentionality in spiritual practices, and the value of obedience and devotion. Encourage members to ensure that all people feel welcome and included in their spiritual community.

- **Intentionality:** Emphasise the significance of approaching worship with reverence and attention to detail, providing guidance on how to view acts of worship as meaningful and significant.

- **Outcome:** By practising inclusive worship, approaching spiritual practices with intentionality, and viewing acts of worship as expressions of obedience, the community grows stronger in their commitment to God, reflecting the principles from the laws about offerings.

**Conclusion:**

- Summarise the key lessons from the laws about offerings, focusing on inclusivity in worship, intentionality and care in spiritual practices, and the value of obedience and devotion.

- Challenge the congregation to apply these principles in their modern worship practices and community life.

- Offer a prayer for guidance, dedication, and a deeper commitment to practising inclusive worship, approaching spiritual practices with intentionality, and viewing acts of worship as expressions of obedience in their spiritual journey.

**Link to Modern-Day Problems:**

◇ **Inclusive Worship Practices:** How can modern believers practise inclusivity in their worship, ensuring that all people, regardless of background, feel welcome and included in their spiritual community, inspired by the inclusion of both Israelites and foreigners in the regulations for offerings?

◇ **Intentional Spiritual Practices:** What steps can believers take to approach their spiritual practices with intentionality and care, recognising the importance of intentionality in worship, inspired by the detailed instructions for offerings?

◇ **Expressing Obedience and Devotion:** How can believers view their acts of worship as expressions of obedience and devotion to God, understanding their value as meaningful and significant, inspired by the sacrificial system?

◇ **Inclusivity, Intentionality, and Obedience:** In what ways can modern Christians practise inclusive worship, approach spiritual practices with intentionality, and view acts of worship as expressions of obedience in their spiritual journey, inspired by the principles from the laws about offerings?

**Offerings for Unintentional Sins**
**Numbers 15:17-29 (NIV)**

1. The Lord said to Moses,
2. "Speak to the Israelites and say to them: 'When you enter the land to which I am taking you
3. and you eat the food of the land, present a portion as an offering to the Lord.
4. Present a loaf from the first of your ground meal and present it as an offering from the threshing floor.
5. Throughout the generations to come you are to give this offering to the Lord from the first of your ground meal.
6. "Now if you as a community unintentionally fail to keep any of these commands the Lord gave Moses—

7. any of the Lord's commands to you through him, from the day the Lord gave them and continuing through the generations to come—

8. and if this is done unintentionally without the community being aware of it, then the whole community is to offer a young bull for a burnt offering as an aroma pleasing to the Lord, along with its prescribed grain offering and drink offering, and a male goat for a sin offering.

9. The priest is to make atonement for the whole Israelite community, and they will be forgiven, for it was not intentional and they have presented to the Lord for their wrong a food offering and a sin offering.

10. The whole Israelite community and the foreigners residing among them will be forgiven, because all the people were involved in the unintentional wrong.

11. "'But if just one person sins unintentionally, that person must bring a year-old female goat for a sin offering.

12. The priest is to make atonement before the Lord for the one who erred by sinning unintentionally, and when atonement has been made for that person, they will be forgiven.

13. One and the same law applies to everyone who sins unintentionally, whether a native-born Israelite or a foreigner residing among you.

**Theological Significance:**

- **Unintentional Sins:** The laws about offerings for unintentional sins underscore the importance of recognising and addressing even unintended wrongs. This reflects the need for vigilance and humility in spiritual practices.

- **Atonement and Forgiveness:** The provision for atonement and forgiveness for unintentional sins highlights God's grace and the means He provides for restoring a right relationship with Him.
- **Inclusivity in Atonement:** The same law applies to both native-born Israelites and foreigners, emphasizing the universality of God's grace and the inclusivity of His laws.

**Modern Interpretation:**

This passage teaches modern believers about the importance of recognising and addressing unintentional sins, the provision of atonement and forgiveness, and the inclusivity of God's grace.

**Key Themes:**

- **Unintentional Sins:** The passage highlights the importance of vigilance and humility in recognising and addressing even unintended wrongs.
- **Atonement and Forgiveness:** The provision for atonement and forgiveness underscores God's grace and the means for restoring a right relationship with Him.
- **Inclusivity in Atonement:** The same law applies to everyone, emphasizing the universality of God's grace and the inclusivity of His laws.

**Modern-Day Examples:**

- **Recognising Unintentional Sins:** Modern believers can practise vigilance and humility in recognising and addressing unintentional sins, understanding their impact on their spiritual lives.
- **Seeking Atonement and Forgiveness:** Emphasising the provision of atonement and forgiveness can inspire

believers to seek God's grace and restore their relationship with Him.

- **Inclusive Spiritual Practices:** Understanding the inclusivity of God's grace can encourage believers to practise inclusivity in their spiritual communities, recognising that the same laws and provisions apply to everyone.

**Questions for Reflection and Discussion:**

1. How does the recognition of unintentional sins highlight the importance of vigilance and humility in spiritual practices?
2. What can we learn from the provision of atonement and forgiveness about God's grace and the means He provides for restoring a right relationship with Him?
3. How can believers practise vigilance and humility in recognising and addressing unintentional sins in their modern spiritual journeys?
4. In what ways can modern Christians understand the inclusivity of God's grace and practise inclusivity in their spiritual communities, inspired by the same law applying to everyone?

**Sermon Notes for Religious Leaders:**
**Title:** "Unintentional Sins, Atonement, and Inclusivity: Lessons from the Laws about Offerings"
**Introduction:**

- Introduce the laws about offerings for unintentional sins in Numbers 15, focusing on the themes of recognising unintentional sins, seeking atonement and forgiveness, and the inclusivity of God's grace.

- Highlight the importance of vigilance and humility,
  seeking atonement, and practising inclusivity in spiritual
  practices.

**Body:**

1. **Recognising Unintentional Sins:**
   - Discuss the laws about offerings for unintentional
     sins, highlighting the importance of vigilance and
     humility in recognising and addressing even
     unintended wrongs.
   - Reflect on how these principles can be applied to
     modern spiritual practices, encouraging believers
     to practise vigilance and humility in their spiritual
     lives.

2. **Atonement and Forgiveness:**
   - Explore the provision for atonement and
     forgiveness, emphasising God's grace and the
     means He provides for restoring a right
     relationship with Him.
   - Encourage the congregation to seek atonement
     and forgiveness, recognising the importance of
     restoring their relationship with God.

3. **Inclusivity in Atonement:**
   - Discuss the inclusivity of God's laws and grace,
     highlighting that the same law applies to both
     native-born Israelites and foreigners.
   - Emphasise the need for believers to practise
     inclusivity in their spiritual communities,
     recognising the universality of God's grace.

**Working Example for Religious Leaders:**

**Example:** "Practising Vigilance, Seeking Atonement, and Inclusivity in Church Life"

- **Scenario:** Imagine your church is encouraging members to recognise unintentional sins, seek atonement and forgiveness, and practise inclusivity in their spiritual communities.
- **Action:** Organise a series of teachings and discussions on the importance of vigilance and humility, seeking atonement, and practising inclusivity. Encourage members to recognise and address unintentional sins, seek God's grace, and include everyone in their spiritual practices.
- **Atonement:** Emphasise the significance of seeking atonement and forgiveness, providing guidance on how to restore their relationship with God.
- **Outcome:** By practising vigilance, seeking atonement, and inclusivity, the community grows stronger in their commitment to God, reflecting the principles from the laws about offerings for unintentional sins.

**Conclusion:**

- Summarise the key lessons from the laws about offerings for unintentional sins, focusing on recognising unintentional sins, seeking atonement and forgiveness, and the inclusivity of God's grace.
- Challenge the congregation to apply these principles in their modern spiritual practices and community life.
- Offer a prayer for guidance, dedication, and a deeper commitment to practising vigilance, seeking atonement, and inclusivity in their spiritual journey.

**Link to Modern-Day Problems:**

◇ **Recognising Unintentional Sins:** How can modern believers practise vigilance and humility in recognising and addressing unintentional sins, understanding their impact on their spiritual lives, inspired by the laws about offerings for unintentional sins?

◇ **Seeking Atonement and Forgiveness:** What steps can believers take to seek atonement and forgiveness, recognising God's grace and the means for restoring their relationship with Him, inspired by the provision for atonement?

◇ **Inclusive Spiritual Practices:** How can believers understand the inclusivity of God's grace and practise inclusivity in their spiritual communities, recognising that the same laws and provisions apply to everyone, inspired by the same law applying to both native-born Israelites and foreigners?

◇ **Unintentional Sins, Atonement, and Inclusivity:** In what ways can modern Christians practise vigilance, seek atonement and forgiveness, and inclusivity in their spiritual journey, inspired by the principles from the laws about offerings for unintentional sins?

**Deliberate Sins and the Sabbath-Breaker**
**Numbers 15:30-41 (NIV)**

1. "'But anyone who sins defiantly, whether native-born or foreigner, blasphemes the Lord and must be cut off from the people of Israel.

2. Because they have despised the Lord's word and broken his commands, they must surely be cut off; their guilt remains on them.'"

3. While the Israelites were in the wilderness, a man was found gathering wood on the Sabbath day.

4. Those who found him gathering wood brought him to Moses and Aaron and the whole assembly,

5. and they kept him in custody, because it was not clear what should be done to him.

6. Then the Lord said to Moses, "The man must die. The whole assembly must stone him outside the camp."

7. So the assembly took him outside the camp and stoned him to death, as the Lord commanded Moses.

8. The Lord said to Moses,

9. "Speak to the Israelites and say to them: 'Throughout the generations to come you are to make tassels on the corners of your garments, with a blue cord on each tassel.

10. You will have these tassels to look at and so you will remember all the commands of the Lord, that you may obey them and not prostitute yourselves by chasing after the lusts of your own hearts and eyes.

11. Then you will remember to obey all my commands and will be consecrated to your God.

12. I am the Lord your God, who brought you out of Egypt to be your God. I am the Lord your God.'"

**Theological Significance:**

- **Defiant Sin:** The passage differentiates between unintentional and defiant sins, underscoring the severity of deliberate disobedience and its consequences.

- **Sabbath Observance:** The punishment of the Sabbath-breaker highlights the importance of Sabbath observance and the seriousness with which God regards His commands.

- **Reminders of Commandments:** The instruction to make tassels on garments serves as a physical reminder to obey God's commands and maintain a consecrated life.

**Modern Interpretation:**

This passage teaches modern believers about the severity of defiant sin, the importance of Sabbath observance, and the use of physical reminders to maintain obedience to God's commands.

**Key Themes:**

- **Defiant Sin:** The passage highlights the severity of deliberate disobedience and the consequences of defiant sin.
- **Sabbath Observance:** The punishment of the Sabbath-breaker underscores the importance of observing God's commands, particularly the Sabbath.
- **Physical Reminders:** The instruction to make tassels on garments serves as a reminder to obey God's commands and maintain a consecrated life.

**Modern-Day Examples:**

- **Avoiding Defiant Sin:** Modern believers can recognise the severity of deliberate disobedience and strive to avoid defiant sin, understanding its consequences.
- **Observing the Sabbath:** Emphasising the importance of Sabbath observance can inspire believers to honour God's commands and set aside time for rest and worship.
- **Using Reminders:** Understanding the use of physical reminders can encourage believers to find ways to remember and obey God's commands in their daily lives.

**Questions for Reflection and Discussion:**

1. How does the differentiation between unintentional and defiant sins highlight the severity of deliberate

disobedience and its consequences?

2. What can we learn from the punishment of the Sabbath-breaker about the importance of Sabbath observance and the seriousness with which God regards His commands?

3. How can believers strive to avoid defiant sin in their modern spiritual journeys, understanding its consequences?

4. In what ways can modern Christians use physical reminders to maintain obedience to God's commands and a consecrated life, inspired by the instruction to make tassels on garments?

**Sermon Notes for Religious Leaders:**

**Title:** "Defiant Sin, Sabbath Observance, and Reminders: Lessons from Deliberate Sins and the Sabbath-Breaker"

**Introduction:**

- Introduce the laws about deliberate sins and the Sabbath-breaker in Numbers 15, focusing on the themes of defiant sin, Sabbath observance, and the use of physical reminders to maintain obedience.
- Highlight the importance of avoiding defiant sin, observing the Sabbath, and using reminders to maintain a consecrated life.

**Body:**

1. **Defiant Sin:**
   - Discuss the differentiation between unintentional and defiant sins, highlighting the severity of deliberate disobedience and its consequences.
   - Reflect on how these principles can be applied to modern spiritual practices, encouraging believers

to strive to avoid defiant sin.

2. **Sabbath Observance:**
   ◦ Explore the punishment of the Sabbath-breaker, emphasising the importance of observing God's commands, particularly the Sabbath.
   ◦ Encourage the congregation to honour God's commands and set aside time for rest and worship, recognising the significance of Sabbath observance.

3. **Physical Reminders:**
   ◦ Discuss the instruction to make tassels on garments, highlighting the use of physical reminders to obey God's commands and maintain a consecrated life.
   ◦ Emphasise the need for believers to find ways to remember and obey God's commands in their daily lives, understanding the value of physical reminders.

**Working Example for Religious Leaders:**

**Example:** "Avoiding Defiant Sin, Observing the Sabbath, and Using Reminders in Church Life"

- **Scenario:** Imagine your church is encouraging members to avoid defiant sin, observe the Sabbath, and use physical reminders to maintain obedience to God's commands.
- **Action:** Organise a series of teachings and discussions on the importance of avoiding defiant sin, observing the Sabbath, and using reminders to maintain a consecrated life. Encourage members to find ways to remember and obey God's commands in their daily lives.
- **Reminders:** Emphasise the significance of using physical

reminders, providing guidance on how to maintain obedience to God's commands.

- **Outcome:** By avoiding defiant sin, observing the Sabbath, and using reminders, the community grows stronger in their commitment to God, reflecting the principles from the laws about deliberate sins and the Sabbath-breaker.

**Conclusion:**

- Summarise the key lessons from the laws about deliberate sins and the Sabbath-breaker, focusing on defiant sin, Sabbath observance, and the use of physical reminders to maintain obedience.
- Challenge the congregation to apply these principles in their modern spiritual practices and community life.
- Offer a prayer for guidance, dedication, and a deeper commitment to avoiding defiant sin, observing the Sabbath, and using reminders to maintain a consecrated life in their spiritual journey.

**Link to Modern-Day Problems:**

◇ **Avoiding Defiant Sin:** How can modern believers recognise the severity of deliberate disobedience and strive to avoid defiant sin, understanding its consequences, inspired by the differentiation between unintentional and defiant sins?

◇ **Observing the Sabbath:** What steps can believers take to honour God's commands and set aside time for rest and worship, recognising the importance of Sabbath observance, inspired by the punishment of the Sabbath-breaker?

◇ **Using Reminders:** How can believers use physical reminders to maintain obedience to God's commands and a consecrated life, understanding their value in daily life, inspired by the instruction to make tassels on garments?

◈ **Defiant Sin, Sabbath Observance, and Reminders:** In what ways can modern Christians avoid defiant sin, observe the Sabbath, and use reminders to maintain a consecrated life in their spiritual journey, inspired by the principles from the laws about deliberate sins and the Sabbath-breaker?

**Summary and Reflections on Obedience**
**Numbers 15:30-41 (NIV)**

1. "'But anyone who sins defiantly, whether native-born or foreigner, blasphemes the Lord and must be cut off from the people of Israel.

2. Because they have despised the Lord's word and broken his commands, they must surely be cut off; their guilt remains on them.'"

3. While the Israelites were in the wilderness, a man was found gathering wood on the Sabbath day.

4. Those who found him gathering wood brought him to Moses and Aaron and the whole assembly,

5. and they kept him in custody, because it was not clear what should be done to him.

6. Then the Lord said to Moses, "The man must die. The whole assembly must stone him outside the camp."

7. So the assembly took him outside the camp and stoned him to death, as the Lord commanded Moses.

8. The Lord said to Moses,

9. "Speak to the Israelites and say to them: 'Throughout the generations to come you are to make tassels on the corners of your garments, with a blue cord on each tassel.

10. You will have these tassels to look at and so you will remember all the commands of the Lord, that you may

obey them and not prostitute yourselves by chasing after the lusts of your own hearts and eyes.

11.   Then you will remember to obey all my commands and will be consecrated to your God.

12.   I am the Lord your God, who brought you out of Egypt to be your God. I am the Lord your God.'"

## Theological Significance:

- **Defiant Sin and Community Standards:** The passage reiterates the severity of defiant sin and the community's responsibility to uphold God's standards. This reflects the collective commitment to maintaining holiness.
- **Sabbath and Holiness:** The incident with the Sabbath-breaker underscores the sanctity of the Sabbath and the seriousness with which God regards His commands.
- **Reminders of Obedience:** The instruction to make tassels serves as a tangible reminder to obey God's commands and maintain a consecrated life.

### Modern Interpretation:

This passage teaches modern believers about the communal responsibility to uphold God's standards, the sanctity of the Sabbath, and the use of physical reminders to maintain obedience and holiness.

### Key Themes:

- **Community Responsibility:** The passage highlights the communal responsibility to uphold God's standards and maintain holiness.
- **Sanctity of the Sabbath:** The incident with the Sabbath-breaker underscores the importance of observing the

Sabbath as a holy day.

- **Reminders of Obedience:** The instruction to make tassels serves as a tangible reminder to obey God's commands and maintain a consecrated life.

**Modern-Day Examples:**

- **Upholding Community Standards:** Modern believers can recognise the communal responsibility to uphold God's standards and maintain holiness, understanding the impact of individual actions on the community.
- **Honouring the Sabbath:** Emphasising the sanctity of the Sabbath can inspire believers to set aside time for rest and worship, honouring God's commands.
- **Using Tangible Reminders:** Understanding the use of physical reminders can encourage believers to find ways to remember and obey God's commands in their daily lives.

**Questions for Reflection and Discussion:**

1. How does the community's responsibility to uphold God's standards highlight the importance of collective commitment to holiness?
2. What can we learn from the incident with the Sabbath-breaker about the sanctity of the Sabbath and the seriousness with which God regards His commands?
3. How can believers recognise the communal responsibility to uphold God's standards in their modern spiritual journeys, understanding the impact of individual actions on the community?
4. In what ways can modern Christians use tangible reminders to maintain obedience to God's commands and

a consecrated life, inspired by the instruction to make tassels on garments?

**Sermon Notes for Religious Leaders:**

**Title:** "Community Standards, Sabbath Sanctity, and Tangible Reminders: Lessons from Obedience and Holiness"

**Introduction:**

- Introduce the laws about defiant sin, the Sabbath-breaker, and the instruction to make tassels in Numbers 15, focusing on the themes of community responsibility, the sanctity of the Sabbath, and tangible reminders to maintain obedience.
- Highlight the importance of upholding community standards, honouring the Sabbath, and using reminders to maintain holiness.

**Body:**

1. **Community Responsibility:**
    - Discuss the community's responsibility to uphold God's standards and maintain holiness, highlighting the collective commitment to maintaining a consecrated life.
    - Reflect on how these principles can be applied to modern spiritual practices, encouraging believers to recognise the communal responsibility to uphold God's standards.
2. **Sanctity of the Sabbath:**
    - Explore the incident with the Sabbath-breaker, emphasising the importance of observing the Sabbath as a holy day and the seriousness with which God regards His commands.

- ○ Encourage the congregation to honour the Sabbath, setting aside time for rest and worship, recognising the sanctity of this day.
3. **Tangible Reminders:**
    - ○ Discuss the instruction to make tassels on garments, highlighting the use of tangible reminders to obey God's commands and maintain a consecrated life.
    - ○ Emphasise the need for believers to find ways to remember and obey God's commands in their daily lives, understanding the value of tangible reminders.

**Working Example for Religious Leaders:**
**Example:** "Upholding Community Standards, Honouring the Sabbath, and Using Tangible Reminders in Church Life"

- **Scenario:** Imagine your church is encouraging members to uphold community standards, honour the Sabbath, and use tangible reminders to maintain obedience to God's commands.
- **Action:** Organise a series of teachings and discussions on the importance of collective commitment to holiness, observing the Sabbath, and using tangible reminders to maintain a consecrated life. Encourage members to find ways to remember and obey God's commands in their daily lives.
- **Reminders:** Emphasise the significance of using tangible reminders, providing guidance on how to maintain obedience to God's commands.
- **Outcome:** By upholding community standards, honouring the Sabbath, and using tangible reminders, the community

grows stronger in their commitment to God, reflecting the principles from the laws about defiant sin, the Sabbath-breaker, and the instruction to make tassels.

**Conclusion:**

- Summarise the key lessons from the laws about defiant sin, the Sabbath-breaker, and the instruction to make tassels, focusing on community responsibility, the sanctity of the Sabbath, and tangible reminders to maintain obedience.
- Challenge the congregation to apply these principles in their modern spiritual practices and community life.
- Offer a prayer for guidance, dedication, and a deeper commitment to upholding community standards, honouring the Sabbath, and using tangible reminders to maintain a consecrated life in their spiritual journey.

**Link to Modern-Day Problems:**

◇ **Upholding Community Standards:** How can modern believers recognise the communal responsibility to uphold God's standards and maintain holiness, understanding the impact of individual actions on the community, inspired by the laws about defiant sin?

◇ **Honouring the Sabbath:** What steps can believers take to honour the Sabbath, setting aside time for rest and worship, recognising the sanctity of this day, inspired by the incident with the Sabbath-breaker?

◇ **Using Tangible Reminders:** How can believers use tangible reminders to maintain obedience to God's commands and a consecrated life, understanding their value in daily life, inspired by the instruction to make tassels on garments?

◇ **Community Standards, Sabbath Sanctity, and Tangible Reminders:** In what ways can modern Christians uphold community standards, honour the Sabbath, and use tangible reminders to maintain a consecrated life in their spiritual journey, inspired by the principles from the laws about defiant sin, the Sabbath-breaker, and the instruction to make tassels?

# Embracing the Journey of Faith

As we conclude our exploration of the Book of Numbers, it is essential to reflect on the rich tapestry of lessons and insights we have uncovered. This book has taken us through the trials, triumphs, and tribulations of the Israelites, offering timeless wisdom that remains profoundly relevant in our contemporary lives.

**Reflecting on the Journey**

Throughout this study, we have witnessed the Israelites' journey, marked by moments of profound faith and instances of doubt and disobedience. We have seen the importance of obedience to God's commands, the significance of community, and the necessity of maintaining faith even in the face of adversity. These stories are not just historical accounts; they are mirrors reflecting our own spiritual journeys.

**Key Takeaways**

- **Faith and Obedience:** The recurring theme of faith and obedience in Numbers teaches us the importance of trusting in God's plan, even when the path seems uncertain. Just as the Israelites were called to follow God's commands, we too are called to live lives of faithfulness and devotion.

- **Community and Responsibility:** The communal aspects of the Israelites' journey remind us of our responsibilities to one another. As members of a faith community, we are tasked with supporting, uplifting, and holding each other accountable.

- **Divine Guidance:** The constant need for divine guidance is a central lesson in Numbers. We are reminded to seek God's direction in all aspects of our lives, trusting that His wisdom will lead us to where we need to be.

### Applying the Lessons

As you move forward, consider how the lessons from Numbers can be applied in your daily life:

- **Personal Reflection:** Regularly reflect on your spiritual journey. Are there areas where you need to exercise more faith or obedience? How can you align your actions more closely with God's will?
- **Community Engagement:** Engage actively with your faith community. Offer support, seek guidance, and work together to uphold the values and teachings you have explored in this study.
- **Seek Divine Guidance:** In all decisions, big or small, seek God's guidance. Trust that He will provide the wisdom and direction you need to navigate life's challenges.

### A Final Encouragement

Remember, the journey of faith is ongoing. The lessons from the Book of Numbers serve as a foundation, but your personal journey continues. Embrace the teachings, apply them in your life, and remain open to the ongoing work of the Holy Spirit.

As you reflect on the insights gained from this study, may you find renewed strength, deeper understanding, and a closer relationship with God. May your faith community be enriched, and may you continue to grow in your spiritual walk, guided by the timeless wisdom of Scripture.

**Prayer for Guidance**

Let us close with a prayer:

"Dear Heavenly Father, we thank You for the journey we have taken through the Book of Numbers. We are grateful for the lessons learned and the insights gained. Help us to apply these teachings in our daily lives, to walk in faith and obedience, and to seek Your guidance in all things. Strengthen our communities, and help us to support one another as we grow in our spiritual journeys. May Your wisdom guide us, Your love sustain us, and Your Spirit empower us. In Jesus' name, we pray. Amen."

Thank you for joining this journey of faith. May the wisdom and lessons of the Book of Numbers continue to inspire and guide you.

★ Dear Reader, Thank you for reading my book.

I highly value your opinion! Please consider leaving a review on Amazon. Your feedback helps other readers discover this book.

Visit the book's page on Amazon, and click "Write a customer review," and share your thoughts. Your review makes a meaningful impact.

If you are reading this book on an eReader then you will see a 1-5 star rating on the final page. It just takes a second to vote but helps us authors out no end.

Thank you for your time and support!

Best regards,

Harper

www.ingramcontent.com/pod-product-compliance
Lightning Source LLC
Chambersburg PA
CBHW031524150726
47990CB00001B/48